AN ELEMENT OF RISK

A Prequel to The Horses Know Trilogy

LYNN MANN

Coxstone Press

Copyright © 2024 by Lynn Mann

Lynn Mann asserts the moral right to
be identified as the author of this work.

ISBN 978-1-7393276-4-4
Published by Coxstone Press 2024

All rights reserved.

No part of this book may be reproduced in any form or by any electronic or mechanical means, including information storage and retrieval systems, without written permission from the author, except for the use of brief quotations in a book review.

This novel is entirely a work of fiction. The names, characters and incidents portrayed in it are the work of the author's imagination. Any resemblance to actual persons, living or dead, events or localities is entirely coincidental.

This book was created without the use of Artificial Intelligence (AI). The use of any part of this book for AI training, machine learning, or any other similar purpose without prior written permission from the author is strictly prohibited.

In memory of Dad and Braveheart

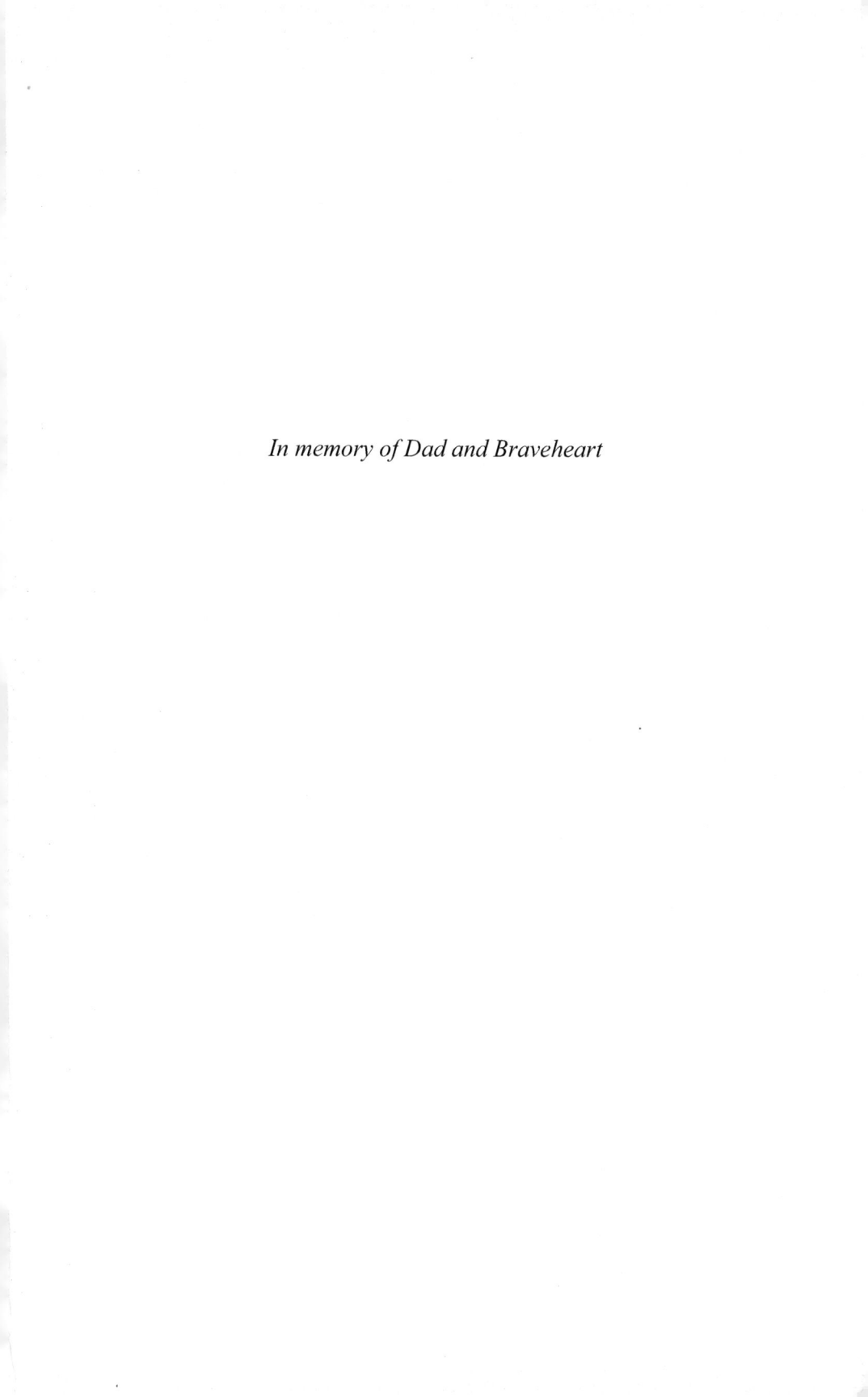

Chapter One

Henry slammed the door behind him with his foot. He brushed his feet vigorously on the mat while blowing on his red, chapped hands.

'Take those boots off and get yourself into the tub,' Ma said, nodding to where our tin bath sat in front of the fire. 'If you'd come straight home with your brother and father instead of stopping to let the Wilson girl bat her eyelashes at you, you'd be clean and warm and sitting down to a hot meal by now, like they are.'

Henry looked at me, rolled his eyes and mouthed, 'Thanks.'

I grinned at him.

Ma stalked over to the bathtub, peered into it, and then turned back to my brother. 'It was your turn to go first, but now you'll have to sit in all the salt and fish guts the other two have washed off, because I'll be damned if I'm going to empty that out, bucket by bucket, then fetch and heat more water…'

'Bucket by bucket,' Henry chimed in with her, grinning at me.

'…bucket by bucket,' she continued as if he hadn't spoken,

'just so you can languish in the fresh water you were no doubt expecting. Come on, over here with you while the rest of us finish our meal with clothes pegs on our noses until you're clean. Honestly, Clara Wilson must have no sense of smell.'

'Leave off the lad, Queenie,' Pa said. 'He's worked as hard as me and Jimmy here, and at eighteen, I'd be worried if he wasn't courting a lass. Our Jimmy'll be slow to come home before long too, just as soon as he works up the courage to flash a smile the Smith girl's way.' He winked at me. 'No need to look so panic stricken, Son. She'll be a grand match for you. Just work on that courage, eh? She'll only watch for our boat to come in for so long, before she turns her attention elsewhere.'

'Expert on the fairer sex, are you, Fred?' Ma said, glaring at him as she sat back down at the table.

Pa chuckled. 'I wish.' He ripped a chunk of bread off one of the thick slices on his plate, dunked it in his bowl of chowder, and scooped out a chunk of fish. He pointed his dripping bread at me. 'I only have one piece of advice for you, Son – no, two. The first is to marry the first girl to take your heart, because she'll be the right one.' His eyes flicked towards Ma and he looked her up and down while she tried not to smile. 'The second is to take a bath whenever your wife tells you to, otherwise you'll never have any sons.'

Henry's laugh from the bathtub joined mine as Ma pulled a hand cloth from her apron pocket and flicked Pa's leg with it. He grabbed hold of it, pulled it out of her grasp, and swirled it around so that it became more of a weapon.

Ma narrowed her eyes, unable now to stop herself from grinning. 'You wouldn't,' she challenged Pa.

He grinned back at her, his eyes bright like they always were when he looked at her, and continued to swirl the cloth by way of reply.

Chapter One

She was up and out of her chair so quickly that it toppled over behind her with a crash, tripping up Pa as he leapt after her. She ran to the other side of the bath tub and leant on the rim, feinting left and right as Pa reached it, so that he couldn't guess which way she would run.

'Oi!' my brother said, moving his hands over his groin.

'Oi nothing,' Ma said breathlessly, her eyes as bright as Pa's. 'There's nothing there I haven't seen hundreds of times before.'

'But I'm a man now,' Henry complained.

Ma darted to her left, towards the drawn curtain that separated my parents' bed from our living room. She darted behind it and wrapped it around herself, but not before my father had flicked the cloth and made contact with her heavily skirted backside. He grabbed her and threw her on the bed, then proceeded to tickle her. She shrieked so loudly that when the door to the wooden, single-roomed house we called home was flung open, Henry and I looked towards it with a grin, expecting any one of our neighbours to run in and demand to know what was wrong.

Instead, our seven-year-old cousin ran into the room followed by a blast of cold wind that, while nowhere near the gale it had been while Pa, Henry and I had been out at sea fishing that day, was still strong enough to thrust the door back against the wall so hard, the house shuddered.

'The press... gang... is... here,' she panted. 'Ma told me to... run and tell you. They've already...' her voice cracked and her bottom lip quivered.

My mother ran to her and grabbed hold of her arms, then loosened her grip and stroked her niece's long, black hair away from her eyes. 'They've already what, Nim?'

'They've already taken... Pa, and they're coming this way.' Nim's face crumpled and she began to cry. Ma picked her up and sat her on her hip as if she were a toddler, before grabbing the door and hauling it closed.

Pa threw the wet bathing towel he and I had already used at Henry – who had stood up suddenly in the bath tub with all thoughts of modesty forgotten – then he bent to lift the corner of one of the thin rugs that covered the wooden flooring of our home.

He pulled it back and said, 'Don't just sit there, Jimmy, clear everything off the table that shows there are four of us living here, and throw it down here.' He lifted the trap door he had uncovered and pointed to the dark hole it revealed.

I gathered two plates and two bowls and practically threw them into the hole, followed by two beakers and spoons. My mother rushed over with our boots and coats, and my father threw in his, Henry's, and my clothes.

'Right, get in, Jimmy. You too, Henry,' my father ordered. 'Quickly!'

Neither of us hesitated. He had drilled us often enough that we knew exactly how deep was the hole and where each of us should sit in order to make room for him to join us. As soon as he did, my mother lowered the trapdoor and there was a rustling noise as she pulled the rug back into position.

'Nim, sit at the table with me, love.' My mother's voice was muffled, but I could still hear the tremble in her voice. 'See, we're having the same chowder your ma makes, and I happen to know it's your favourite. When the men come, we'll need to pretend you're my daughter, and you and I live here alone and are in the middle of eating our tea. Do you think you can do that? You won't need to speak, just eat and act like I'm your ma.'

I tried to slow and quieten my breathing, and heard Henry and Pa doing the same. Henry's teeth started to chatter and, sitting close beside him as I was, I could feel him shivering. I felt around for our coats, and my hand closed on what felt like one of them. I

Chapter One

tugged at it until Pa shifted, then pulled it from beneath him and gave it to Henry.

'Thanks,' he whispered.

'Shhh,' Pa whispered curtly.

All three of us jumped as the door crashed open and booted feet pounded into the room.

'Who the hell are you?' Ma shrieked. 'You have no business in my home. Get out before you frighten my child more than you have already.'

'Where's your husband?' a man barked.

'Dead. Went fishing one day last winter and never came back. Didn't you hear me? Get out of my house.'

There was a rapid thudding of footsteps as men rushed to all four corners of the room. Wooden curtain rings rattled together as the fabric that concealed my parents' bed was yanked aside, and there was a bang as the lid of the bedding trunk was dropped shut. One pair of boots trod slowly, heavily towards the table. There was a screech as a chair was pulled back and a soft thud as someone sat on it. I could picture Ma standing, arms folded beneath her bosom and her chin stuck out as she always did when she was angry.

'If your husband's dead, why does that bath water smell of sweat and fish guts?' The man who addressed my mother spoke with authority and I imagined him sitting at our table as if it were his.

'That was... that was my bath water,' Ma said. 'I have to go fishing while my sister has little Nim here for me. Someone has to provide for us both now her pa's not around.'

'I'll provide some of what you're missing, love,' a voice said from over by the door, and there was a chorus of laughter.

Pa stiffened beside me, and I grabbed his arm.

'Now there's a thought,' the man at the table said. 'If you don't have a man about the house, you'll be wanting to catch up on some fun, won't you? Eh? Come and sit on my knee.'

Pa exploded through the trapdoor, his rage giving him the strength to heave it and the rug out of his way as if neither were there. Henry and I were only a second behind him. All three of us launched ourselves at the heavily bearded man sitting before Ma, leaving the cap that he had pulled down low over his eyes to flutter to the ground nearby.

'Fred! Boys, no!' Ma screamed.

Strong hands grabbed me and pulled me off the bearded man before I could punch the leer off his face for a third time.

'What have we here now, then? Strapping young lad, you are, aren't you?' a voice growled in my ear. 'You'll be a fine addition to His Majesty's navy.'

I tilted my head forward and then snapped it back into his face as hard as I could, satisfaction at the crunching sound of his nose breaking overriding the sharp pain that my action caused me. He released his hold, and I hurled myself at a short but heavyset man who had just punched Henry in the gut while another held his arms behind his back. It was as if I were a fly hitting a tree; I bounced off him and landed on my back. The sole of a boot appeared above my face... and then everything went black.

～

I was being carried – no, dragged, I realised groggily; my unbooted feet were trailing in the sand. The icy wind bit at my hands and feet and penetrated my shirt and smock as if they weren't on my back, and perversely, the only warmth giving me comfort from the cold was that emanating from the hands of the two heavily garbed men who were dragging me by my armpits.

The sound of waves crashing ahead brought me around

further. I was being press-ganged! So, presumably, were Henry and Pa, if they were even still alive; we all knew that the thugs who kidnapped men to serve on warships were the roughest men on our side of the law and often went too far in their efforts to subdue their victims.

I struggled violently in the failing light, hoping to shock my captors into letting go of me. The one on my left held fast, but I succeeded in wriggling out of the grip of the man to my right... only to find that my legs wouldn't support me. As I fell to the ground, dangling from my left arm as it was gripped even harder by the stronger of my two captors, I caught sight of Henry being dragged by two more men, one of whom was grunting with the effort of each step. My brother's head lolled on his shoulders and his body was slack, but I decided he had to be alive or they'd have left him behind.

A hand grabbed me under my right armpit and hauled me up onto my feet. 'Do that again and I'll brain ya,' a gravelly voice said in my ear.

All I could think about was that Pa had to be on my right, because I hadn't seen him to my left. I gathered what little strength I had and lurched upward slightly, tilting my head to the right. Around fifteen men were walking meekly in a line, attached to one another with rope. Even at a glance, I could see that none had Pa's slight limp from when he got his foot caught in a fishing net and broke his ankle years ago.

'Pa?' I croaked. I tried to swallow and grimaced at the flash of pain in my head. 'Pa?' I said more loudly. 'Pa?'

One of my captors laughed. 'Your pa ain't comin' to rescue you, lad. He was a strong 'un, but not the brigh'est. If he'd fought less savage like, he would've bin alongside you now and had a chance of goin' home to your ma when his service was done. As 'tis, he'll be six foot under by nightfall and your ma will still be alone. You and your brother 'ave 'is temper and 'is strength, but if you've got any sense at all, you'll use your brains more'n he did. Do your time and then you can go 'ome to your ma and whatever girl is sweet on you.'

Pa was dead? Dead? They killed him? Rage rumbled in my stomach and spread into my arms and legs, burning them from inside and giving me strength I would never have guessed I had. I wrenched myself free of both my captors and lashed out at the one who had told me of Pa's demise. I caught him with a back-hander across his face before a sharp pain at the back of my neck sent me back to blackness.

∼

The next time I came to, it was dark and the wooden floorboards upon which I lay were moving. I sat up and vomited, holding my head in my hands in a vain attempt to quell the flashes of pain that penetrated its steady but intense throbbing. I wiped my mouth on my sleeve and tried to open my eyes further than they wanted to, in the hope that they would become accustomed to the dark.

Waves slapped against the sides of the boat in whose bilge I realised I was sitting, and someone sobbed nearby. I got to my feet and shuffled towards the sound. 'Henry?'

'He's in the same cage as you, Jim,' a familiar voice said wearily.

'Uncle Jacob?'

His voice was resigned as he said, 'Yes, it's me, lad. Your aunt sent Nim to warn you. I'm sorry she didn't make it.'

I crouched down, still holding my head, then felt around for my brother. 'She did make it. She warned us and we hid, but the men were threatening to molest Ma, so we showed them what happens to anyone who thinks of doing that.'

Chapter One

'Nim made it? Was she there when the men came?' Panic strengthened my uncle's voice. 'Was she harmed?'

My hand found the rough fabric of my brother's coat. 'She was there, but she wasn't harmed while I was conscious. They didn't want her or Ma, not really, they just wanted us.'

Uncle Jacob sighed. 'It's a pity you didn't see fit to remember that at the time; now your ma and my Riva and Nim have no one. You and I'll just have to endure what's coming in the hope we can get back to them some day.'

I felt for my brother's arm and shook it. 'And Henry.' I knelt down and lowered my face to where I judged his must be. 'Henry, wake up.'

'He'll not be doing that, Jimmy lad. Not after the beating he took when they brought us all down here. You should rest while you can.'

I felt for my brother's cheek and slapped it, wincing at the fresh pain in my head that my sudden movement caused me. 'He's strong. Me and him, we're like Pa, even the press gangers said it. Come on, Henry, wake up.' I shook his arm again.

It occurred to me that something hadn't felt right when I slapped him. I put my hand back to his cheek and withdrew it suddenly. He was cold. Too cold. I found his arms and rubbed my hands up and down them.

'Henry. HENRY.'

'Jim, stop it. I told you, he'll not wake. He came to just as they threw you both in your cage. He thought you were dead and he went berserk. One of the men went even more crazy, and the others couldn't pull him off your brother until it was too late. They threw him in there with you as a warning in case you might see fit to follow his example. You have to face it. We're sailors in the Royal Navy now, and there's nought we can do about it. All we can do is try to stay alive until the king wins his war and we can all go home.'

~

I didn't follow his advice. Shock and grief fuelled my temper and wouldn't allow me to. When the hatch to the deck was finally pulled open and light flooded in, allowing me to see the mess the press gangers had made of my brother's body, my rage was fuelled further. When the door to my cage was opened and I was beckoned out to follow my fellow slaves up to the deck where I would no doubt have been given my orders, I came out fists first despite being unsteady on my feet.

It was only once I was tied shirtless to the mast of the ship that was now our prison, and the first mate's lash tore its first strip from my back, that I woke up.

I sat up in bed, gasping and shaking, my nightshirt soaked through with sweat, my head pounding and a stinging pain in my back. My bedroom door creaked open and light from my mother's lantern flickered on the grey stones of my bedroom wall as she hurried to my side. She put the lantern on my bedside table and pulled me close.

'Henry and Pa are dead,' I sobbed. 'My brother and my pa are dead and now Ma's all alone.'

'Devlin, you've just had one of your dreams, that's all,' my mother whispered. 'Your brothers are alive and well and asleep in their beds, which is a miracle considering how loudly you just screamed, and your father's on his way. You're in bed, at home, and you're safe.'

'But the press gangers kidnapped me...'

'They didn't. They don't exist,' my mother whispered, holding me close and rocking me from side to side despite my fourteen years.

A wave of nausea quickly turned to an urgent need to void my stomach of its contents and I pushed my mother away from me urgently before leaning over the side of the bed and vomiting noisily onto the stone floor by her feet.

My mother's hand shot to my forehead, making me wince and flinch away from her. 'You don't have a fever. Did you eat anything after dinner last night? Something that might have disagreed with you?'

I shook my head. 'I don't think so. And the press gangers ARE real. One of them stamped on my face and knocked me out, then when I came around, another clubbed me over the back of the head. When I came around again, I was sick, and now I've been sick again. I think I have a concussion. That's what Shif called it yesterday, when he was trying to get me to feel like I had it in order to see if I could find the herbs that would help it.'

'Our Master Herbalist asked you to identify the herbs that would ease concussion symptoms during your testing?' my mother said. 'That sounds a little difficult, no wonder you didn't show any aptitude for herbalism. Maybe I'll have a little word with Shif and see if he can't re-test you.'

'What's more concerning is that Devlin thinks he has a concussion because of a dream,' my father said as he followed his lantern light into my bedroom. 'Son, your scream sent chills through me. You were probably sick as a result of feeling so afraid. We all know how real dreams can feel.'

I flinched at the extra light and held my hands up in front of my face. 'The first mate whipped me. My back hurts.'

'That's it, I'm going to get Shif,' my mother said. 'He's not right, Lennon.'

Father sighed. 'I'll go.'

He left the room, followed by Mother, who returned shortly afterward with a glass of water and a mop and bucket. She cleaned up the mess I had made whilst I sipped at the water, then gently helped me out of bed and to the chair by the fireplace. Twice, she had to hold me more firmly as dizziness had me swaying on my feet. She stripped my bed of its sweat-soaked sheets and remade it with fresh ones, then helped me out of my sodden nightshirt and into a clean one, making very sure to run her hand over my back and show me it was clean of the blood I was sure must be there. She was just tucking me back into bed when footsteps sounded on the stairs.

I was again forced to hold my hands in front of my face to ease the pain darting behind my eyeballs as light from Shif's lantern preceded him and my father into my room. Shif put his lantern on my bedside table next to my mother's, and I clamped my hands over my eyes tightly.

There was a shuffling of feet and then Shif said, in the gentle voice that had soothed so many during his years as Coastwood's Herbalist, 'You can open your eyes, Devlin, I've moved the lanterns further away.' His knees cracked as he knelt down on the wooden floorboards beside my bed.

'So, you're experiencing sensitivity to light,' he said, 'and your father tells me you've been sick. How does your head feel?'

'It hurts.'

'Any dizziness?'

'Yes,' my mother said from behind him. 'I had to help him to the chair by the fire. And his back hurts.'

I nodded, wincing at the pain in my head and neck as I did so.

'Lift your nightshirt, lad, so I can see your back.' Shif leant around me as I did as I was told.

I bent an arm up behind me and pointed. 'It hurts there, where I was whipped.'

Chapter One

Out of the corner of my eye, I saw Shif glance up at my parents.

'In his dream, like I told you,' my father said and Shif nodded.

He ran his fingers across my back, following my finger, and I sucked in a breath through gritted teeth.

Shif sat back on his heels and stared at my back, and I supposed he was attempting to pick up the energy vibration of my injury in the way he had described to me while testing my aptitude for herbalism.

After a few minutes, he shook his head almost indiscernibly and asked me, 'What day is it today?' Then he grimaced. 'Or, I should say, what day will it be when the sun comes up in a few hours' time?'

My mother put her hand on his shoulder. 'We're sorry to have called you out in the small hours, Shif, but as you can see, he isn't right.'

My father nudged her and said, 'Shhhh.'

I frowned. 'Um, my second testing day? I think?'

Shif nodded slowly, his eyes never leaving mine, then held a hand up in front of my face and said, 'Keep your eyes on my forefinger.'

I could see that he was moving it slowly to my right, but it also seemed to stay where it was. My eyes flicked back and forth between the two versions of his finger. I thought I heard someone saying my name from far away, and I frowned at the distraction from my task.

'Devlin.' Shif's voice was clear and firm as he said my name again. I blinked and looked into his eyes, seeing worry in them. He nodded. 'Okay, you're back with me. You should lie down now, and rest.' He raked a hand through his long, grey hair and got to his feet, pushing down hard on the side of my bed to support himself. He moved towards the door and beckoned to my parents to follow him out.

I felt tired and groggy and desperately wanted to do as he had told me, but I also wanted to hear what he was going to tell my parents. When the last of them reached the bottom of the stairs, I got out of bed, stood still until the room stopped spinning, then staggered across the room, careful to avoid the floorboards that I knew would creak. I was relieved to reach the doorway and rested there a moment, my hand grasping the doorframe and my head resting against the cool grey stone wall. When I trusted myself to walk further without falling, I moved to the top of the stairs and, clenching the wooden handrail attached to the wall with one hand and the bannister with the other, wobbled my way down six of the stairs. I sat down just as another wave of dizziness hit and caught my mother's voice as it drifted out of the kitchen.

'Are you absolutely sure, Shif? He was fine when he went to bed, and when I found him, he was sitting up, tangled in his bedsheet. He'd literally just woken up; he wouldn't have had a chance to hit his head on anything.'

'There's no mistaking it,' Shif said softly. 'I can't find anything wrong with his back, but, however he got it, he definitely has a concussion.'

Chapter Two

I had always known that my time with Ma, Pa and Henry was real. I knew what it was like to dream at night, and I knew that when I was with my other family, I wasn't dreaming; my brain wasn't processing things that had happened during the day, as my parents had repeatedly tried to convince me was the case when I told them where I had been. Now I had proof; the concussion I had sustained as a result of the press gangers' beatings had followed me into my waking world.

'Has anything like this happened before?' Shif asked my parents.

'He's dreamt about being part of another family since he was small,' my father said. 'As he's grown older, it's like the family he dreams about has grown older with him. In fact, I feel as if I know Fred, Queenie and Henry personally. He's always insisted his "other family", as he calls them, are real. He's described their house and village, even the beach and coastline where they supposedly lived, in intricate detail, and he's dreamt of being in fights with other lads, such as we would never allow to happen.

He's never woken up with physical symptoms consistent with what happened in his dream though. How is that even possible?'

Shif sighed and then there was silence. Eventually, he said, 'The human mind is an amazing thing. I suppose it's possible that if it believes something strongly enough, it could cause the body to experience it physically.'

'But why does Devlin believe his dreams are real?' my mother said. 'And why have things suddenly got so much worse? I mean, he's actually got a concussion from dreaming? The timing couldn't be worse, with him testing for the Skills.'

'Maybe that's it,' Shif said. 'I tested him for herbalism yesterday. Maybe in training his mind to reach for the herbs, I've somehow opened up a pathway between the mental and physical that's allowed aspects of his dreams to manifest physically. I pushed him harder than I normally do because I had a strong feeling he has an aptitude for herbalism, but that something was blocking him, almost as if part of his mind was resisting my suggestions and holding him back.'

'He said you asked him to create the symptoms for concussion in his mind and then find the herbs that would ease them,' my mother said. 'Could this be a delayed reaction to your suggestion?'

'I suppose it's possible, but he actually has the symptoms, Mowaya,' Shif replied. 'When we train Apprentices to feel as if they have the symptoms they're attempting to find cures for, they don't believe they have them to the extent that the symptoms actually manifest.'

'So, what if he dreams he's been injured more severely?' my father said. 'What if he dreams he's killed? Do you think he could go to sleep one night and never wake up?'

There was silence and in my mind's eye I could see Shif

staring with unfocused eyes, as our friend always did when he was thinking.

Eventually, he said, 'The truth of it is that I don't know. I do think it's best that he doesn't test for any more Skills just now. In any case, he should rest up for a week or two to recover from his concussion.' I heard the metal clasps of his herb bag popping open. Shif continued, 'I'll leave you a herbal preparation that will ease the trauma to his brain and help him sleep. I'll let the other Testers know he's poorly and won't be in for testing just yet. You'll need to monitor him closely for the next twenty-four hours, and if his symptoms get any worse, fetch me straight away.'

'But shouldn't we keep him awake?' my mother said. 'What if he goes straight back into the dream and something happens that makes him think he's hurt even more badly?'

The sound of Shif snapping the clasps of his bag shut sent a flash of pain through my head, and I let go of the bannister railing to which I had been clinging, in order to hold my head in my hands. I toppled forward and just as I was about to lurch headfirst down the stairwell, a hand grabbed the collar of my nightshirt, and an arm wrapped around my shoulders from behind and pulled me back onto the stair.

'When you've just achieved your first successful eavesdropping session,' my elder brother whispered into my ear, 'you don't want to give yourself away by throwing yourself down the stairs. I'm proud of you and so will Kap be when I tell him. Come on, let's get you back to bed before you're discovered, then in the morning, you can tell me and Kap what was so important that Shif's here in the middle of the night, and my whiter-than-white little bro' is pulling a sneaky.'

Twenty years old and burly due to five years working on my father's fishing boat, Joplin easily pulled me to my feet, where I stood swaying, fearful of turning around and going back up the stairs in case I fell. I panicked at the sound of the back door closing behind Shif; my parents would be making for the kitchen door and then the stairs. I tried to turn around but was overcome with dizziness and fell back against the bannister. Once again, it was Joplin's brawny arm that saved me.

'Whoa there, Dev, what's up with you?' he whispered. He clamped his arm more tightly around my waist, hoisted me against his hip, and lifted me up the stairs. At the sound of my parents whispering in the hallway below, he hurried along the landing to my room, trailing my feet along the floor, and deposited me on my bed. 'Was Shif here for you?' he asked me.

I couldn't answer him. The light from the lantern my mother had left in my room was penetrating my eyelids even as I clamped them shut, causing stabbing pain, and I feared I would vomit again.

'Dev? What's wrong?' Joplin asked me.

'I'll fill you in on that later, Joplin.' My father's voice preceded him into the room. 'Back to bed now. We'll need to be up again in a few hours to catch the tide. Put your head around Kaplin's door on your way back to your room, and if we've woken him too, tell him the same thing. Off you go.' Uncharacteristically, his tone left no room for discussion and my brother, also unusually, did as he was asked without comment.

My father squeezed my shoulder gently and said, 'Rest now, Devlin. I'll be back as soon as I can tomorrow.' My eyes still squeezed shut, I heard him pad out of the room.

Mother took my hands and pulled me gently to my feet, then supported me while she pulled the sheet and blanket back further. 'You shouldn't have tried to get out of bed,' she whispered. 'You heard Shif, you need to rest. Sit down now and swing your legs under the sheets while I hold them up.'

When I had done as she said, she took one of my hands and

Chapter Two

folded it around a beaker, telling me, 'Drink this. Shif said it'll help you sleep.'

I drank the cool, earthy-smelling potion and then sucked in my cheeks at its slightly bitter aftertaste. My mother took the empty beaker from me, pulled my bedding up to my chin and tucked me in tightly, as she had when I was little. 'Sleep now,' she whispered and kissed my forehead.

She sat down on my bed and I was aware of her weight and warmth by my legs as I drifted away from the waking world.

∽

Shif's potion did indeed help me sleep, in fact, when I awoke, the sun was pouring through the gap between my bedroom curtains with an intensity that told me I had slept away most of the morning. The events of the night came back to me, and I was relieved that the brightness of the sun's rays was causing my eyes no pain or discomfort whatsoever. I sat up, rubbing them.

Immediately, my mother's face was in front of my own, her brown curls loose around her face instead of swept back by the brightly coloured clips she usually wore, and the skin beneath her worried, brown eyes swollen and so dark, it was almost black. 'How are you feeling, Devlin? You didn't dream again, I'm sure of it. How's your head? Are you feeling sick? Dizzy? At least you can open your eyes properly now, that's a relief.'

I blinked. 'I'm fine, Mother.'

'You're a long way from fine, my son, but it's a relief to know you're feeling better. I'll fetch you something to eat, then you'll have some more of Shif's potion and get straight back to sleep. Rest is what you need, Shif said. Plenty of rest.' As she made for the door, I noticed she was still wearing her nightdress. Further, despite having woken up lying in exactly the same position as when I had gone to sleep, my bedding was rumpled on one side of me and there was a depression in the pillow to the side of the one my head had made.

My mother had slept with me as she hadn't had cause to since I was four years old and had returned from my first visit to my life with my other family. Then, I had woken screaming as a result of Henry having been punched in the face by another boy. His nose had poured with blood, convincing me he was dying, and I had been inconsolable.

My fireside chair was by my bed, its cushion flattened and my mother's shawl draped over one of its arms. I supposed she had risen to see my father and brothers off, as she always did when they left for a day's fishing, and, rather than getting dressed and setting about her daily routine as one of our village's Bakers, she had then come back to watch over me. Rarely one to fuss and always one to encourage independence in her sons, her attentiveness told me the extent of her concern. I felt impelled to put her mind at rest.

I pulled back my sheet and blankets, swung my feet to the floorboards and slowly, tentatively, stood up. I felt completely normal; all the night's pain, dizziness and nausea had disappeared. I walked to the door, along the landing, down the stairs and into the kitchen, to find my mother stirring a pan of soup.

'What are you doing out of bed?' she said, bustling over to me and attempting to turn me around to go back out of the room.

I shook myself out of her arms and said, 'I'm fine, Mother, really. I didn't get my concussion here, so maybe that's why the symptoms haven't lasted long; I've obviously slept them off.'

She rubbed her chin with the tips of her fingers as she thought. Finally, she said, 'There's nothing obvious about any of this, Devlin. I can't tell you how relieved I am that you're feeling better, but you still need to follow Shif's advice and rest for the next few weeks.'

'But his advice was based on what he knows of people who've had concussion physically, not mentally like I did.'

My mother narrowed her eyes. 'You seem to know an awful lot about it. Did you hear our conversation with Shif after we left your room last night?'

I cursed myself inwardly and scrambled for an answer that would stop her questioning me further. 'He taught me all about it when he tested me,' I blurted. 'He wanted me to feel like I had it so I could find the herbs that can help it. I told you last night, remember?'

'I remember. I very much doubt he told you his theory of how you managed to get it in your sleep though, seeing as at that point, it hadn't happened.' She sighed. 'Oh, Devlin, I'm sorry you heard us. We thought we were talking quietly enough, but obviously not. You mustn't concern yourself with anything we said, we were just thinking out loud. As it happens, I had an idea while I was watching you sleep. I'm going to ask Shif to make you a sleeping potion that will stop you dreaming, then this kind of thing can never happen again.'

I nodded. Henry and Pa were dead, and Ma likely would be by the time I made it back to her, if I ever did. There was nothing for me in my other life except pain and suffering. I bit my lip as hot tears spilled down my face, and the thought of sleeping peacefully was suddenly very appealing.

My mother returned to the stove and poured some soup into a bowl, which she placed on the table. 'Here you go, love. You can sit down here and have it before I get you back up to bed.'

∼

I found I was more than content to spend the next two weeks in bed, even knowing that my friends were going through testing without me and that by the time I was up and about, they would know the Skill in which they would apprentice when we all left school the following year, or would be considering which Trade to choose instead. Although I didn't feel the slightest bit unwell physically, my mother's continued insistence that I observe Shif's advice and rest gave me time to grieve for the family I had lost.

At Mother's request, the Herbalist created a potion that had me sleeping so soundly, I was dead to both my worlds until my eyes opened. When I was awake, however, I replayed over and over in my mind my last hours with my other parents and brother. I sobbed under the sheets whenever I relived seeing Henry dead at my feet, or receiving the news that Pa had been killed and realising what that meant for Ma. I told myself again and again that there was nothing for me in that world anymore. That I had a family in this world who were alive and well, and I had to leave my other life behind. Mercifully, when my two weeks of rest were up, I was almost as sound mentally as I knew myself to be physically. I thought I was, anyway.

I ate my breakfast alone at the kitchen table; Father, Joplin and Kaplin would already have cast their nets out at sea and Mother was at work in her bakery, having returned to it the week before. Though the school term had ended the previous week, I had a full schedule for the next seven days; today I would be re-tested – at my mother's insistence – to see if I showed an aptitude for herbalism, then on every day that followed, I would undergo testing for another Skill until I had been tested for all seven.

As I scooped porridge onto my spoon, I remembered having felt strangely uncomfortable as I made my way to Shif's house for testing two weeks before, and even more uncomfortable as I tried to follow his instructions and extend my mind to the herbs he had laid out on the table in front of me – it was as if part of my mind knew how easy it was to sense which of them could do what, while the other part didn't want to. I kept getting the briefest sense of which herb would ease each of the range of conditions Shif asked me to conjure up in my mind, but by the time I opened my mouth to say which one it was, the sense was gone, along with my memory of which herb it was, to be replaced with a sense that I'd had a narrow escape. I had been frustrated and relieved in turn, and increasingly confused as a result, as had Shif. When he finally told me I had done enough for the day and that unfortunately, he couldn't recommend that I apprentice for herbalism, he looked as disappointed as he was confused.

'In all my years as a Tester for herbalism, I've never spent so long with a potential Apprentice only to find myself unable to offer an apprenticeship,' he told me, raking his fingers through his hair until they snagged in the cord with which he had tied it back. 'Do you know why you're fighting yourself, Devlin? Are you even aware of it?'

I shook my head in answer to his first question, hoping he would take it as a reply to both of them. He stared at me for a few moments, then patted me on the shoulder and dismissed me. I had made my way home more slowly than normal as I tried in vain to find the answer to his first question.

As I swallowed my last spoonful of porridge, I wondered whether he was feeling as much trepidation at repeating the process as was I. I decided to leave early for my testing with him and take the long route to his cottage via the beach. Unlike the rest of my family – and to the amusement of my brothers – I'd always had an inexplicable aversion to being out of my depth in the sea, but I liked to walk barefoot through the shallow water and felt the need to do something I enjoyed in order to distract me from how I suspected the rest of the day would unfold. There was also the possibility that some of my friends would be there now that the school holidays had begun, though I suspected most of them would still be in bed so early in the day.

I washed my bowl, spoon, and the pan in which I had made my breakfast, and left them by the sink to dry. Suddenly looking forward to feeling the sun on my face after two weeks indoors, I hurried into the hallway, buckled on my sandals and stepped onto the cobbled path outside the front door.

The sky was cloudless and the palest, softest blue. The warm rays of the early morning sun had an edge to them that promised far greater heat as the day progressed. The sound of waves tickling the shale of the beach and the gentle breeze that wafted past my nose carrying the scent of seaweed, informed me what I would see when I reached the bluff from which I would take the well-trodden path down to the sand. The sea would be the clear, azure blue it always was on a calm day, and dotted with white and grey gulls content to bob quietly around on its surface rather than fly above it, shrieking their raucous cries. Fronds of brown seaweed would reveal the extent of the water's reach before it had retreated over the almost white sand to the tiny stones it was agitating now.

On any other day, I would have felt a surge of happiness and hurried on my way. Now, I found myself rooted to the spot, my mouth dry and my heart thumping as sweat broke out on my forehead. I couldn't even bring myself to close the front door behind me.

'Morning, Devlin, it's good to see you up and about again,' a voice called.

I blinked and noticed our next-door neighbour waving from the cobbled street along which she was pushing a small barrow full of lettuces.

'Um, thanks, Phyllis, I mean Mrs neighbour, um, no, sorry, I mean Mrs Sharman,' I said, my face flushing and sweat now running down my back.

'Are you quite alright, dear?' she asked, putting down the handles of her barrow and reaching for the handle of our front gate with a gnarled hand.

The thought of being pinned in our front doorway by Phyllis and interrogated as to my past and current condition galvanised me into action. I reached behind myself and slammed the door, then hurried down the path, opening the gate before she could.

'I'm fine, thank you,' I said. 'I was just thinking what a nice day it's going to be. I'd better get going or I'll be late for testing.'

I squeezed past her, trying not to look at the hair growing out of the enormous wart on her chin about whose sudden appearance my brothers had cheerfully forewarned me a few days previously.

She patted me gently on the cheek. 'Just remember, Devlin, there's more to life than the Skills. Show aptitude or don't, it's up to you. Choose the way you want your life to go.'

'Um, okay, thanks Mrs Sharman.' I turned and walked away from her, so caught up in trying to make sense of what she had said that I barely heard the spoken greetings or saw the waved ones that were directed my way. It was only when I reached the bluff and my eyes feasted on the scene my senses had promised me that I let go of trying to reconcile Mrs Sharman's assertion with everything else I had been told about the Skills. As I looked down on the sea lapping at the beach between it and the grassy cliffs of our coastline, the panic I had felt earlier returned.

I couldn't move. Each breath of salty air seemed to carry with it the scent of the sweaty, unwashed men who had dragged me away from my home. Every splash of seawater on the beach was accompanied by the sound of those men grunting with the effort of their labour. Each caress of my face by the warm breeze transformed into a slap of the icy wind that had witnessed my kidnap.

I shook my head and rubbed my eyes. That didn't happen here. I left that experience behind when I woke up two weeks ago. This beach was safe. I was safe. A twang in my stomach corroborated the fact that deep down, I didn't believe it. Ma and Pa hadn't been able to keep me safe – in fact, the whole of our village had been cowed by a relatively small gang of men with large fists, heavy batons and strong intent. How could I be safe anywhere when Pa and Henry, two of the strongest people I had known, had been overpowered so easily? When I had been beaten, taken from my home and whipped?

I turned away from the sea, unable to look at it or the beach any longer, let alone walk the way I had planned to Shif's cottage. I ran back towards the village as fast as I could, followed by a sense of menace that I couldn't shake off, even when the familiar paddocks of the nearest cottages came into sight. I ran alongside them, trying but failing to take comfort from the sight of sunflowers lining the fence of one, brightly coloured pea flowers climbing up frames in another, and fruit bushes laden with berries in one further along.

By the time I reached the last paddock, I was running flat out and heaving with the effort, yet couldn't think of slowing my feet. They pounded onward at a tangent to the coast, taking me further inland towards the lone cottage at the edge of a forest that dared approach the coastline no further, in which Shif lived and worked. When I collapsed on its doorstep, finally feeling the sense of menace fade away, I felt a profound relief that Shif had asked the village Rock-Singers to build it there, decades before I was born.

'Well now, what have we here?' Shif's voice was almost drowned out by the thumping in my ears, but grew steadily louder. 'Devlin? You're a little early, lad. I've only just finished my

Chapter Two

morning forage and have yet to break my fast.' A full basket of herbs appeared on the step beside me, along with a pair of booted feet. 'Are you alright?' He crouched down beside me, his knees crunching sickeningly. 'Look at me, lad.' When I did, he frowned. 'You're not ill, you're frightened. What's got into you?'

I couldn't bring myself to tell him. I couldn't begin to describe the terror that the beach and sea had evoked in me, let alone try to convince him it was warranted; he knew of my dream and as far as he was concerned, that was all it was, regardless of the fact that I had woken from it with physical evidence of that which had befallen me whilst I slept. I was panting so hard that I thought I would faint, which saved me from having to fashion any sort of reply.

Shif got to his feet and, putting a hand under each of my armpits, said, 'Come on, up you get. I have a brew that will calm…'

I pulled away from the hands that would drag me away from my village and shuffled frantically backwards along the ground. I couldn't let them take me. I had to escape, to get back to Ma.

'Devlin.'

I blinked away the darkly bearded, heavily garbed man standing in front of me so that clean-shaven, grey-haired, lightly clothed Shif stood in his place. He had both of his hands out in front of him, as if attempting to calm one of the wild animals of the forest.

'I'm sorry, lad,' he said. 'I know better than to touch a scared animal, but one is never too old to make a mistake. I'll go on in and put the kettle on, and you just follow when you have a mind to. There's no rush.'

It was some time before I felt able to accept his invitation.

Chapter Three

Shif wasn't in his consulting room when I finally stepped into it. The basket he had been carrying sat empty on the wooden workbench that stretched across the far wall, and of the herbs it had contained, there was no sign. The door to his kitchen stood open as it never had when I had been to see him as a patient or to collect preparations for my family or neighbours, or when he had tested me for eligibility as an Apprentice Herbalist. I tiptoed across the large flagstones of the consulting room, as always feeling strangely reassured by all the jars and packets of dried herbs, and pots of living ones, that lined the grey stone walls upon shelves rendered invisible by the density of their loads.

When I reached the doorway, the sound of a teaspoon being tapped against the rim of a mug preceded my vision of the same. Shif pushed the mug across a small, circular table towards me and nodded to one of the chairs tucked beneath it. 'Take a seat,' he said, 'and drink this. You'll soon feel a lot better.'

'But what about…'

'Your testing?' Shif said. 'I don't think there's any merit in proceeding with that just yet, do you?'

I pulled the chair out from under the table and sat down. I sniffed at the steaming mug. 'What's in it?'

'I wonder if you can tell me,' Shif said, sitting down with a mug of his own and a pile of buttered toast.

I screwed up my nose. 'It's green.'

'Since most plants are, that doesn't narrow it down much, does it?' At the look of consternation on my face, Shif smiled. 'I'm teasing you, lad. Didn't I just say I wouldn't test you just yet? I won't tell you what it's made from in case you find yourself an Apprentice with a need to work that out for yourself, but I will tell you it's a tried and tested remedy for calming the mind.'

'I'm not crazy,' I blurted.

Shif looked at me levelly for a while and then said, 'Did you know that the most talented minds are often the most sensitive ones?'

I shook my head and looked away, unable to meet his gaze any longer.

'So then, you also won't know that in order for their talents to be free to be expressed, those minds need to feel safe. Protected.'

My eyes flicked back to his.

He smiled. 'Drink your tincture.'

∞

When I arrived home that afternoon, my parents were sitting at the kitchen table, waiting for me. Their mugs and the glass teapot favoured by my mother were all empty. Mother got to her feet and looked at me expectantly.

Father said, 'The fact that I'm home ahead of you makes me

think Shif held on to you for a good reason? A happy one? Your day went well?'

I couldn't prevent a grin from stretching across my face. 'It went really well. He didn't test me for herbalism, he taught me to draw. See here.' I flopped the large sketchpad Shif had given me onto the table in front of them and opened it to the first page, where there was a pencil sketch of my left boot. My parents looked down at it and then back up at me.

'Is this some kind of joke?' my father said.

I flicked to the next page of the sketchpad, where I had begun a sketch of the nearest of the wide-girthed oak trees that stood behind Shif's cottage. It was incomplete, since Shif had insisted I draw every part of the tree – even the veins on each individual leaf – in the minutest detail, but I was proud of how realistic I had made the trunk, lower branches and leaves appear, even in the absence of any colour.

'He said to tell you that my mind needs training before he or anyone else can test me,' I said, 'so that's what he's doing. He's happy to help me as often as I want him to – every day if need be, now that school's finished for the summer – as long as I promise to stay out of the way and be quiet when he's with his patients. He said there's no point in me seeing any of the other Testers until I can focus my mind better, and that drawing will help with that.'

'You've never had any trouble focusing on anything before,' my mother said. 'You never had any trouble at school... is this because of your latest dream?'

I shook my head. 'I failed my herbalism testing the day before I had the dream.'

'Shif must think you have potential to be going to so much trouble,' my father said thoughtfully. He looked at my mother. 'He knows what he's doing. And like Devlin said, school's out and it's not like he has anything better to do.' He looked back at me and said hopefully, 'Unless you want to help out on the boat with me and your brothers this summer? You could go to Shif's once we're back on land instead of staying to help us with the catch?'

I felt dizzy at the thought. Where my brothers had leapt at his offer to help on the boat during school holidays as soon as they reached double figures, and had enthusiastically chosen to follow him into his Trade, I'd refused his offer every time he'd made it since I reached ten years old. Whereas previously, I'd felt a sense of dread at the thought, this time I had to sit down before I fell down. All I could do was shake my head by way of reply, swallow down the terror that made my stomach clench and my legs tremble, and try to block out the memory of being caged with my brother's body below the deck of the boat that had taken me away from everything I had known and loved.

My eyes came to rest upon my sketchpad, and without thinking, I drew it to me while fumbling in my pocket for the pencil Shif had given me. As soon as I had it in my hand, I saw the oak tree in my mind, its branches still while its leaves rustled peacefully in the summer breeze. I added more leaves to the drawing, my hand a frantic blur of activity as my mind offloaded the image to which it had grasped as tightly as my fingers were now holding my pencil.

When I finally stopped drawing, I looked up from the completed tree to see my parents sitting on either side of me. Steam wafted gently from the spout of the teapot and the mugs before the two of them. My mother was clasping hers so tightly that her fingers were white.

Her face was equally pale as she said, 'That was, um… that was amazing, Devlin.'

'Shif taught you to do that in less than a day?' Father said.

'He told me to look at my subject with curiosity and dedication,' I said, repeating the exact words Shif had used. 'Then he told me to look away and see it in my mind, and let my fingers transfer what I could see to the sketchpad without thinking of anything else, and definitely without trying. The boot took me a long time as I kept losing the image of it in my mind and having to study it all over again, but the tree was easier. I can still see it now.'

Father waved his hand over my drawing. 'Clearly.'

'It's a beautiful drawing, Devlin,' Mother said. 'In fact, it's stunning. I wouldn't have believed you'd drawn it if I hadn't just witnessed it, let alone at the speed you did it. But why did you suddenly start drawing when we were in the middle of a conversation? It was like something came over you and you forgot where you were, or that we were even here.'

'I just…' I swallowed and looked down at the tree. 'I just suddenly felt like I needed to.'

I looked back up at them both. 'This is what I need to spend this summer doing, like Shif said. Nothing else.'

Father's brown eyes filled with the same disappointment they had held every time I refused to help on his boat, but when Mother reached out and squeezed his hand, he nodded slowly.

She smiled weakly at me. 'Why don't you run along and let all the other Testers know you'll be deferring your testing until Shif thinks you're ready?'

I got to my feet obediently, relieved to feel my legs steady beneath me once again, and made for the door.

'On your way home,' Father said, 'stop by the boat and tell your brothers to hurry if they're still there – I'll not let them get in the habit of being back late for dinner because of allowing themselves to be distracted by the Carling girls.'

The boat would be tied to the pier. And on the sea. I reached the door and grabbed hold of its frame, feeling dizzy again. My legs buckled, and I panted as Father's words transported me back

Chapter Three

to Ma scolding Henry for stopping off on his way home to chat up Clara Wilson, just before the press gangers arrived to shatter our lives. I shook off the hands that grabbed me and tried to run.

'Devlin!' Father's voice brought me back to myself. He took hold of my arms again and half dragged, half carried me back to my chair, where I sat panting. 'Go and get Shif,' he said to Mother.

'No,' I said. When Mother showed no sign of slowing her rush for the door, I shouted, 'NO!'

She hurried back to me and knelt in front of my chair, taking my hands in hers. 'But you're not well, Devlin.'

'Shif already knows what's wrong with me,' I said, my voice shaking, 'and his remedy is here.' I nodded towards my sketchpad. 'I'm okay. I just can't go near the boat. Or the sea. Or the beach.'

'Because of your dream?' Father said. 'But that's all it was; a dream. Nothing's going to happen to you if you go to the beach. And nothing's going to happen to you if you go to the boat.'

'YOU DON'T KNOW THAT!' I shouted and began to sob. 'I thought I was safe before. So did Pa and Henry, and look what happened to us all.'

'That was a dream, Devlin,' Father said, his voice quiet but with a harder edge to it now. 'You're fourteen years old, and you have to get to grips with what's real and what isn't.'

Mother squeezed my hands again. 'Devlin, look at me.'

I blinked away my tears and did as she asked. She took a handkerchief from her skirt pocket and wiped my face, telling me, 'You don't need to go near the boat. Your father can go and chivvy your brothers along. Just go and let the Testers know you won't be testing for the Skills for a while, okay? Can you do that for me?'

I nodded and she hugged me, then got to her feet, drawing me up with her to mine. I retraced my steps to the kitchen door in the silence that followed. It was only when I had walked the length of the hallway and opened the front door that the low hum of my parents' voices reached me. I didn't hang around to try to hear what they were discussing, for I knew. I didn't know, however, as I stood on one doorstep after another, thanking each Tester in turn for agreeing to test me belatedly and letting them know that I still wasn't ready, that it wouldn't just be a while before I'd test for the Skills – it would be never.

Chapter Four

By the time the summer days were noticeably shorter and the first leaves in Shif's forest had faded from a bright, vigorous green to one that was almost yellow, I had filled twelve sketchpads with drawings. Some of their pages were covered with a multitude of small sketches, some just one or two, and others contained the likeness of a single subject. All of my drawings, however, revealed the extent of the curiosity and dedication I had afforded all my subjects, a fact about which Shif was constantly delighted whenever he examined my work.

My mentor's approval and intermittent company were all that had made my summer of nightmares bearable after he refused to continue providing me with the sleeping potion that kept them at bay, telling me that its long-term use would do more harm than good and refusing to be swayed by either my or my mother's protestations.

I would go for a week or two without having a nightmare, then I might live through what I knew was my enslavement and torture on the warship HMS Royal Sovereign night after night for several weeks. During my – or, as I was in my nightmares, Jimmy's – experiences, I learnt to sail as part of a crew of one hundred and thirty-four, and, just as importantly when aboard a warship, to scramble; to leap into action at a moment's notice and instantly understand and follow orders whenever the situation required it, so that all on board could live to see another day. I also learnt what it was to be constantly cold, hungry and exhausted; to be beaten regularly; and to be terrified within seconds of waking from the sanctuary of exhausted slumber, both of the enemies of our nation and of those aboard the ship who would tolerate no hint of disobedience.

When Joplin and Kaplin learnt the reason for me waking them, night after night, with my screams, they thought it was hilarious, especially when I was in agony from injuries I was adamant I had sustained whilst asleep. But when I described aspects of sailing that I couldn't possibly have known without firsthand experience, they became confused and asked questions in order to make a liar of me, all of which I answered correctly and without hesitation. When I went on to describe battles at sea and the parts I had played in them, all far beyond anything they or my father had experienced as sailors of a simple fishing vessel, they were stunned. Then when I tried to warn them of the dangers of leaving dry land and begged them, sobbing, never to sail again, the uncomfortable glances exchanged between them were quickly replaced by grins and laughter, and the teasing returned.

They nicknamed me "Snail" when they heard about my increasing tendency, while out on errands for my mother, to rush to the safety of home at the mere suggestion by passing friends that I might want to join them on the beach or even to picnic with them in what should have felt to me like the safety of the hills a little further inland. The only way I could calm myself after arriving back home in a panic was to grab my latest sketchpad and a pencil, and draw my way out of it.

I couldn't contemplate leaving the safety of the village for any other reason than to run – flat out so that I always arrived gasping – to Shif's cottage. Whenever I arrived there, with or without notice, it was as if Shif had known when the exact moment of my arrival would be; a mug of steaming, calming tincture always sat waiting for me on the step before his closed door if he had a patient with him, or on the kitchen table if he were alone.

He never commented on my mood or appearance, even when, as the summer was fading, I turned up early one morning in my pyjamas, having bolted from the kitchen around whose table my brothers had been sitting, teasing me about the dangers they might face at sea that day.

'You've left your pad and pencils behind,' was all Shif said before leaving me sitting, gasping, at his kitchen table. He returned shortly afterward with a new sketchpad, his own box of pencils, a knitted pullover that was far too big for me, a pair of boots that were also too large, some thick socks, and a towel. He nodded in approval as I lowered my empty mug to the table. 'Good lad, that'll help. Dry your feet now, and put the socks and boots on. The pullover too, there's a nip in the air.'

I did as I was told, despite the warmth of his kitchen. He saw me glance at the fire roaring in the hearth and said, 'We'll not be stopping in here. Your ability to observe and memorise details has improved to the point that it needs challenging further than the drawing of stationary or barely moving objects will allow. We're going into the forest, and I expect you to fill a pad with sketches of the animals we'll find there by the time we come back out.' He raised a hand as I opened my mouth to protest and said, 'Don't tell me you can't fill a sketchpad in a day because at the speed you can draw now, you'll do it easily.

Now, I have a day of herb collecting ahead of me, so get the pullover and boots on and then get this down you.' He placed a plate piled high with toast on it beside the butter and jam already on the table, then fetched a knife and slid it across the polished surface to me.

I just sat and looked at him, my heart thumping painfully and my mouth suddenly too dry to eat. He pushed the sketchpad towards me along with his pencil box. 'Get drawing, lad. I expect you to put every bit of your considerable talent into producing a sketch of me, and I want it finished by the time I'm standing back here, washed and dressed.'

I noticed for the first time that, like me, Shif was in his pyjamas, however he'd still had tea and breakfast prepared and waiting for me. How, yet again, had he known I was on my way?

I jumped as he said, 'Staring into the distance won't get that sketch done, or your breakfast eaten.' He waved his hand from his face down towards his feet and grinned. 'Take in my beauty and then get to work. You don't have long.'

My terror of leaving his cottage for the unknown faded as I filled my mind with the image of him standing before me. I took in every crease and button of his white pyjamas with their yellow stripes, every tiny hair on his as yet unshaven chin, and every long, grey hair hanging loose around his shoulders. His eyes were bluer than I'd had cause to notice before, and although equidistant from his red, bulbous nose, they were slightly different in size and shape. The corners of his mouth crept an equal distance up his face when he smiled, and he had a dimple on his chin…

∽

Shif snatched my sketchpad from under my hand without giving me a chance to take in my completed drawing of him. He frowned and then chuckled. 'You know, this is a good reminder to me to be very careful what I ask for.'

I blinked. An empty plate sat on the table beside me. I licked my lips and tasted butter I couldn't remember smearing on toast that I couldn't remember eating, yet which the butter on the knife, crumbs on the plate and full feeling in my stomach told me I had.

Shif tore the sketch from the pad and waved it around. 'This is truly excellent. Never draw me again though, lad, my pride won't survive it a second time.' He handed the pad back to me and said, 'Bring this and a pencil with you – in fact, bring the whole box of them, it'll save you having to keep stopping and sharpening the same one.' He put his hand on my shoulder and clasped it firmly, compelling me to rise from my chair and walk ahead of him towards the door. 'From the moment we step outside, I want you on the lookout for something to sketch.'

Lookout. The word snatched at my mind and took me back to the nightmare that was never far from my waking world.

'Jimmy, get up to the crow's nest and keep a lookout. Anything gets close enough to fire its cannons on us, an' I'll have your hide.' The first mate's voice and the stench of his breath reached me as easily as the warmth from Shif's hand as he grasped my shoulder. He tightened his grip and propelled me to the kitchen door, through his consulting room and onto the step where he turned me to face the trees.

'There you go. There's a bird right there waiting for you, lad.' Shif released his grip on me and pointed, his finger in front of my face so I couldn't help but follow its direction. 'You'll have to concentrate hard, because she won't be on that branch for long. See how the feathers on her back are a darker brown than those on her chest? You'll need to find a way to distinguish the two shades from one another with a box full of grey pencils.'

The bird moved. As she hopped sideways along her branch,

the light caught a hundred different aspects of her. When she opened her wings and flew, it caught a thousand more, all of which filled my mind to the exclusion of all else…

'Page two complete.' Shif's voice was full of approval as it brought me back to my surroundings. I could have sworn only seconds had passed, yet my hand felt stiff and my sketchpad heavy in my hand. When I blinked, the lines and smudges with which I had covered its second page resolved into five detailed sketches of the bird at different stages of flight. 'Go on, into the forest with you.' He didn't give me a chance to think, to panic, to freeze; he grasped my shoulder again and guided me between the trees at a steady pace, despite my tripping and stumbling in boots that were too big for me. 'Another bird. See him? To your right.'

I drank in the shine of the bird's tiny black eyes and the way he tilted his head to one side as he stared back at me. The red feathers on his chest stood out starkly against the narrow band of grey surrounding it and the white of his abdomen and brown of his head and back, giving me no problems whatsoever despite having no coloured pencils to record his likeness. In fact, I barely needed to concentrate on his colouring at all; it was his expressions and body positions that required most of my focus, since they were great in number and he switched between them constantly during the seconds he was nearby.

By the time I became aware of my surroundings once more, I had covered two pages of my pad with his likeness, and Shif's hand was no longer upon my shoulder. A rustling behind me preceded the sound of his voice. 'Keep going, lad, you're not short of subjects in here.'

I felt a sudden hunger that had nothing to do with my stomach. I scanned the trees and bushes around me and felt a surge of excitement when movement caught my eye. My feet moved of their own accord, no longer tripping and stumbling despite their badly fitting protection and the multitude of tree roots erupting out of the forest floor, as I hurried after the yellow and black insect that buzzed ahead of me. The few seconds during which it stopped to explore the purple flower of a large bush were enough for me to register its features within my mind and then cover half a page with sketches of its tiny yet resplendent, intricately assembled body.

As soon as I had finished, my eyes flicked to my left in an attempt to locate the animal my ears assured me was there. The few seconds during which it was visible before it disappeared into the undergrowth were enough for me to register the exact brown of its fur, the length of its ears, the fear in its black, bulbous eyes, the white fluff of its tail and the strength in its hind legs as it hopped away. She, not it, I realised suddenly. I didn't have a chance to wonder how I knew her gender, as my hand demanded that my mind provide it with a constant supply of information as it sped across the page.

The moment I had emptied my mind of everything it had recorded of the rabbit onto the paper, I followed a sudden sense that a much larger animal browsed the lower branches of a tree some distance away. He wouldn't be there for long and if I didn't reach him quickly – and ever so quietly – my eyes would miss out on the chance to load my mind with what I knew would be nothing short of magnificent.

I flipped to a new page as I hurried between the trees and had a fresh pencil in my hand by the time my feet obeyed my sense that the time had arrived for utmost stealth. I crept from tree to tree without making a sound, finally hovering behind one close to where the animal browsed. I could smell him now; the heady musk of a powerful male in his prime. My hunger to see and capture him on paper was greater than any physical hunger I had ever felt – even that which plagued me in my nightmares.

I peered around the tree, knowing that while the light breeze carried my scent away from him, and my sudden ability to move through the forest without sound had prevented him from knowing of my approach, the sight of me would cause him to take flight.

He was every bit as breathtaking as I had known he would be. I feasted on the image of brown fur, rippling muscles, intelligent eyes, and twin bones extending from his skull into a double threat of the damage he could inflict were he cornered or denied a mate…

~

I blinked as my sketchpad was prised out of one painfully cramping hand and my pencil from the other. Two large baskets sat on the ground beside me, one heaped high with different leaves and the other neatly packed with bark from what must have been more than a dozen types of tree, judging by the range of colours and textures. I was sitting at the base of the tree around which I had peered hours before, judging by the sun's position high above me. My stomach announced its expectation of lunch with a loud rumble. I got to my feet and brushed the forest floor from the pullover whose length had ensured my comfort as I sat drawing.

Shif finished leafing through my sketches and slapped the cover of the pad shut before handing it back to me. 'Well, I think we can call it a day, lad. You've surpassed even my expectations, filling a pad in just a morning, not to mention covering most of its sheets with a stag, of all beasts. Want to tell me how you found him?' He looked at me intently and I suspected he already knew.

'The same way you knew the first bird we saw was female and the second was male, I think,' I said. 'And the same way you always know when I'm on my way to you and have tea ready?'

His eyes crinkled at their corners as he smiled. 'I wondered how long it would take you to figure it out. All you need, in order to know lots of things, is to sidestep your brain.'

I frowned, trying to relate what he had said to the morning that had just passed by without me even noticing it. It was only then that I realised I had no idea where I was, and therefore no idea how far I was from the safety of his cottage or my home. I turned around, desperately looking for a way that might take me to either.

Shif tapped the cover of my sketchpad, making me jump. 'Let's head back to the cottage, shall we? You've discovered the extent of your talent for sketching, now it's time for you discover how well you can paint. You can start with the birds.' He slid back the cover of the pad in my hand and pointed to the sketches of the little brown bird on the top page. 'You channelled your observations of her into these. When you stand in front of a canvas with a paintbrush in your hand, you'll need to dive back into them and interpret the shades of grey as the colours your mind held while directing your hand. Make a start on that now while you're following me.' He picked up a basket in each hand and strode off the way I supposed we must both have come.

As I stared at the sketches I had done what seemed like days ago, I calmed down and a question arose in my mind. 'How did you find…' I realised the answer before I could get it all out. Shif had found me the same way I found the stag when I had been caught up in the process of sketching. Suspicion dawned. Shif had encouraged me to spend my summer sketching in order to prepare my mind for Skills testing. Did being able to find the stag mean I was now ready? I stumbled after him, again catching the toes of my overlarge boots on roots and creeping plants as I hadn't whilst pursuing the stag. 'Are you going to test me for herbalism soon?' I asked and promptly tripped and fell flat on my face.

I pushed myself onto my knees, spitting out the rich brown

mulch that made up the forest floor. Shif extended a knobbly hand and pulled me to my feet, chuckling. 'No, lad.'

Relief flooded me and I couldn't put my finger on why. 'The summer holidays are nearly over though. I'll be back at school in a few weeks, and I still won't know what I'll be doing when I leave in a year's time. My parents won't be pleased.'

'And how about you?' Shif said, grabbing a handful of my pullover and shaking it so that most of the mulch clinging to it fell back to where it belonged. 'Are you pleased?'

'About not being tested? Um, yes. Yes I am.'

'Because?'

As soon as I thought about it, Herbalism seemed to loom over me, its unfamiliarity as scary as drawing felt safe. But it was more than that. I was happy when I was observing and being curious. I was calm while my fingers were moving a pencil around a page. It felt like a different part of me was in charge when I was transferring everything I could see onto paper, from the normal part that had me constantly anxious. I bent down and picked up my sketchpad with a shaking hand.

'Because, Devlin?' Shif's voice was as kind as ever but carried a note of firmness, which, along with his use of my name, told me he wanted an answer. An honest one.

I looked down at the sketchpad in my hand. 'I'd rather draw. And paint. I'm good at sketching and I know I'll be good at painting, because I can already see the paintings that'll come from these; I can picture them in my mind as easily as I can see their subjects when I look at my sketches.' I raised my eyes to meet his. 'But I have to train in a Skill or a Trade.' I gulped.

'You know, there was a time when there were no Skills,' Shif said. 'No Skills and no Trades. They only came into being when people discovered how to do them and found they were better at their new talent than anything else. I don't need to test you for herbalism because I already know you have an aptitude for it – more than aptitude, actually; if you had the inclination, you could be one of the most talented Herbalists The New has ever known. But you don't, and that means you would be a barely adequate one. In fact, if I were to test you, I doubt you'd pass. Those who show an aptitude for the Skills are those who have the will for them, in my experience.'

I frowned, his words prodding my mind until it dredged up a memory of the conversation I'd had with Phyllis from next door that had so flummoxed me. *Show aptitude or don't, it's up to you. Choose the way you want your life to go.* That was what she had said.

'So why do we test for them at all?' I said. 'Why don't we all just choose what we want to do?'

'We're all doing that constantly, lad, we just refuse to believe it.' Shif shook his head and chuckled. 'We humans are a funny lot, there's no doubt about it. Why do you think I prefer to live with the animals and trees rather than in the village with the rest of you?'

'Everyone thinks it's so you're closer to where you get most of your herbs from. But it's really because you think we're all crazy.' I chuckled with him.

'I'm just as crazy a lot of the time. The animals and trees just stop it being all the time.' Shif straightened his face. 'I wasn't going to do this just yet, but since you're currently still under their influence, I'm going to ask you to tell me what you choose to do. There are no rules here, and no expectations. All that exists here in the forest is truth.'

'I choose to draw and paint. But doing that isn't a Skill, it isn't even a Trade…'

'Sensing and finding subjects who call to you to capture their likenesses for the good of us all, recording the details of life that you see and we miss, producing permanent reminders of the beauty of the world around us, moving us with your talent – that is very definitely a Skill.' Shif held his hand out to me. 'Congratulations, Devlin, at being the first to practise the newly recognised Skill of artistry.'

'Um, but it isn't recognised,' I said. 'It's something people do in their spare time.'

'Not the way you do it, they don't,' Shif said, his hand still outstretched. 'I can sketch as well as the next person, but my art just shows what my eyes see. Yours shows what your soul perceives.' His voice broke slightly as he added, 'Your sketches can move a person.' He cleared his throat and continued, 'I can't wait to see what your paintings can do. Your Skill is recognised. By me. And I'm just the first who will do so.'

I shook his hand.

Chapter Five

I took to carrying a sketchpad and pencil with me whenever I left home; not only because I recognised sketching as a necessity for coping with the panic that was never far away when I was beyond the safety of our cottage, but because the hunger for new subjects that had wakened within me in the forest became insatiable.

When I saw friends approaching, I would immediately start sketching anything I could see, giving me a reason not to go with them to wherever they invited me, as well as keeping my mind away from the terror that threatened to take hold of me at the very thought of doing so. When the sound of the sea's waves lapping on the shore reached my ears, I would stop in my tracks and sketch rather than running for home. When I woke in the night, screaming with terror and agony from the most recent injuries inflicted upon me aboard HMS Royal Sovereign, I would reach under my bed for the pad and pencil I kept hidden there and offload everything from my mind onto the paper. By the time I turned the page to a fresh one so that I'd never have to see the record of my nightmare again, the fear and pain it had evoked in me had been expelled, and I was able to go back to sleep.

While I never transferred the contents of my night pad to canvas, I used all the sketches of observations I made during the day to create painted "works of art", as Shif called them, at such a rate that during the remaining two weeks of the summer holidays, I exhausted his supply of canvas.

'You'll need to go to the Weavers' workshop tomorrow and ask them for another roll,' Shif told me as he stretched his last segment across the frame that would hold it at the right tension for me to paint on it. I flexed my fingers, keen to put it on the easel that had been his but he had insisted was now mine, and start painting the image from the sketchpad beside me that felt alive in my mind and eager to get out. 'But before you do that,' he continued, 'you must tell your parents which Skill you'll be contributing to the village. They can't hear it second hand as a result of the Weavers' gossiping.'

'What if I don't tell the Weavers the canvas is for me?'

Shif grimaced as he pulled the last corner of the fabric into place on the frame. He affixed it with a staple and gave it to me. 'Who would you tell them it's for?'

'Um, you?' I clutched the frame much more firmly than was necessary.

'And when they ask how I came to use a roll of canvas that I only collected three weeks ago and they know full well would normally last me at least a year, maybe as long as two?'

I hesitated.

'Telling untruths is hard work, as well as counter to how your parents raised you,' Shif said. 'You paint with your heart and soul, lad. If your art is to be the whole truth – and trust me, it'll lose its magic if it's anything else – your conscience must be clear.' He

Chapter Five

took hold of the frame again, gently prised it from my grip and rested it on the easel. 'Devlin, look at me.'

I found it difficult to raise my eyes to meet his, but he waited in silence until I did and then said, 'You're the bravest person I know. You have more than enough courage to tell your parents how you intend to spend the rest of your life.' His eyes told me that which he never had; he knew my nightmares were far more than normal nightmares.

'What if they won't accept that being an Artist is a Skill, or even a Trade?'

Shif turned and rummaged through the canvases piled on a nearby table. He selected two and held them up, looking from one to the other for a few moments before handing one of them to me. 'Show your parents this and tell them I dare them, or anyone else, to dispute it.' His friendly wink did little to ease my anxiety, but I took the painting from him and rolled it up. He nodded at the waiting blank canvas. 'Get going with that first, and you'll feel more than up to the challenge. Do you have all the colours you need?'

I put the rolled canvas on top of the others and bent to check the vials of paints sitting on a shelf below the window, out of reach of the sunlight pouring through it. I compared the colours in my head with those I knew I could create on my palette by mixing contents of the vials and said, 'Yes, thank you.'

Shif glanced at the sketch that lay tantalisingly by my easel and nodded in approval. 'Get going, lad. I'm looking forward to seeing the results of this one.'

∽

Had the paint been dry, it would have been my latest painting that I would have been clutching to my chest as I walked home that evening; not because it was the one I would have chosen, but because Shif had assured me it was my best yet. In fact, he had been on the verge of insisting I take it while still wet, regardless of the fact that dirt and dust would have stuck to it and should the dark clouds overhead have chosen to divest themselves of their contents early, it would have been ruined.

'I've known your mother since she was your age, and you've captured everything about her in that portrait,' he had said wistfully, watching over my shoulder as my hand swept over the canvas with its final few strokes. 'I can see her as she was then, how she is now and every year in between, and I have absolutely no concept of how you've managed it. This isn't just Skill, lad, it's genius.' His voice cracked slightly and I turned in surprise to see him standing with his hand over his heart. He transferred it to my shoulder and said, 'I'm prouder of you than I can say, and your parents will be too, when they see this. I almost wish I was coming with you, so I could see the look on your father's face.'

I tried to persuade him to come with me regardless of the fact that I refused to risk the portrait by taking it home before it was ready. Since we had denied one another's requests, I walked home alone and it was the painting he had previously selected that I carried rolled up inside my coat.

My footsteps slowed as I approached the village. Smoke drifted from a few chimneys as the first fires were lit in hearths that had been empty since the end of spring. I shivered and buttoned my coat as the nippy wind that had prompted the fires reached me. I shuddered at the smell of salt it carried, from which I had been spared by the strong earthy smell exuding from the forest by Shif's cottage. Were it not for the painting cocooned in my non-waterproof coat and the spots of rain that began to slap the top of my head, I would have stopped to sketch the patterns made by the smoke leaving the chimneys before being dashed to

Chapter Five

nothing by the sea breeze. As it was, I quickened my pace to a jog, then further to a fast run as the rain came down in earnest, silently thanking Shif for the waterproof cover he had fashioned for the sketchpad currently slung over my shoulder.

By the time I stood dripping on the mat inside the front door of my home, my scalp stinging from the ferocity of the rain, it was dark outside, though it should still have been light. My mother came hurrying out of the kitchen, wiping her hands on a towel that she then flung over her shoulder.

'Let's get you out of that coat and into a nice, hot bath,' she said, her arms outstretched in anticipation of stripping me where I stood.

I shook the strap of my sketchpad cover down my arm and leant it against the wall, relieved to see water droplets running off its waxed coating.

Kaplin's head poked out of the kitchen. 'Bath? Me and Jop were at sea all day and we never got offered a bath.'

Mother waved a hand over her shoulder at him, still intent on disrobing me where I stood. 'You're seventeen years old and perfectly capable of running yourself one whenever you care to. Besides, it was dry when you came in.'

'It wasn't dry on the sea,' Kaplin protested. 'I got soaked pulling the last net in. Just because I was dry when I got home didn't mean I didn't suffer when I was wet. I could be brewing a cold right now.'

My mother yanked my coat down my back in an attempt to persuade it down my arms, to which it seemed to be glued. I flung the rolled up canvas, over which I had stooped in order to keep it dry, as far away from me as possible so it would remain free of water.

'If you get a cold, then you'll also be perfectly capable of nursing yourself better,' my mother said with a grunt as she increased the effort she was putting into her battle with my coat. 'You're a Fisherman and as your father has told you over and over, being able to look after yourself so you don't miss a day's fishing is every bit as important as being able to sail and fish.'

Kaplin's eyes followed my canvas as it rolled down the hallway towards him. 'What's that?' he said, all thoughts of being mothered forgotten.

'It's nothing you'd be interested in,' I said. 'Just something Shif wants me to show Mother and Father.'

Kaplin looked at me appraisingly. 'If you say I won't be interested, then I'm thinking I'll be more than interested.' His body joined his head in the hallway just as, with a final yank, my mother freed me from my coat.

I ran to where the canvas had come to a stop and picked it up between my thumb and forefinger. I held it out in front of me so I wouldn't drip on it, and turned to face my mother so that Kaplin was behind me and couldn't grab it.

My mother slapped her hands to her sides in exasperation. 'You're dripping all over the hall. And look at those muddy footprints after your father just mopped the floor. Anyone would think we both enjoy clearing up after you lot.'

I thrust the canvas at her, my desperation to avoid it being commandeered by Kaplin and as a predictable consequence, Joplin, greater than the fear I had felt at telling her and Father about the future I had chosen for myself. 'Shif told me to show you this and tell you he dares you to dispute I'm to be an Artist,' I blurted out.

Mother looked at me as she took it, her frown of worry appearing that always darkened her face at any mention of my nightmares or the strategy I had developed for coping with their consequences. She held a hand up to Kaplin as he skidded to a stop beside me, and shook her head and glared at him as he reached to grab it from her. When he lowered his hand, she slowly, carefully – almost unwillingly – unfurled the canvas.

Her frown softened and then disappeared altogether. Her eyes filled with tears and she put a hand to her heart just as Shif had done earlier in the day, allowing one side of the canvas to curl in on itself. She looked from it to me. 'You did this?'

I nodded uncertainly. She touched a hand to my cheek and held it there for a moment before hurrying past me towards the kitchen, my wet, muddy shivering forgotten.

Kaplin looked after her and then stared at me. 'What is it? What did you do?' When I didn't answer, he gave a sharp sigh of frustration and ran after my mother. 'What did Snail do? Let me see.'

I stood, rooted to the spot in the complete silence that followed. When it continued without interruption, I bent down to unlace my boots. I pulled them off unhurriedly and put them on the rack by the door, then padded across the grey flagstones of the hallway, leaving wet footprints and a trail of drips in my wake.

I reached the kitchen doorway to find my parents and brothers poring over my painting, each of them holding a corner of it flat against the kitchen table. At the sound of my wet socks slapping on the kitchen floor, they all turned to look at me. I frowned and checked behind myself, not recognising the way my family were regarding me and thinking for a moment that someone must have let themselves into the house and made their way to the kitchen behind me. There was no one there. I turned back to my family to find my father holding up the painting of the stag for me to see.

'How did you…' He shook his head and tried again. 'When did you…' He stared at me, waiting for me to answer the questions he had been unable to complete.

'I found him by following a feeling I had,' I said. He stared at me blankly. 'I painted that from some sketches I did of him when I was in the forest with Shif. He was collecting herbs and bark, and I was sketching things that move instead of things that stay still. It's much harder because I have to observe everything about them instantly and then let it all out of my mind and onto the paper through my hand before I forget. When I filled a sketchpad in a morning, Shif said it was time for me to learn to paint. We went back to the cottage, and he showed me how to mix the paints he makes on a palette to get the exact colours I want, and how to stretch a canvas over a frame and treat it so I can paint on it. That was a few weeks ago. He wanted me to show you that painting. Actually, he wanted me to show you another one more, but the paint was still wet.' I looked at my mother. 'It's of you.'

She put a hand to her heart again and her other hand shook as she reached out to the painting my father was still holding up. She gently traced the outline of the stag with her forefinger, as if stroking the actual beast himself. 'He was scared of you, but he trusted you at the same time,' she whispered. 'He's gentle by nature, but he'll fight to the death if he has to. He's young and has a lot to learn, but he's also wise, as if he was born that way. I've never seen him before, but I feel like I know him. I even know he's alive right now. How is that possible?'

'Shif reckons it's a Skill,' I said. 'He told me he's recognised it formally as one, so that makes it one, and it's how I'll be contributing to the village. As an Artist.'

Kaplin opened his mouth to speak, but I quickly added, 'And he dares anyone to dispute it.' The younger of my brothers closed his mouth.

'Seriously, Snail,' Joplin said, pointing to the painting, 'you did this? Shif didn't do it and tell you to pass it off as yours to get you out of testing? Everyone knows he's taken you under his wing.'

I felt my cheeks heating in anger at his accusation that I would lie, then gulped as I remembered my earlier intention to do exactly that in order to avoid announcing my chosen profession.

'Of course he did it,' my mother snapped. 'I can see Devlin in that painting as easily as I can see the stag.' She turned back to me. 'And you say you've just finished a portrait of me?'

I nodded, my teeth chattering with the chill that was seeping through to my bones. 'When Shif saw it, he said he could see you at my age, your age now, and every age in between.'

Mother put a hand on Father's arm. 'Run Devlin a bath and see he stays in it until he's warmed through. I'm going to Shif's.'

He put his hand on hers and held it there as rain hammered against the window. 'Not in this storm, you're not. You'll be in no better state by the time you get there than Devlin is.'

She pulled away from him. 'I have to see it, Lennon. Look at the stag again and try to tell me you don't understand.'

Father sighed. 'Mowaya, please stay here. I'll go to Shif's and fetch the painting. I assume it's a similar size to this one?' He looked at me quizzically.

'It's smaller. I had to fit it on Shif's last piece of canvas.'

Father nodded. 'So then, if I wear my cape, I can hold it underneath. I won't let it come into contact with me or the cape; I promise the painting will reach here intact.' He stared at Mother until she nodded, then quietly let out the breath he had been holding.

It was always entertaining for my brothers and me to watch him try to talk her out of something on which she had set her mind, yet neither of my brothers drew attention to the fact, or even grinned at, Father's obvious relief that for once, he had succeeded. Instead, they watched him hurry out of the room, then Joplin turned back to the painting now held by my mother, and Kaplin turned to me.

'So if you're an Artist, how will you be contributing to the village, exactly? I mean, we can't eat your paintings, can we? Or drink out of them or sit on them.' He turned back to the painting.

I tried to remember what Shif had said when he had been trying to convince me I should be an Artist, but for the life of me, couldn't. 'Um, I'm not sure.' I felt a familiar heaviness in my heart as I waited for my brothers' teasing to start. They remained silent.

'Devlin's rendered the two of you speechless,' Mother said. 'That's contribution enough to the village, don't you think?' The corners of her mouth twitched as she held her hand out to me. 'Come on, upstairs with you now and into the bath. If you're going to be The New's first Artist, you can be a clean, dry and warm one.'

I took her hand and allowed myself to be led towards the kitchen doorway through the rare and continuing silence. A quick glance over my shoulder revealed Joplin now standing close by one of the lanterns that hung on the kitchen wall, his nose only a hand's width away from my painting whilst the candlelight flickered over it, with Kaplin peering over his shoulder.

My mother squeezed my hand and whispered. 'Shif was right. About everything.'

Chapter Six

I followed Mother up the stairs. 'What do you mean? How was Shif right?' I asked her.

She turned and smiled down at me. 'He was right to teach you to draw and have you spending the summer getting so good at it, and he was right to recognise your talent as a new Skill, because that's exactly what it is. There's absolutely no other word for it.' She held both of her hands out to me and pulled me up the last step onto the landing beside her, where she hugged me. 'I've been so worried about you, Devlin. Your father and I both have. We know you're still having nightmares and they're causing you pain, no matter how quickly you stifle your screams, but Shif said…' Her breath caught in her throat.

I pulled away from her. 'What did he say? What else was he right about?'

She swallowed. 'He just said to leave you be – that you're the only one in your head and you'd find your own way through what's bothering you. He said if he saw you in pain or distress, he'd give you something that would help, but beyond that, we should trust you to find a way to cope with what's happening to you. It hasn't been easy for either of us and if we didn't trust Shif as much as we do, we'd have ignored his advice, but I'm so relieved we didn't. These last few weeks, I've noticed you shining so much brighter, despite your nightmares, and now I know why. You've discovered a talent like nothing I've ever seen or heard of, and I couldn't be prouder of you. My son, an Artist!'

She hugged me again before pushing me away and brushing at the front of her blouse and skirt, as if doing so would somehow dry the water that now soaked her almost as thoroughly as it did me.

'I know, into the bath with me,' I said, and made for the bathroom door. I turned back to Mother as a thought occurred to me. 'There's a sketchpad hidden under my bed.' When she lifted her eyebrows, I added, 'The sketches in it aren't from here. I can't look at them, but you can. If you want. Just put the pad back when you've finished and make sure it's open at a new page, so it's ready for when I need it.'

She disappeared into my room in a flurry of skirt, all concern about her wet clothes forgotten. Glad of the opportunity to run my own bath, I turned the hot tap until it would turn no more, and the cold tap just half a turn. I stripped quickly, relishing the prospect of the hot water – which I knew my mother would consider overly hot if I gave her a chance to test it – stinging my skin as I sank into it, and was soon delighting in the sensation.

I languished in the bath until my head pounded with its heat and I feared I would faint. I sat up, leant towards the edge of the bath and slithered over its rounded edge onto the floor. When my head stopped spinning, I stood up and, grinning at having survived another of my "extreme baths" as my brothers called them, rubbed myself dry with a towel. It was only as I was wrapping it around my waist that I realised my mother had been

Chapter Six

quiet for an awfully long time. I dumped my wet clothes in the wash basket and tiptoed along the landing to my bedroom, concerned about what I would find when I got there. There were only sketches in the book – disjointed outpourings of my observations and emotions – and not the paintings that really brought them to life, so they shouldn't have bothered her too much... should they?

I peered around my bedroom door. My mother was standing by the side of my bed with my sketchpad in her hands. She had lit the lantern on my bedside table, and its glow softened the greyness of the stone walls and seemed to hold at a distance the harsh beating of the rain against the windows. Had its light not flickered, causing the resulting shadows to move in unison, I would have believed for a moment that it was time that was standing still rather than just her, for she was completely motionless.

I waited by the door, unsure of what to do. I could see grey lines on the page she was studying, so if I approached her, I would risk seeing that which I knew I absolutely couldn't risk seeing. But she was staring at the page with an intensity that unnerved me, and she had been in my room and presumably standing in that spot for too long for everything to be okay.

'Mother?' I ventured finally.

She jumped and the look on her face as she turned to me was one of pure terror.

I rushed to her side without further thought and took the pad from her without looking at it. I threw it back under my bed. 'I'm sorry, I shouldn't have told you about my sketches. They're just how I cope with my nightmares, like Shif said, and I thought you might want to see them, but I was wrong. Mother? Talk to me.'

She looked down at me with eyes that weren't her own. 'Jimmy?' she said. 'So it's true, you're alive. I had a feeling you were. And you're with your uncle, that's good to know. But what about Henry?' As her eyes filled with tears, I recognised them.

'Ma?' I whispered.

She bit her lip. 'I'm glad you're with your uncle. If I thought my sister would believe me, I'd tell her Jacob's alive and you and he are looking out for each other, but she'll tell me this was just a dream.' She stroked my hair from my eyes. 'You're looking well, my Jimmy, despite what they've done to you. You always were a strong lad, like your pa.' She took hold of my chin so firmly it hurt. 'You stay alive, do you hear me? You stay alive and you come back to me. You're all I've got now.'

'I will, Ma,' I said. 'I promise.'

She nodded and pulled me to her. Where Mother's hugs were always soft, warm and comforting, Ma's was hard and desperate. The pain of being wrenched away from her flooded through me as if it had just happened, and I hugged her back every bit as fiercely, not wanting to let her go. I lost track of how long we stood so, and it was only when the front door slammed that we broke apart.

'I'm back,' Father called out. 'It took me twice as long to get home as it did to get to Shif's, the wind was that fierce off the sea. Come and take the painting from me, will you, while I get out of this cape? It was worth fighting the weather for, there's no doubt about that.'

Mother wiped her face. 'What... just... happened?'

I managed a half smile. 'You were there with me. In my other life. You were my mother there, just like you are here. You recognised me and Uncle Jacob from my sketches and it made you remember.'

She shook her head slowly. 'I was there with you?'

My brothers' voices joined my father's in conversation downstairs. Mother looked towards the door and then back at me. 'They can't know about this, they won't understand. I don't understand.' She shivered and Ma flicked across her face briefly as she remembered living Ma's life. Feeling Ma's grief. She swallowed hard. 'Your father will just be scared for me as well as for you if he knows about this.'

'Mowaya? Where are you?' Father called out. 'You need to see this.'

'I won't say anything,' I told Mother. 'I promise.'

I followed her out of the room and down the stairs.

'Not dressed yet, Devlin? You're shivering again,' Father said. He gestured to Joplin to hold up the painting that had again rendered both my brothers speechless and said, 'The stag had me convinced that Shif knew what he was doing, having our boy draw and paint all summer, but this – well! The whole village will be lining up to be painted when they see this.'

Mother gasped and grabbed hold of my hand. She squeezed it so hard, I would have yelped had I not returned the gesture with equal intensity. Mother looked out of the painting as a young girl, the mature woman she was now, and every other version she had ever been of herself. Including Ma. Having just lived through her, Mother recognised her. And having just seen her in Mother's eyes, she practically screamed to me from among all the other aspects of Mother I had painted into the portrait, so that I did too.

'That's her,' she whispered almost imperceptibly to me, her lips barely moving.

I nodded. 'It's you.'

'Of course it's you, Mowaya, the likeness is incredible – in fact, it's more than incredible, it's astonishing,' Father said, looking between his wife and the painting. 'It's you and... so much more that I can't even begin to describe. Will you do me next, Devlin? Since this storm is showing no signs of abating, you could do your sketch this evening and the painting tomorrow?'

'He's back at school tomorrow,' Mother said, sounding a little more like herself.

'I still have to go to school?' I said, rubbing my arms to try to stop shivering.

'Of course you do,' my mother replied. 'You're fourteen. You'll do your last year at school while your mind becomes accustomed to the idea of the Skill you'll be training in, just like all your friends. It'll give everyone else in the village a chance to get used to the idea too.'

'He won't be training though, will he?' Father said. 'There's no one to train him. Shif told me that Devlin's far surpassed his own ability to draw and paint, and there may never be another Artist as talented in our lifetime. Our son is a Master Artist before he's even left school!'

'So then, he can paint and draw in his spare time for the next year. Then, when he's old enough to be a Master Artist, he'll truly be one,' Mother said stubbornly. Her voice softened as she said, 'Devlin, go and get dressed, then you can sketch your father while your brothers and I cook dinner.'

Chapter Seven

By the time I left school a year later, every living room in the village had at least one of my paintings hanging on the wall. Since I wouldn't be serving an apprenticeship, my parents asked Shif, as the only one to have given me any kind of training, to perform my qualification ritual for me.

He stood before me in our living room, looking unusually smart and well groomed, his hand on my shoulder. 'Devlin Bakewell, following a successful if non-existent apprenticeship, I declare you not only a qualified Artist, but a Master of the Skill of artistry. Congratulations to you and your family.' I thought I saw a tear in his eye, but he winked it away.

Joplin's hand appeared between us and stroked Shif's smooth cheek. 'So this is what it takes for you to risk a close shave,' my brother said. 'Or are you hoping Dev will sketch you to mark this joyous occasion, and you're wanting to look your best?'

I pushed Joplin's hand away and punched him lightly in the gut. 'Shut up, Jop. As it goes, I was hoping to sketch all of you together for a painting to mark the day.'

'All of us?' Mother said, handing a glass of ale to Shif. She hugged me and whispered, 'You know I'm not comfortable being painted. Not since... well, you know.'

'No one else can see Ma in your portrait,' I whispered back. 'They can see different sides to you they can't put their finger on, but no more than that.'

'Your father knows something changed the day he brought the portrait home.' Mother whispered urgently. 'He knows there've been occasions when I've gone running into your room during the night and woken you before you've even started screaming. He just doesn't know it's whenever you're with Jimmy, or that it's her who has me running to you before I'm properly awake myself, because she somehow knows when you're living as her son and needs me to watch you sketching so she knows what's happening to him.'

'You don't have to be scared of her.'

'I'm not scared of her. I'm scared that if you paint me now, I'll have to see how she's doing after another year of worrying about Jimmy. About you. I'll have to feel her pain and exhaustion, and I'm not sure I have the strength.'

'Is anyone else allowed to congratulate our son, love?' Father's voice caused us to jump apart from one another exactly as it had ten months previously.

'Sorry, Len,' she said, the tremble in her voice so slight as to be barely perceptible. She gestured to me. 'May I present our son, the Artist.'

Father drew me into a warm embrace and then passed me my first glass of ale. He lifted his own glass, and Shif, my mother and brothers followed his lead. 'To our Devlin, the first Master Artist of The New,' he said.

'The first Master Artist of The New,' the others echoed and

took a sip of ale. My brothers then drained their glasses and belched loudly in unison.

'Anyone would think we'd practised that,' Kaplin said proudly.

'Anyone would think that at eighteen and twenty, you'd have grown out of it by now,' Father said, then surpassed their belches with one of his own. All three of them laughed and clinked their empty glasses together in mutual congratulation.

As always, I was left on the outside of the closeness they shared. Borne out of their blood tie but solidified by their mutual love of, and time working together on, the sea, I knew I couldn't hope to be included in it. I caught my mother's eye and realised for the first time that I didn't mind; the bond between her and me was so strong, it spanned lifetimes. She smiled at me faintly, as if she knew what I was thinking.

'You know, you've sketched or painted each of us before, lad,' Shif said. 'But you've never painted yourself. How about a self-portrait to mark the day, instead of one of us lot? One your parents can keep so they can see you every day once you're off travelling, sharing your Skill with the other villages?'

My stomach clenched so violently, I thought I would vomit. I looked to Mother for reassurance, only to find Ma looking back at me, her face frozen in panic. I glanced at my father and brothers, all three of whom were racing to drain their refilled glasses of ale, then at Shif, who looked between my mother and me with relaxed interest. He tilted his head briefly in my mother's direction, and I followed his lead and moved to stand closer to her.

'You have a Skill that is, as far as we know, unique,' he said quietly to me. 'It shouldn't remain that way. If there's the slightest chance you could inspire others to discover a similar level of artistry within themselves, then for the good of all in The New, I really feel you should try.' He paused until Ma tore her eyes away from my face and met his. 'Sketching your way out of the village will enable you to leave, lad,' he said whilst holding her gaze. 'The portrait of yourself that you'll create today will help your mother to let you go.'

It was Mother who shook her head and looked pleadingly from Shif to me.

'It's necessary for both of you,' Shif said quietly but firmly.

As was so often the case, I had a feeling he knew far more about our situation than he had been told; I hadn't divulged to anyone what had been happening between Mother and me since she first saw the sketches of my nightmares, and I knew from the fear and confusion darkening her expression that she hadn't either.

Her face was Ma's again as it hardened. 'No mother should have her son taken away from her.'

Shif showed no sign of having taken her sternness as a rebuke. He laid a hand gently on her arm. 'But every mother should know when it's time to let him go.'

Ma's face softened back to Mother's. She shook her head again, frantically now. 'Devlin's fifteen. He's far too young to be setting out on his own.'

'Some of his friends are packing their bags as we speak, ready to set off in the morning for villages whose Masters have spaces for Apprentices. It's time for Devlin to go.' Shif's tone was gentle and respectful, but carried his absolute certainty that he was right.

I felt dizzy with panic. Though I could hear Joplin telling Kaplin and Father a joke, I couldn't make sense of it and their consequent laughter sounded far away... and suddenly it was far away.

I put a hand to my jaw, my head ringing from the punch that the second mate had just dealt me, and spat a bloody tooth out onto the wet, wooden boards of HMS Royal Sovereign's deck. A wave broke over her gunwale and landed on top of me, taking the air out of my lungs and stinging my skin with its frigidity.

'If you're not back on your feet by the time I count to three,' the second mate growled, 'I'll take the greatest pleasure in knocking out a few more of those beau'ies.'

'I never knew you could count, Sam,' the first mate called from his place at the wheel.

The second mate laughed, revealing a maw of jagged, blackened teeth. He cracked his knuckles and replied, 'I counted well enough the times I put you down 'afore you finally stayed down, last time we wrestled.'

I scrambled to my feet while his attention was elsewhere and returned to my task of pulling at the rope I had left dangling when he knocked me off my feet, at a speed I hoped would protect me from another clout.

'Devlin.' The voice was faint and unworldly, and spoke a name that wasn't mine, yet I knew it called to me. I found it comforting and clung to it... and found myself standing back in the living room with Shif's arm around my waist, holding me upright, and Mother standing in front of me, her face less than a hand's width from mine. I rubbed my aching jaw and, relieved to feel all my teeth still there, searched her eyes for Ma, but it was definitely Mother who had hold of my arms and was gently shaking me. She put a hand to my cheek. 'Oh, thank goodness.'

She risked a look over her shoulder to where my father and brothers were continuing to drink and make merry, then leant closer to Shif and whispered, 'His nightmares are one thing, but he's never collapsed with his eyes open before – at least, not while he's been at home. Has he with you?'

Shif shook his head. 'It won't usually happen somewhere he feels safe. It's because he's panicking at the thought of leaving Coastwood.'

'So it could happen at any time he doesn't feel safe?' Mother said loudly and flinched. She checked over her shoulder again to make sure the others weren't paying attention, then added more quietly, 'Like if he's off travelling on his own?' She drew me to her side. 'He's not leaving.'

Relief helped my head to clear. Mother was on my side. Shif looked from one of us to the other, his eyes full of patience as he waited for one of us to relent. The longer it went on, the less I could bear it. I had an idea.

'You said I should try to inspire others to find artistry in themselves,' I said to him. 'So then, I should do that here, in our village first, before moving on to another one.'

He looked solely at me now, his eyes kind but penetrating where they had been soft. 'There isn't one person in this village that hasn't had ample chance to be inspired,' he said. 'If it was going to happen here, it would have by now.'

'How do you know?' I said. 'I wouldn't have known I had it in me if you hadn't given me a sketchpad and pencil and told me I should learn to draw, then shown me how to paint.'

'I just gave you the prompting you needed,' Shif said. 'The drawings and paintings adorning the walls of every cottage in this village are more than enough of a prompt for those who see them every day. Has anyone asked you to teach them to sketch or paint? Has even one person in Coastwood asked you any questions whatsoever that would suggest they're interested in emulating your example?'

I thought about it and reluctantly shook my head. Then I had another idea. 'But everyone is different, aren't they? Maybe some just need more prompting than others. I could stay here and run artistry classes for a bit, see if that does it – for the kids at school and anyone else who wants to paint.'

'That's a wonderful idea,' Mother said before Shif could reply.

'You could put a notice on the village noticeboard, offering to run classes for children over the summer holidays. Goodness knows how many parents will be grateful to you for taking their children off their hands for a few hours a week. Isn't that a great idea, Shif? Inspiring young minds to consider expressing themselves in such a beautiful way? And if they do well, the parents themselves might be inspired to give painting a go.'

Shif sighed. 'I can't force you to let the lad go, Mowaya, any more than I can force you, Devlin, to leave. All I can do is advise it, which I'll do again, very strongly. The longer this situation goes on, the harder it will be for you both to rectify it.'

Mother held me to her side even more tightly. 'Devlin might never need to leave. When the next Herald visits the village and takes away the news that we have The New's first Master Artist here in Coastwood, Devlin could be inundated with requests for apprenticeships, and everyone knows it's the Apprentice who travels to the Master and not the other way around.'

'If a Herald had arrived here with that news, would it have given you even the tiniest hint of exactly what it is that a Master Artist can produce?' Shif said. 'Do you think there's the faintest chance that even one so eloquent as a Herald can describe the emotions, knowledge, wisdom and history contained within Devlin's paintings?'

Mother was silent.

'If they could,' Shif continued, 'there would be no need for the paintings at all, and you and I both know, Mowaya, that The New has that need.'

'What need is that, Shhhhhhhhhiff?' Joplin said, hanging an arm around the old man's neck. 'More ale?' He turned and yelled, 'More ale for Shhhhhhhhhiff.'

Father handed our friend a glass of ale. 'Come on, Shif, you're falling behind. Another for you too, love?' he said to Mother.

She picked up her almost full glass, drained its contents and held it out to him. 'Yes, for once, I think I need… I mean, I think I'll enjoy a second.'

Father raised his eyebrows at me. 'What about you, Devlin?'

'Come on, Snail,' Kaplin said, slapping me on the back with one hand and holding my abandoned glass in front of me with the other. 'Down your first and start on a second, it'll bring you out of your shell.'

The thought terrified me and I pushed the glass away. 'No thanks.'

It would be many years before I would touch another drop of ale.

Chapter Eight

Mother was right. Within hours of pinning my offer to teach artistry on the village noticeboard, I was inundated with parents knocking on our door, wanting to book their children into the two classes I had proposed. I soon realised I would have to run more classes a week in order to accommodate them all, and in fact, would need to run at least one a day in order to keep the class sizes manageable and cater for so many age groups. Not only that, but where I had intended to teach the classes in our kitchen, I would need to use the village hall. I hadn't spent much time there and felt shaky at the thought of doing so.

I spent the next week sketching my way to it, all around the outside of it, and inside its large, light, airy space from every angle. By the time the day arrived when I would run my first classes there, I still felt uncomfortable but consoled myself with the thought that at least the hall was further from the sea than was my home.

Mother was more than delighted when my classes were well attended and dropped in at the end of every single class with a tray of cakes and biscuits to "reward the children for their concentration and effort". She had no idea whether her rewards were deserved, because she never asked and I never volunteered that information. We were both just relieved that we could justify to ourselves – if not to Shif, who refused to comment either way on the subject – my continuing presence in the village.

We were even more relieved when, as the end of the summer loomed, the headteacher of the school asked whether I would enrol as a Teacher for the new school year. Apparently, my young age was no reason to delay him offering me the appointment when my dedication to my Skill was abundantly clear. I accepted gratefully, happy to not only have a valid reason to delay my departure from the village even longer, but that my reason for staying was a position in a place I knew well and afforded me a feeling of safety, security and consistency.

Shif wasn't invited to the celebration dinner Mother organised on hearing of my appointment. She said it was because we should celebrate straight away, that evening, and there was no time for any of us to go and get him. She shushed down Kaplin's offer to run at top speed to fetch him, and Father's suggestion that we hold the celebration the following evening so that Shif, without whom his son wouldn't be a Master Artist, let alone the youngest Teacher ever to have been appointed in the village, could attend. I should have spoken up for my friend and mentor, and I knew it. But I also knew I couldn't bear the lack of enthusiasm that would accompany his congratulations, or the levelness of his stare.

I hadn't visited his cottage since my qualification ceremony. When I had seen him in the village, I avoided him when I was alone and spoke as little as possible to him when we were in company. The longer the situation went on, the greater became the distance between us… and the less vibrant became my art.

I could see it in the images I was creating, but more

Chapter Eight

importantly, I could feel it. Where there had been an urgency, a flow to my hand's movements when I had used to sketch or paint, as the summer went on and I lingered in Coastwood, my speed at sketching and painting had gradually waned. My desperation to hunt out new subjects for my art became more of an interest than an urge, and an increasingly vague one at that.

I threw myself into creating plans for the lessons I would be teaching at school, as the Headteacher – whom I felt strange to be addressing as Hal rather than Mr Fuller – advised, and tried to ignore the fact that the only time I sketched with the speed or talent of which I had proven myself capable was on waking from my continuing nightmares.

~

It didn't occur to me that Shif might come to the art exhibition I organised at the end of my first year as a Teacher, and I was mortified when he entered the school hall, for not only were my students' works on display, but so were some of mine that Hal had insisted I create especially, one being a portrait of him.

I tried not to watch my mentor as he slowly made his way around the hall, often stopping to talk to proud parents gesturing enthusiastically at their child's creations before extricating himself and continuing his slow perusal. I couldn't help it; whether out of the corner of my eye, over the top of the heads of my students as they chattered happily to me and one another, or in my peripheral vision, I couldn't stop myself hoping I would see approval on Shif's face or in his demeanour.

I saw it in neither and felt myself becoming increasingly desperate. Where I had planned to stay out of his eyeline and hailing distance, I lingered where I was, chatting distractedly to parents and students alike as he continued his slow approach.

When he appeared beside me, I realised my mistake; I had come to a stop in front of the portrait I had painted of Hal.

I had tried to convince myself it was good, because it was. My ability to scrutinise a subject and my eye to hand co-ordination were both as sharp as ever, to the extent that – as so many parents had already told me – at first glance, the painting had its viewers believing that Hal himself was staring out of the wall. But the dullness in Shif's eyes where there had always been a sparkle when he looked at my work, and the fact he no longer felt the urge to reach out and touch the painting as he had with those I had done up until he pronounced me an Artist, told me he felt about it exactly as I did. Something was missing.

'It's good, lad,' he said. He waved a hand around the hall. 'They're all good.'

The lack of enthusiasm in his voice shook me into blurting out, 'But something's missing. What is it? What's missing from my painting?'

He didn't meet my gaze. 'Your soul.'

My mouth was suddenly parched. I told myself that was why I didn't argue with him, but deep down, I knew it was because I had no argument to offer. Shif stood patiently beside me, still regarding the portrait.

'How do I get it back?' I said eventually.

He turned to face me, the faintest spark of brightness in his eyes. He touched a finger to my chest. 'It's right there, where it's always been. But the longer you resist your calling, the more you'll stifle it. You'll always be a good painter, lad, but there's a difference between skill and Skiiiiiiill.'

The extended pronunciation of his last word left me in no doubt of his meaning; as far as he was concerned, I no longer had the right to call myself an Artist, let alone a Master of the Skill. I felt sick all of a sudden, as if my lunch were suddenly as out of place in my stomach as Shif believed me to be in Coastwood.

I swallowed repeatedly until I felt better, ignoring two parents who were trying to strike up conversations with me until they gave up and left me be. When I was no longer afraid of seeing my lunch for the second time that day, I turned back to Shif to find him gone; it seemed his slow circuit of the hall had come to an end.

'Devlin?' Another parent placed herself in front of me.

I just about managed to smile at her. 'Hello, Mrs Green.'

'I just wanted to thank you for all the help you've given my Kally this past year. She hates her other lessons, but she loves artistry. I've just been looking at all the paintings she's done this term, and I can't believe how good she is!' The short, plump woman grabbed my hand and shook it with both of hers. 'You have a wonderful future ahead of you as a Teacher, and all of us in Coastwood know how lucky we are to have you.'

I smiled weakly at her and her twelve-year-old daughter, who had sidled up beside her while she was talking. Kally flushed red and shyly returned my smile before being dragged by her mother back to the section of the wall that was covered in her paintings.

I should have been as happy as I knew Mother would be when I told her how much my classes were enjoyed and appreciated, and I tried to be, but my heart felt as heavy in my chest as it had been light until I began teaching. I plodded to the centre of the hall and scanned the paintings stuck up on the walls all around me. None of them showed me what I wanted to see. None of the children I was teaching would be an Artist.

Panic swirled around in my chest. It burst down my torso to my legs, causing them to tremble, and erupted into my throat, causing it to constrict so that I felt as if I would choke.

What about the adults of Coastwood? I focused on that

thought to the exclusion of all else. I had thought of offering classes for them, but so far, I had only taught children. What if I ran evening classes for the adults of the Trades? Just because they hadn't shown aptitude for any of the other Skills, it didn't mean they wouldn't for artistry. And if they did, I would be following my "calling", as Shif had referred to it. I would be able to paint with my soul again; I would be a Master Artist once more.

~

I ran evening classes for four years, during which I was constantly on the alert for any sign that I had reached the souls of my adult students and set them free to sense subjects awaiting their scrutiny; that I had inspired in the villagers the ability to sketch and paint to their soul's desire, despite no longer being able to do it myself. I never saw any sign whatsoever. In fact, most of the adults, despite their enthusiasm for, and enjoyment of, the classes, could sketch and paint no better than my students at school. I repeatedly tried to convince myself that some people just needed longer than others to find their talent, right up until the night that stripped me of any capacity to care.

I was late to eat that evening, as I always was on the three evenings a week that I ran classes in the village hall. Mother and Father usually waited to eat with me, but on that evening, Joplin and Kaplin had stopped by for dinner with their wives and Joplin's baby son, and my family had long since retired to the living room to chat in greater comfort. As I sat in the kitchen, eating alone, I listened to the chatter and laughter that drifted along the hallway while Father, Joplin, Kaplin and Kaplin's wife shared their customary after dinner glass of ale, and a familiar feeling of despondency stole over me. I convinced myself yet again that my presence in the village was justified – that any day, one of my

Chapter Eight

students would suddenly find it within themselves to sketch without thinking, to paint without doubting – but where I would usually have then been able to force myself to think of other things, on that evening, I couldn't seem to.

Tomorrow would be another day. Another day of trying to explain to school children how to see all the different aspects of their subjects when, in fact, there was no way of explaining how one can see that of which the eyes are incapable; of encouraging them to let their hand move across the page without directing it; of showing them by example how to bring a sketch to life using paint, when I was no longer capable of producing more than the tiniest spark of talent.

When my despondency was accompanied by a sense of foreboding, I began to panic, assuming my ability to convince myself that I had good reason to stay in the village had expired, and finally, I had no option but to leave.

No. Only Shif and Mother knew of my calling, and Mother would never want me to go. I could go on avoiding Shif and his obvious disapproval, and just teach at the school where my classes were among the most popular. I had no reason at all to dread the following day, and also none to fear going to bed – despite still having nightmares, they weren't as frequent as they had once been and I was always fine once I had expelled them to my sketchpad.

I finished my stew, washed my bowl, cutlery and mug, and went upstairs. I wasn't in the mood for my brothers to ask for the hundredth time when I was planning to start courting, or remind me that at twenty, I was older by three years than either of them had been. All I wanted was to have a bath, go to bed and hopefully have a nightmare-free night so that I could sleep away the feeling something terrible was going to happen.

For the first time in years, I ran a bath with almost as much cold water as hot. I told myself it was because I wasn't used to bathing so soon after eating, but I knew deep down that wouldn't normally be enough to divert me from my usual "extreme bath". On entering my bedroom, I found myself not only pulling my bedroom window tightly shut but bolting it, as if a storm were raging outside when, in fact, the cool autumn air would have kept my sinuses clear and ensured a better night's sleep.

I tossed and turned and was still awake when my brothers and their families finally left, and my parents came up to bed. I pretended to be asleep when my father poked his head into my room and whispered, 'Goodnight, Devlin.'

When Mother came in and hovered silently by my bed, my feeling of impending doom intensified. I sat up and whispered, 'Are you alright?'

She sat down beside me and gripped my arm. 'I feel strange, like something awful is going to happen, only I can't think why that should be. I had an urge to come and see if you're okay, which made me wonder if it's coming from her.'

'Ma?'

Her lack of reply was answer enough. I hesitated, unwilling to add strength to my own feeling by speaking of its existence. Mother released and re-gripped my arm over and over, like a cat kneading a cushion.

'I have the same feeling,' I finally admitted. 'But why would we both be feeling it if it's from her?'

She took a sharp inward breath and then breathed out slowly and deeply. 'Why would we both be feeling it if it wasn't?'

She was hurting my arm, so I prised her hands off it and took them in my own. 'I don't know.'

'Jimmy?' Her voice was Ma's now, as was the strength in her hands as she squeezed the blood out of mine. 'What's happening, my boy?'

I didn't need to fall asleep. Suddenly, I was there, staggering

Chapter Eight

across the wet and violently rocking deck of the warship that was, at that moment, very definitely at war. I leant further into the ferocious wind that appeared as hellbent on sinking the ship as were the gunships whose cannons propelled a seemingly endless supply of missiles in our direction, and, ignoring the screams of the injured men over whom I was forced to clamber, reached for the rope up which I had been ordered to climb in order to help drop the sails. My hand was frozen and contained as little strength as the rest of me, so I could barely grip the rope, let alone climb up it. The whistling of a cannon ball over my head should have galvanised me into action, but my starved, beaten, exhausted body was unable to respond to my sense of danger.

The ship lurched violently, throwing a wall of water up into the air where it seemed to hang motionless for an impossible amount of time. I used what little strength I had to twist my hand around the rope and then allowed it to take my weight so that it tightened around my wrist. I closed my eyes just before the water hit me.

Pain exploded within my body. I opened my mouth to scream but instead inhaled icy, salty water. I was deaf to the roaring of the waves, the howling of the wind, the screaming of men and the thunder of cannon fire; all I could hear was the pounding of my heart and the multitude of air bubbles squealing past my ears as they tried to escape the water holding us all captive. All I could feel was the agony of my broken wrist and dislocated shoulder.

Then the water ceased its sudden attack, pouring innocuously down the steeply tilting deck to merge with the sea and leaving my injured wrist and shoulder to take my full weight. I coughed up the water that had invaded my lungs and shook my head to clear it from my eyes and ears. I barely had time to register the absence of the injured sailors who had littered the deck before the pain in my wrist and shoulder announced itself all over again. I tried to grip the deck with my feet in order to stand, but couldn't find the strength. For the first time in this particular battle, the scream that pierced my ear drums was my own as I hung helplessly from my injured arm. I looked around desperately for someone who might help me, but of those who had likewise tethered themselves to the ship, some drooped unconscious, others screamed as loudly as I, and many appeared to be dead.

I tried again to gain purchase on the slippery deck and walk my feet underneath myself, and this time managed to take a small step with each foot… before slipping and jolting my weight through my wrist and shoulder all over again. My scream was taken from me by the wind as soon as it left my mouth, rendering it as insignificant as I had been since being taken aboard the HMS Royal Sovereign.

The crack of a cannonball hitting the main mast of the ship would no doubt have been ear splitting had the wind chosen that moment to relent. As it was, it was still loud enough to reach my ears despite the wind's efforts to divert it. Despite the agony it caused me, I couldn't prevent myself from raising my head in order to witness the damage.

It was as if time slowed down and deadened my senses to everything but the sight of the ship's mast fracturing into two main sections and a multitude of splinters, all of which seemed to hang in the air around the cannonball that had created them – which itself seemed intent on remaining in mid-air to witness the carnage it had wrought. Then time released its hold, and I watched with interest the splinter that appeared to pick me out of the chaos. It headed straight for me, not even swayed from its course by the relentless, buffeting wind. I knew, with no inkling of how, that I belonged to it and it to me.

I abandoned my pain. I ignored my exhaustion. And for the first time since I had woken aboard the warship, I forgot my grief, for I knew it would soon end. I welcomed the shard of the ship that had caused me so much misery, not even flinching as it pierced my chest, for the pain that would end my suffering was a blessed relief.

My eyes closed slowly and even as blood gurgled out of my mouth, my lips relaxed into a smile.

'JIMMY!'

My eyes shot open and tried to pick Ma out of the darkness that was rapidly closing in on me. How could she be on the ship? She should go, it wasn't safe.

'Jimmy, please, pull the splinter out. You have to pull the splinter out or you'll die.'

I couldn't see her anywhere. I smiled again. She wasn't here; I was imagining it. She was safe at home. I allowed my eyes to close… and saw her face. She was paler than I had ever seen her, and she was sucking in her cheeks and chewing on them as she did when she was scared.

If I died, Ma would be alone. I promised I'd make it back to her, but I never would if I allowed myself to die. She'd always be alone.

I opened my eyes and tried to grasp the splinter with my free hand, but where it had appeared so tiny when it was liberated from the mast, I found it to be thicker than my arm. I couldn't get hold of it any better than I'd been able to grab the rope that was less than a quarter of its thickness, let alone pull it out.

I was overcome with guilt and sadness. 'I've let you down, Ma.' I coughed on the blood that flowed out of my mouth with my words. 'I'm…' I coughed again. 'I'm sorry.'

My eyelids were too heavy to remain open. As they drifted shut, I exhaled for the last time. Ma's stricken face was the last thing I saw.

'Jimmy? Where've you gone? Oh, my boy. My boy. My boy.'

Ma had hugged the air out of me many times through Mother, but she had always hugged Jimmy. Now that Jimmy was gone, it was me to whom she clung with no regard for the injuries her son had left in my wrist, shoulder and chest. I had to expel my experience onto my sketchpad before my injuries killed me… yet I suddenly realised that, unlike those with which I had woken before, these didn't appear to be causing me any pain.

I wriggled out of her clutches and pushed her away as gently as I could. She picked up my sketchpad from where it lay at her feet and, with a shaking hand, held it near the lantern she must have lit when I slipped into Jimmy's world. Her other hand went to her mouth and stifled a grief-filled moan. I gently pulled the sketchpad out of her grasp and immediately dropped it as I caught sight of a blood-soaked Jimmy hanging from his wrist with a stake through his blood-soaked chest.

'I sketched while I was dreaming this time?' I whispered.

Mother's face was her own as she said, 'You didn't fall asleep.' Then it was Ma's face, then Mother's, then Ma's again.

I stood up. 'Ma, let her go. Jimmy's gone.' I stooped to pick up the sketchpad, turned the pages back to the first scene of my nightmare, and showed it to her. I gulped as Jimmy's life became real for me again, but turned to the next page, and the next, and the next, until I was back at the sketch of his death. 'He's gone,' I whispered.

My legs gave way and I sat down heavily on my bed, my left arm at an unnatural angle to my body and my left hand hanging limply. Mother was beside me in an instant.

'Devlin?'

I coughed, and blood sprayed into my lap.

Chapter Nine

Mother shrieked, 'No! This doesn't happen anymore. Jimmy's injuries don't have a hold on you once you've sketched them.'

'I looked at the sketches again this time though,' I croaked and coughed up more blood. 'I took them back in.'

'LENNON!' Mother shrieked.

Father staggered into my room, rubbing his eyes.

'Get the Healers. All of them!' Mother said. 'We need a Tissue-Singer, a Bone-Singer and Shif. HURRY!'

He stopped abruptly at the sight of blood in my lap and dripping from my chin, then turned and thundered down the stairs in his nightshirt. The front door slammed behind him moments later.

'Lie back,' Mother said, 'and let me lift your nightshirt.'

I shook my head frantically and tried to fend her off from helping me.

'Devlin, this is no time to be shy, I've seen it all before,' Mother said, her voice trembling almost as much as her hands.

'Hurry and lie back so I can see if you have a wound as bad as Jimmy's. I know you've had nothing more visible than mild bruising to show for his injuries before, but you've never coughed up blood either.'

'I can't... shoulder,' I gurgled through the blood welling in my throat.

Mother glanced at my dislocated limb and dismissed it. 'There's nothing I can do about that, and I can't worry about it.' She wrung her hands together and then, without warning, grabbed both of my shoulders and pushed me backwards, squinting against the blood that erupted out of me with my yell. 'I'm sorry, sorry, sorry, sorry...' She repeated her apology over and over as she lifted my nightshirt and wrenched it upwards until my torso was bare.

Her eyes widened. She bent down and grabbed my sketchpad with a bloody hand, and looked from the sketch at which I had left it open, of a dead Jimmy hanging from his left wrist with a stake through his chest, to me. I didn't dare look down when she put a hand to my chest and tenderly touched the spot where Jimmy had been impaled. She withdrew it quickly when I flinched, and when I coughed again, she put an arm behind my back and sat me upright so I wouldn't choke.

'How... bad... is... it?' I said.

'Nowhere near as bad as Jimmy's wound, but bad enough.' She didn't remove her arm, but hugged me to her almost as tightly as Ma would have, despite my gasp of pain. She stroked my forehead with her other hand, despite it being slick with blood. 'Hold on, Devlin, please just hold on. There's nothing that the Healers can't fix, you just have to stay with me until they get here. Shif will be a little while, but you know Wrent and Killie live close by, so just hang on.'

I nodded, hoping that both the Bone-Singer and Tissue-Singer of whom she spoke would already be on their way. I wanted to tell Mother not to worry, that I'd never leave her as Jimmy had been forced to leave Ma, but I suddenly felt exhausted. And very cold.

'Devlin, stay awake,' Mother said, rubbing my legs now. She pulled my sheet and quilt over my shivering body. 'Don't you close your eyes. Come on, stay with me.' My cheek stung as she slapped it, and my eyes opened in reflex.

There was a crash downstairs as the front door was flung open. Panic laced my father's voice as he said, 'Don't take your shoes off, you need to get up to him right away. There was blood everywhere when I left, so the light knows how much there'll be now. Hurry, Killie. Up the stairs and to your right.'

Mother shook me gently. 'Just a bit longer, Devlin.' Her voice broke and when she spoke again, it was thick with Ma's grief. 'You can't leave me.'

I couldn't stop my eyes from closing, but before I succumbed to the darkness waiting to consume me, Coastwood's most newly qualified Tissue-Singer filled my vision.

'Thunder and lightning.' Killie and I had often sat next to one another in classes at school, and though her voice was familiar to me, the horror it carried was not. Her small, cold hand clasped mine and she took a sharp breath in and out, then a softer, slower one. Her voice was calm and confident as she said, 'Dev, it's me. I know you're hurting and you must be scared, but I'm here now and I'll sort this. Try to relax so that all of your strength is available to your body as it heals.'

She hummed a deep, harsh sound that was almost a growl, and almost immediately, I felt something shift within my chest. I relaxed and allowed the darkness to take me.

∼

It was almost a month before I was strong enough to stand unaided. Of Jimmy's chest wound, there was no sign, and my shoulder and wrist were as sound and strong as ever; Killie and Wrent had fulfilled their roles admirably. Shif, of course, had been amazing too. Though Killie's strength and talent as a Tissue-Singer had left him with no wound to poultice or heal, his tincture had ensured that I slept with a peaceful mind, so I could regain the strength that Jimmy's injuries and their subsequent healing had taken from me.

Killie and Wrent checked in on me every week, but Shif came every day. Sometimes I slept through his visits, but I would often wake to find him sitting next to my bed, leafing through the sketchpad in which I had recorded Jimmy's last minutes. He always put it under the bed as soon as I woke, and immediately spoke of other things. When he could see I was tiring, he would take his leave, promising to return the following day.

It was his hand that hovered beneath my left elbow while Mother's hovered beneath my right as I finally stood, wobbling on my feet by my bed.

'Can you take a few steps, lad?' he asked.

Mother said, 'I think he should sit back down. He's still so weak.'

'And he won't get strong if he doesn't move around,' Shif said gently. 'You won't fall, lad, your mother and I'll support you if need be. How about walking to the door and back?'

I nodded but immediately stopped; my head felt so heavy upon my shoulders that I felt I would overbalance. Twenty-two painfully slow steps later, I collapsed back onto my bed.

'Well done,' Shif said. 'Tomorrow, we'll do that twice. By the end of the week, we'll have you sitting downstairs by the time your father and brothers get in from fishing, then you can all set about getting some colour back into your cheeks. Never have I seen a fishing family with such pale faces.'

'It's been such a shock,' Mother said.

'For the two of you more than the other three,' Shif said, looking between us both.

Mother and I shot each other a look, unsure of what to say. As always, Shif spared us the trouble of having to worry about it.

'There are some things that are too difficult to speak about,' he said. 'Too strange to find the words for. It was clear to me that at least some words needed to be found in order to satisfy Killie and Wrent's concerns about how you came about your injuries, Devlin, and your father and brothers' worries that the same thing might happen again. The words needed to be true but unspecific enough that your affairs would remain your own, so I took the liberty of perusing the sketchpads under your bed until those words came to me. Killie and Wrent will not question you, nor will they reveal to anyone else what happened here. Their job is done, but I won't feel discharged from mine until I know you feel in a position to cope unaided with what happened.' He paused and looked between Mother and me several times, his eyes finally settling upon me. 'My sleeping preparation has made sure you haven't dreamt for the past month, but as I told you the last time you needed it, it's unwise to take it for too long. It's time for you to sleep unaided. Do you think that'll be a problem?'

It was only then, when I allowed myself to think about Jimmy for the first time since almost perishing from his injuries, that I realised I felt different inside. Jimmy's death had severed my awareness of him, leaving in its place an echoing well of sadness, despair and... fear. The bursts of panic I had always felt at leaving the village – at being taken from my mother – were now an overwhelming terror. I had been right to fear leaving Coastwood. My artistry students may no longer be a strong enough reason for me to stay, but what happened to Jimmy definitely was. I would stay where everything was predictable and nothing could harm me.

'Devlin?' Shif said.

I managed to unclench my jaws and say, 'His life's over. I won't be with him in my dreams again.'

Shif nodded slowly. 'I hoped that was the case. Mowaya, how about you? Has anything changed?'

Mother's face shifted so that it was Ma who answered him. 'Everything has changed.' She looked at me and her face hardened. 'Who are you? You're not my Jimmy.'

Shif quickly stepped between the two of us and said to her, 'Jimmy's gone. You know he has. You won't find him here again.'

Ma stepped to the side and looked past him at me, but he stepped in front of her again. 'You won't find him here again,' he repeated. 'Not ever.'

It was Mother who sobbed as she crumpled into his arms. 'I feel her pain as if it's mine. Please don't try to talk Devlin into leaving once he's better, Shif. I've just been through losing one son, I can't lose another.'

Shif stroked her hair as he held her close. 'And that's why it's even more important now for the lad to go. You can't keep feeding a fear that's strong enough to have reached out to you from another lifetime. The only way to banish it is to starve it.'

Mother pushed him away. 'What do you know of it, Shif? You don't even have a wife, let alone a child. What do you know of worrying about someone other than yourself?'

'You aren't worrying about Devlin, Mowaya,' Shif said calmly, as if she hadn't just insulted him to his face. 'You're worrying about how you'll feel when you don't know where he is or what he's doing.'

'With good reason!' she shrieked, putting her hands on her hips. 'Look what happened to Jimmy.'

'And look how it's still affecting you, lifetimes later.' Shif spoke as if he were observing the weather. 'The only way you'll feel better than you are right now is by finding your courage and letting Devlin go.'

I scrambled to my feet so I could look into his eyes when I spoke. 'I don't want to go. You said it yourself, I have no Skill in artistry now. All I can do is sketch and paint and help others to enjoy doing the same. Anyone in the other villages can do that, they don't need me.'

At last, Shif's face clouded. 'You still have the Skill, lad, you've just buried it under a mountain of fear and insecurity.' He stepped away from Mother and me. 'I can see I've outstayed my welcome. You know where I am if you need me. Until then, I'll be hoping that you're faring well in my absence, and working towards following my advice.'

∽

Shif never lost that hope. He received no invitations to our home in the fifteen years that followed, despite my father's confusion and repeated – but unanswered – demands for my mother's reason for his banishment, and she and I avoided the Herbalist whenever we could whilst out and about. When we couldn't, he would lift a hand and smile in greeting, then raise his eyebrows as if hoping for us to confirm my departure. I could never bring myself to meet his eyes, and would hurry about my day, which was every bit as predictable as my refusal to leave my mother.

I had found, once I was strong enough to leave the house after recuperating from Jimmy's injuries, that the fear that had plagued me since first dreaming of his kidnap and enslavement was no longer something that came and went according to my situation. It had become part of me, along with the sadness and despair he had taken to his death. Jimmy's feelings were embedded so deeply within me that I couldn't step aside from them, I couldn't comfort myself from them, and I found it difficult to bear living with them.

My fear of leaving everything that was known to me became a pathological fear of anything unknown. My need to carefully consider whether a given course of action could bring the unknown into my life became a compulsive avoidance of any situation that might involve a measure of surprise. My horror at any situation where I might not have choices open to me became an obsessive need for control over my life. The only measures that gave me any degree of relief from Jimmy's legacy were cleanliness, tidiness and routine.

I rose at dawn every day regardless of season, weather or work schedule. I adhered to a strict hygiene ritual that ensured I was always immaculately groomed and dressed, and always in the same uniform; once I had felt a measure of comfort in an outfit comprising a white shirt, brown trousers and brown boots, they were all I would wear, with the addition of a brown pullover, cloak and wide-brimmed hat when the weather called for them. I walked the same way to school every day; taught the same lessons day in, day out, week in, week out, year in and year out; ate the same food for lunch; walked the same way home and refused to leave the house again until the following morning. I spent the evenings chatting or playing games with my parents, or working on my own paintings.

I stopped showing my art to anyone, for as far as I was concerned, it could barely be viewed as such. My paintings were accurate recordings of what I saw, but that was all they were. They weren't capable of evoking fascination in viewers trying to understand how they were seeing far more deeply into the subject than if they had observed it in real life. They wouldn't cause anyone to reach out and touch them as if the subject were right there, before them. No one would be inspired to do any more than glance, nod in approval and appreciation of my skill – which I was only too aware had lost its capitalisation – and move on to other conversation. I had lost the ability to sketch and paint at a speed that was infinitely faster than that at which my brain could operate, with the result that my brain was far too involved for my work to be worthy of someone with the title of Master Artist. My paintings were as boring, predictable and depressed as was I, and try as I might, I couldn't resurrect them.

Sometimes, in my desperation, I would consider going to see Shif for help. I never considered for long; there was no time in my strict schedule to go and see him and no way Mother would allow him into the house to visit me – and besides, I knew what his advice would be. My mind would slam down before I could acknowledge it to myself, and I would throw myself into the next task in my schedule until its familiarity calmed me.

My brothers gave up trying to tease me into courting. My father gave up trying to understand my mother's and my steadfast refusal to explain why we couldn't abide Shif, and our apparent inability to understand that my still living at home whilst in my thirties was unusual.

It was on my thirty-fifth birthday that I came closest to giving up on life. As always, I rose at dawn. As always, I got to the bathroom before my parents, ran an extreme bath filled with the exact amounts of complementing scents that soothed me, and languished in it for seven hundred beats of my heart. I spent a further three hundred and fifty heartbeats scrubbing myself clean and washing my hair, then dried myself during the hundred heartbeats that followed. I combed my hair and shaved, folded my towel from corner to corner and hung it on the rail so that its two ends hung at the same level, and dressed from the pile of clean, pressed clothes I had placed on the stool behind the door before going to bed the previous evening. I returned to my room, made my bed and, after a quick check that everything was in its place, went downstairs to the kitchen. Since I couldn't abide surprises, the exact same gifts – unwrapped so I could be sure they were as expected – awaited me on the kitchen table as on each previous year since the meltdown I'd had on my twenty-first birthday. I stood, perusing them for far longer than on any other birthday. I waited and waited for the relief that always followed a momentary spike of anxiety that someone may have forgotten my need for order and predictability, but it didn't come.

I sat down heavily on one of the wooden kitchen chairs that were pulled up to the table, despite the fact that it was past time for me to be toasting the four slices of bread I would eat with butter and jam, and I was still there when Mother entered the kitchen.

She rushed to my side. 'Devlin, what is it? Did someone get you the wrong grade of canvas? Are the shades of the paints not quite right?' She began lifting and replacing each paint pot in order to check. When I didn't answer her, she put her hands on my shoulders and gently shook me. 'Devlin, tell me, what's wrong? Are you ill?'

I couldn't answer her. I couldn't even bring myself to shake my head. Doing so was pointless. Everything was pointless.

From nowhere, I felt as if something seized hold of me deep inside and pulled so hard, I almost fell off my chair. I grabbed the table in order to right myself, my heart pounding and my stomach lurching as if it would expel food that wasn't there.

Mother ran to the stairs and called up to my father. 'Lennon, run and tell Shif that Devlin isn't well – he just nearly fainted. I think he needs a pick-me-up; he's been pale recently. Tell Shif that and bring back whatever he thinks will make him better.'

'Or I could just go and fetch Shif back here so he can form his own diagnosis and prescription,' Father called back.

'You know I won't have him here,' Mother yelled. 'He gives advice where it isn't wanted and…'

Her voice seemed fainter all of a sudden as my internal attacker grabbed me again and pulled even harder, so that this time, I did fall off my chair. Panic forced bile up into my throat, which I expelled over the flagstones. Mother came rushing back in and yelled over her shoulder, 'He's fallen off his chair now, and been sick. Hurry, Lennon.'

It was as if my head were suddenly gripped by a vice attached to an elastic rope intent on recoiling. My arms and legs couldn't help but paddle along the ground in order to keep my body with my head as I was pulled towards the eastern wall of the kitchen. When I reached it, I just about got my hands to it in time to prevent my forehead smashing into the grey stone.

Mother grasped my shoulders and shrieked, 'Devlin, stop! Please, just talk to me. Tell me what's wrong? What's happening?' Her voice changed to one I hadn't heard in fifteen years. 'Is it my Jimmy? Jimmy, are you back with me?' Ma's voice was weak, as if much of her life force had been sucked out of her, but her hands and arms were as strong as ever. She wrenched me away from the wall and turned me to face her. 'Jimmy?' Desperation strengthened her fingers as they pinched my chin and forced it upwards until my eyes met hers – which quickly filled with tears. They ran down her face and weren't replaced as Ma fled. Mother's face was her own once more as she whispered, 'Devlin? If it's not Jimmy making you do this, who is it?'

'I'd warrant it's his salvation.' Shif's voice startled us both, as much by its lack of strength as his words. We turned towards the kitchen doorway, where he stood with my father peering over his shoulder.

Mother pulled me to her with so much force, I was able to relax my efforts in keeping myself away from the wall. I felt her heart pounding against my arm as she said, 'Lennon, I asked you to bring something back to invigorate our son, not terrify him. Shif, you know very well you're not welcome here. Please leave.'

Father stepped in front of Shif. 'Our friend, the man who has kept us healthy since we were children and our sons likewise, was just at the end of the street. Despite our lack of welcome for more than a decade, he was happy to come and help when I asked him to. The least you can do, Mowaya, even if you still refuse to explain your behaviour towards him, is to let him help Devlin as, astonishingly, he seems keen to do.' He turned to Shif. 'You know what's wrong with him?'

Shif hadn't taken his eyes – which I noticed were now cloudy where they had been bright – off me. 'You seem very drawn to that wall, lad. Something pulling you towards it, is it? Something reached inside you, grabbed hold and won't let go?'

Despite myself, I couldn't help nodding hopefully. 'You can give me something to stop it?'

He shuffled slowly but determinedly towards me, despite Mother holding her hand up to him, warning him to stay away. He took an age to crouch down in front of us and lower both hands to the floor to support himself, so that he could peer at me beneath her hand.

He nodded to himself and smiled through the deep wrinkles now lining his face. 'No. There's no stopping this, and even if I could, I wouldn't.'

'You see!' Mother said, an edge of hysteria to her voice. 'I told you, Len, he doesn't want to help us, he just wants to see us both suffer.'

Chapter Nine

'Shif?' My father's voice was uncertain. 'What's happening to him?'

Shif's milky eyes never wavered from mine. 'There's nothing wrong with him. Just the opposite, in fact. I'm as sure as I can be that he's being tugged.'

It was as if he had spoken the words in a foreign language; one whose sounds I recognised but couldn't seem to understand.

'Tugged?' my father said disbelievingly.

'NO!' my mother screamed.

Whatever it was that Shif had diagnosed, and I couldn't bring myself to comprehend, was clearly serious, yet his mouth widened into a smile of delight. How could that be? And how was it he looked so tired, so… ancient?

As if to compound my sudden realisation, Shif staggered as he tried to straighten his legs out of his crouch.

My father rushed to his side and took hold of his elbow to steady him. 'Are you alright? Do you need to sit down? Do you need something to eat? Drink?'

Shif smiled as he shook his head. 'No, thank you. As it happens, I'm feeling better than I have in years.'

Chapter Ten

None of us spoke for some time. Mother's hold on me was as unrelenting as my urge to run through the wall like it wasn't there. Father looked from me to Mother and then Shif, then back to me, time after time, as if Shif's words made no more sense to him than they did to me. Shif busied himself by putting our kettle on to boil and then selecting and mixing herbs from the pouch he never left his cottage without. By the time the kettle whistled with steam, his preparation was ready and waiting in the teapot. He left it to steep for a few minutes before adding cold water and pouring it through a strainer into three mugs, two of which he handed to Father and me. He held the last before Mother, his hand shaking with the effort.

She broke the silence by saying, 'Oh, for goodness' sake.' She grabbed the mug from him and put it on the floor beside her.

Shif pulled a chair out from under the table, sat down and stretched out his legs, crossing them as if settling down for a snooze but instead staring at me with as much curiosity as that

Chapter Ten

which he had encouraged me to harness when observing subjects I planned to sketch. His eyes may have been less vibrant than my distant observations of him had allowed me to realise, but they were no less penetrating.

Father took a sip from his mug and then lifted it to Shif. 'This is good, thank you.'

Shif smiled at him, then returned his gaze to me. My urge to affix myself to the wall waned slightly and partially focused itself upon the mug in my hand. I lifted it to my lips, but Mother's hand blocked it from reaching them.

'Don't drink it,' she hissed. 'You know what he wants. You know what he's trying to do to us.'

Panic lanced through me and I tried to lower the mug... but couldn't. I had to drink Shif's preparation and not just because I felt drawn to, but because whatever was assaulting my mind would increase its assault if I didn't; I could feel it.

I took the mug in my other hand and gulped a mouthful from it before Mother could stop me. The rich aroma of herbs filled my nostrils even as their vibrant flavours vied for attention from my taste buds. Though Shif had taken care to cool the preparation before pouring it, my mouth and throat still stung from the heat it left in its wake, causing me to gasp.

Mother tried to grab the mug from me, telling me, 'You see? No good can come of drinking that.'

'Lennon said you wanted a preparation to give Devlin energy, and that's what I've made for the three of you,' Shif said calmly, still watching me. 'You've all been stuck in something of a rut for a while, and now that events have overtaken you, you'll need some help to come to terms with the fact. I promise you, Mowaya, all the preparation will do is give you enough energy and strength to get through the next few hours.'

Mother looked at him for a while without speaking. Then she grabbed her mug from the flagstone upon which it had been cooling and drained its contents. 'There. Will you go now?'

'Mowaya!' Father said in an uncharacteristically stern voice. He took the chair next to Shif as Mother tightened her arms around me.

Shif ignored them both and continued to stare at me. I took frequent sips from my own mug, as much to block him from view as because I found myself craving its contents. When I had sucked the last drop from it, I set the mug on the floor, unsure of what to do. I felt better for having drunk the preparation, but not so much that I trusted myself able to resist being dragged back to the wall if I tried to move away from it.

Shif waited until my gaze wandered back to his and then said, 'You're being tugged by a horse, lad. Best not to fight it, eh?'

I tried not to understand his words, but unlike when he had spoken them before, my mind was now clear. If a horse were truly calling for me, it would want me to leave Coastwood and go to it – that was what I had been taught at school. I couldn't do that. Fear pierced my body as if I had inhaled shards of glass, making me gasp. I shook my head violently and croaked, 'Tugged? It can't be that.'

'Of course it can't,' Mother said. 'You're just tired. You've been overdoing it lately.'

Father rolled his eyes and shook his head slowly. He knew as well as Mother and I that I overdid nothing – in fact, I underdid everything wherever possible, to the extent that I had backed myself into a corner I found depressingly impossible to escape. He asked Shif, 'How can you be sure?'

Shif grinned. 'I've seen it before, back when I was a lad. There I was, holding my hand out to Mace the Metal-Singer for the hand trowel my old man had ordered from him, listening to him complain about how long he'd had to wait for Carpenter Haber to make its handle, when he froze where he stood and his eyes glazed over. Then it was like his feet took on a will of their own and he ran towards the wall opposite the door. He stood in front of it for a while, pushing at it, like his hands were the only thing stopping him from going straight through it, and when he turned around, he had a smile on his face such as he never usually wore. He understood what an honour it is to be chosen by a horse, you see. He handed me the trowel and told me he wouldn't be making any more of them for a while, because he was going to join the Horse-Bonded. He had his Quest Ceremony the following day, left to find his horse, and didn't return to the village for two years. When he did, his Bond-Partner was with him.'

Though Shif's eyes never left mine, their focus seemed to withdraw somewhere inside himself as he murmured, 'She was a sight to behold. Sanguine, that was her name. She was as elegant as he was awkward, as bright as he was dull, and as perky as he could be sullen. That first time they visited here, the differences between them couldn't have been more marked, but by the second time they came, years later, it was hard to tell where she ended and he began.'

Mother's breath caught in her throat and she coughed, bringing Shif back to the kitchen from his memories and his focus back to me. 'Even if I hadn't seen it before, I would have known what's happening to Devlin,' he said. 'Look at his face.'

Mother yanked me around to face her. Her eyes widened and hardened into Ma's and then narrowed without softening, back to her own. 'No. This can't be.'

Father crouched before me and likewise peered at me. 'What about his face?' he said. 'I don't see anything different.' Unlike Mother and, it seemed, Shif, he never had been able to see when I was sharing my mind with another.

Mother's reaction alone would have confirmed to me that Shif's observation of my situation was accurate, yet as with my decision to drink his herbal preparation, it wasn't her response I found myself trusting. I knew he was right because I could feel it. I could feel that someone had taken hold of part of my mind and claimed it as part of their own.

'We'd best get ourselves prepared for your Quest Ceremony, lad,' Shif said, his arms trembling as he pushed down on the table in an effort to get to his feet. 'You could be travelling for some time before you find your Bond-Partner, and I'm hoping you'll sketch at least part of your way there, so if you'll allow me, I'll add some sketchpads and pencils to those you've been gifted for your birthday.' He waved a hand to where my gifts lay untouched on the table. 'Obviously, I'll supply all the herbal preparations you might need too. I've got a lot to do, so I'd better get going.' His steps were stiff and awkward as he walked over to where I knelt on the floor. He offered his hand for me to shake. 'Let me be the first to congratulate you, lad. I couldn't be happier for you.'

Mother bound my arms to my sides with the ferocity of her embrace. 'You couldn't be happier to have finally found a lie you think will split us up, you mean,' she hissed.

Shif sighed. 'You can't fight what's happening to Devlin, Mowaya, it's so much stronger than the fear you've allowed to hold you both captive. Please, make this easier on yourself and the lad by allowing the clarity and strength my preparation is giving you to help you find your courage. There's more in the pot by the kettle, and I've left more in a tub on the draining board, ready for brewing. I'll make up a load more when I get home, and it'll be waiting for you whenever you need it.' His hand trembled as he continued to hold it out to me, but his gaze was no less steady.

I wanted to shake his hand. The pull on my mind lessened so that

Chapter Ten

I only had my mother's hold out of which to wriggle. I managed it and clasped Shif's hand. The years immediately fell away from us both, transporting me back to when he was congratulating me on my qualification as a Master Artist. I had long forgotten how excited I was then, how full of curiosity and purpose – how alive I felt. My old self fell away from me when Shif let go of my hand, leaving me only too aware of the lethargic, depressed shadow of myself I had become.

The pull on my mind increased steadily until my hands were needed at the wall again. I could hear the grin in Shif's voice as he said, 'I believe you know what you need to do to prevent that. I'll be waiting to hear when your Quest Ceremony will take place. In the meantime, remember there'll be plenty more of my preparation ready and waiting for all of you when you need it. Mowaya, Lennon, I'll take my leave.' His hand clasped my shoulder. 'See you soon, lad.'

Mother waited until the front door clicked shut behind Shif, before saying, 'Devlin, you shouldn't believe anything he said. You're overtired and overwrought, that's all. Get up now and come and sit at the table while I make your toast. Or you can make it, like normal?' she added hurriedly. She sounded so afraid, so desperate, I actually tried to believe her and do as she said, with the result that I spun back to the wall so fast, I didn't have time to brace myself from it.

I blinked through the blood that trickled from the resulting gash in my forehead. 'Shif was right, Mother. I'm being tugged. When I admit it, the pulling decreases and when I try to pretend it's not happening, it gets worse.' My voice sounded different from normal; stronger, though I felt anything but. I didn't have time to consider why that was, as the tugging suddenly decreased in strength, allowing me to turn away from the wall and face my parents. 'I'm being tugged by a horse,' I repeated. I looked from my father's smiling face to my mother's panic-stricken one and whispered, 'What are we going to do?'

∼

As always, Shif's faith in me was misplaced. Where he had expected to be invited along with the rest of the village to my Quest Ceremony within a day or two, I allowed Mother to forbid Father from even telling anyone I was being tugged. Where Shif had trusted we would avail ourselves of his help in the form of the preparation that would help us accept the change being foisted upon our family, only Father collected any from him – and Mother and I steadfastly refused to drink it. And where he'd been confident that I would heed the learning he had witnessed in me and embrace the pull of another's mind on my own, in fact, as the days passed, I persuaded myself that standing or sitting with my back to the eastern walls of our house was preferable to going outside them for any reason whatsoever.

Whenever my stamina faded and I considered succumbing to the tugging that plagued me every second of every day and night, the thought of what it would mean were I to do it – enduring the unknowns of a Quest Ceremony, leaving the village in a direction decided by another on a journey of indefinite length, with no routine or choices and where anything could happen to me at any time, knowing all the while that Mother would be distraught without me – fuelled my terror and kept me by the wall.

After four days and nights, I was exhausted. Fear paralysed me whilst tearing me apart inside as it tried to pull my mind away from the will of the horse that had chosen me. All I could do was sit on my bed with my back to the eastern wall of my bedroom, my head spinning with the fight going on inside it, my stomach spasming with terror and hunger, and close my eyes against the world that seemed hellbent on tormenting me.

Mother rarely left my side, despite Father begging her repeatedly to eat and sleep. She sat next to me, holding my hand and repeating, over and over, 'Our bond is stronger than any other, my son. We won't lose each other again, whoever tries to come between us.'

Much of the time, I was only aware of the words she was saying as being those upon which she had transfixed herself. Sometimes, though, I really heard them and when I did, when they settled in my exhausted, torn mind with real meaning, they didn't feel right. But I didn't have the energy or the wherewithal to ponder them further.

It was a further week before Shif visited our cottage, his voice preceding his footsteps up the stairs, and, strangely, accompanied by a clattering noise outside. I no longer had any concept of whether it was day or night, let alone whether what I could see and hear was real, so thought little of the noise until Shif burst into my room with the energy of a man half his age. 'Do you hear that noise, lad? She's here! Your horse is here! How about that? I've never heard of a horse coming for her Bond-Partner before; tugging usually results in the chosen human going to find their horse. But she's here! She's come for you! How about that?'

I knew he was telling the truth, for the part of me that had been so desperate to travel east was finally still. I heaved a sigh of relief. It was over. I had won. If I had to be bonded to a horse, then so be it, but I would do it here, with Mother. I squeezed her hand weakly as it lay in mine.

'It's okay, Mother. She's here. I'm not going anywhere.' I suddenly felt unclean, as if the words I had murmured were soiled and unworthy of me.

Only in your absence will she be able to navigate the pattern she brought into her current incarnation. Only by leaving will you be able to shed the pattern you brought into yours.

I smiled weakly. The words that appeared in my head were so gentle, so warm, it was as if I were being caressed by the softest, most soothing summer breeze. Then I registered their meaning and my stomach lurched, causing me to dry retch over my lap.

Come to me.

I shook my head. She couldn't make me. She had already tried, and she had failed.

Stifled By Dread. Come to me.

Stifled By Dread. The words reached inside me to the depths of my soul and resonated with the truth that resided there. Those three words encompassed my whole life. They were me and I couldn't resist the one who used them to call me to her.

It felt strange to shuffle to the edge of my bed whilst unhindered by the urge to get as far east as possible, as quickly as possible.

Mother's hand shot out to my arm. 'Where are you going?' She slurred her words as if she were drunk.

Shif gently took her hand in his and said to me, 'Your father and I will look after her. Go to your horse, lad.' His milky, watering eyes sparkled as he whispered, 'She's exquisite.'

I knew it. I could feel it. With my mind full of the horse's beauty, I glanced back at Mother and was shocked by what I saw; the woman who had been at my side, barely eating, drinking or sleeping as she kept vigil over me, appeared to have aged by at least ten years.

I took a step back towards her, but Shif showed me the palms of his hands. 'There's nothing wrong with her that a decent meal and plenty of sleep won't cure. Go to your horse.'

My father nodded in agreement with Shif and flicked his fingers at me, his face slack with relief as Mother finally allowed him to help her up from my bed. I caught sight of myself in the mirror by the bedroom door on my way out and barely recognised the gaunt face looking back at me. The shock that tried to hold me in place fled from the words that were once again placed in my mind.

Come to me.

For the first time in nearly twenty years, I moved willingly, if disbelievingly, towards the unknown.

Chapter Eleven

The street was packed with villagers across its width and as far along its length as I could see, yet it was as if the horse and I were the only ones there. Her silence drowned out the excited shouts and chatter. Her gentle gaze excluded everyone but me. Her dark beauty seemed to extend beyond her physical body and reach out to me so that I couldn't help walking down the cobbled front path to where she stood with her head hanging over the gate.

She was tall and slender, with a glossy black coat. Her refined head could have been chiselled by the finest Sculptor, from her pricked, delicate ears to the gently protruding pools of warmth that were her eyes, and her narrow velvety muzzle. Her mane and tail comprised long, fine black hairs that sparkled in the summer sun, and her long, fine legs were supported by dainty, compact hooves, the front two of which she had placed neatly side by side.

I had been near horses who had visited Coastwood with their Bond-Partners before and had painted them many times, but all I had done was capture their likeness. I had observed none of them as I did this one, for just as she reached out to me, I reached back to her with my mind – and my soul. I couldn't help smiling as I felt the part of myself resurface that I had buried for so long.

My fingers itched to pick up a pencil, yet I couldn't move. Her breath soothed my skin and the calm gentleness that oozed from her made me feel safer than I had since I was a child. I lifted a forefinger to her nose and she sniffed it slowly, carefully, as if she had never scented anything like it – as if she were breathing me into her being. Her eyes drew me in even further, and I became lost in everything she was.

She was in a given place one moment and another the next, for no reason other than she was always where she needed to be. When she was thirsty, she found water. When she was hungry, she moved towards food. When she sensed danger, she moved away from it and when she sensed its absence, she would eat or rest. When she came across the unfamiliar, she was curious, and when she came across that which she recognised, she rediscovered it with enthusiasm. She was as content when the sun was warm on her back as when the chilly rain battered her. She accepted surprise by employing flight, and lack of control over her environment by employing grace. She moved through life with elegance and confidence, and she wanted me along with her for the journey.

I tried to disentangle myself from her at the realisation that although I had rarely felt safer than in her presence, I had never been more at risk… but I couldn't, and not because she held on to me or trapped me in any way – because I found that when it came to it, I didn't want to.

Stifled By Dread.

Risk. The name I chose for her was as true as that which she had chosen for me. I shuddered, sensing something solidify between us. There was no going back.

You should nourish your body and rest, she informed me. *Then we will leave.*

No. I can't do that.

Risk blinked slowly, her long, black eyelashes brushing the tiny, delicate hairs of her lower eyelids before revealing the soft warmth of her eyes once more. *The act of incarnating into a physical body affirms a soul's desire to experience that which would otherwise merely be conceptual. You have discovered that eliminating new experiences from your life has eroded your desire to live it.*

The heat of shame instantly burned my face as Risk identified so precisely the feelings that, until that moment, I had refused to acknowledge to myself. I took a step back from her, terrified of her ability and willingness to confront that which I preferred to avoid.

Now that you have discovered such, Risk continued, *we will embark on a life of varying experience.*

No. I can't do that, I repeated.

You already have. In accepting our bond you have concluded your period of discovering that which is not helpful to you. Now you will experience that which is.

But I can't leave Coastwood. I can't leave my mother. I already know that isn't helpful to me; the last time I did it, I died.

You have chosen to leave physical incarnations more times than you currently remember. Some of them you left because you had learnt all you could from your situation. Some you left in order to take experiences with you that would provide opportunities for learning in subsequent incarnations. Others you left because in so doing you would provide a learning experience for someone else. You left the incarnation to which you refer for all three reasons. The resulting opportunity for learning is sizeable and therefore carries much potential.

I didn't want to understand the words that drifted so lightly and yet so confidently into my mind, let alone believe them, but I couldn't seem to avoid doing either; the connection between me and the horse who stood so elegantly before me steadied my mind so that I couldn't sidestep that which I found unnerving.

My knees buckled as I realised I could no longer delude myself as I had grown so used to doing, and I put out a hand to steady myself. I had been aiming for the gate, but instead found Risk's shoulder. The connection between us intensified, and I felt as if I were floating in her warmth. I couldn't help wondering how one who was so gentle and caring, so beautiful inside and out, could have caused me so much pain and turmoil during the past week.

I merely woke your soul to the agreement it made with mine. The pain and turmoil you experienced were of your own creation. That which you avoid or resist only ever increases in strength. That which you accept loses its ability to affect you so that you may move forward unencumbered.

There are some things that are impossible to accept, I told her. *Being taken from my family? Being forced to work for men who murdered my father and brother? Being beaten and tortured? Being killed in a war I never chose to fight in?*

Have your feelings about your experiences allowed you to live a fulfilling incarnation this time around?

No, but that's not the point! I wasn't sure how I was shouting in my mind, only that I was.

It is exactly the point. Risk swished her tail at a biter who had landed on her belly, then was motionless once more. *Nourish your body and rest,* she repeated. *I would do the same. Then we will leave.*

I had a sudden sense of her hunger, thirst and fatigue after days of travel with little opportunity to rest. Desperate to ease the discomfort she had sensed me inflicting upon myself, she had closed the distance between us at a pace that had punished her body, yet she stood before me as patiently as if she had just arrived from the nearest pasture.

I stepped away from her and was immediately deafened by the shouts and squeals of children, their parents scolding them, and questions shouted to me in a continuous and unrelenting flow.

'You look terrible, Devlin. Are you ill?'

'What's happening? Why is the horse here?'

'Where have you been for the last week? My Polly said you haven't been taking your classes at school.'

'Where are your parents?'

'What are you going to do with a horse who doesn't appear to have a Bond-Partner? Are you going to take her to The Gathering?'

'Should we see if her Bond-Partner's out there somewhere? Maybe they're injured and she's come to get help?'

'Devlin? DEVLIN! Don't just stand there with her, DO SOMETHING!'

I held my hands up to my ears, trying to block them all out. I wanted to run from them, to retreat into our cottage where I was safe and slam the front door behind me. But I would be leaving a part of myself outside, I suddenly realised. Suddenly, the cottage no longer felt the safest place to be. Without thinking, I put my hand back to Risk's shoulder. I raised my other hand and waited for the noise to die down.

'I've been ill, but I'm feeling better,' I said in my classroom voice. The remaining chatter stopped and there was silence. 'This is Risk. She tugged me but I was unable to go to her.' I coughed as the lie tightened around my throat. 'I couldn't find a way to go to her,' I corrected myself. 'She's my Bond-Partner and she needs food, water and rest. Clear a path, please, so I can take her round the back, to our paddock.'

'Bond-Partner?'

'Risk?'

'Tugged?'

'Don't people normally have a Quest Ceremony when they get tugged?'

I smiled down at the child who had strung a sentence together when the adults surrounding her had only managed to utter the odd stunned word.

'Yes, they do.'

'When will you have yours then?'

'Um, I don't know. Maybe when I leave.' The panic that shot through me at my own words was matched in strength by my certainty that leaving the village with Risk was inevitable. I felt as if the sea, which I had avoided so rigorously for so long, had reached out to me, taken me into its depths, and was carrying me away on the strongest of tides which I couldn't hope to resist. Yet strangely, the terror I had always associated with such an event felt as if it were being held away from me by the safety net that had closed around me the moment I laid my eyes upon Risk.

I blinked. A pathway had opened up through the crowd of villagers, yet Risk was still standing by the gate, waiting for me to accompany her to the paddock.

'When are you leaving?' a parent of one of my students asked. Before I could worry that she was cross with me for announcing my intention to abandon my pupils, she smiled and said, 'How long do we have to prepare for your Quest Ceremony?'

A loud gasp made me turn to where my parents and Shif were now standing on the front step. My mother sagged against my father and Shif stood with his arms crossed, smiling.

'Um, that's something I need to discuss with my family,' I

replied, then raised my voice. 'We'll let you know when my Quest Ceremony will be, and we'll see you then.'

I opened the gate, careful to keep my hand on Risk's shoulder. *Come with me.*

Always.

~

'But you can't go, Devlin, you know you can't,' Mother said, gripping my hand so tightly, I could barely feel my fingers. 'I can't lose you again.'

It still felt strange that although I was every bit as terrified at the thought as she, Risk's presence – both in my mind and just in front of me, where she grazed in the evening sunshine whilst our chickens clucked and pecked around her feet – held my fear at a distance, as it had since her arrival the previous day.

'You won't be losing me. I'm not being taken by murderers and sent into danger, I'll be with my Bond-Partner.' The words felt strange as I spoke them. 'I'll be with Risk.'

'You'll be AT risk, and you know it. You don't know where you'll be going or what you'll find there. You don't know who you'll come across or what they'll do to you. You don't even know how to look after yourself; you don't know how to hunt, which plants are safe to gather, how to find water or where it's safe to sleep.'

She was right. The terror that hung at a distance edged closer and tendrils of it poked through the gaps in the safety net around my mind. I couldn't leave.

The setting sun was suddenly blocked from view as a black, velvety muzzle appeared in front of my face, blowing warm air laced with the scent of freshly chewed grass. The gaps in the net closed, squeezing out my fear, even as Mother squealed, jumped to her feet, and pulled at my hand, trying to get me to stand up alongside her.

I chuckled as I resisted her. 'You have nothing to fear from Risk,' I said, stroking my horse's nose between her nostrils. 'She's helping me. She'd never hurt me, or you.'

'She's already hurting me,' Mother whispered, wiping away the tears now spilling over her lower eyelids with the back of her hand.

It will serve her to remember a time when she was afraid and yet trusted herself. Risk's eyes were pools of warmth and safety as she regarded us both.

'Um, Risk said... no, that's not it, she didn't say anything. Not out loud, anyway.' I frowned and then tried again. 'Risk thinks it will help if you can remember a time when you were scared but trusted yourself.' I felt a rush of warmth and approval from my horse as I passed on her advice.

'Right now!' Mother said. 'I'm terrified right now, and I completely trust myself that my instincts are right. You. Shouldn't. Leave.'

Survival instincts are useful when a body's integrity is at risk. They are a hindrance to its long-term health if they are repeatedly listened to over the voice of its soul.

The voice of its soul?

Birthing your siblings was difficult for your mother. When your birthing time was approaching the Healers wanted to stimulate your early arrival to lower the risk of her leaving her incarnation prematurely. She listened to the voice of her soul. She knew you weren't ready to be born and ignored her instinct to preserve her own life at the cost of yours. You both survived because she trusted herself.

I spoke Risk's counsel out loud for my mother. I couldn't have foreseen the effect it would have on her. Her fear deserted her like water draining from a sink after its plug is pulled. She sank back down to the ground, her hand releasing its grip on mine and falling into her lap.

'Mother? Are you alright?'

She looked at me dazedly, her mouth opening and closing without sound.

'Do you need some water?'

She shook her head.

'Then what? What is it?'

She reached a shaking hand to my cheek and I grasped it and held it there. Risk lowered her head and rested it, ever so gently, on the top of Mother's head. I sat and waited.

Eventually, she said, 'You're breathing but you're barely alive, Devlin. How did we get to this point? How did I let this happen?' Her eyes pleaded as she added, 'Can you forgive me?'

I wrapped my arms around her and whispered into her ear, 'What for?'

She didn't answer. She was limp in my arms. I held her away from me. 'Mother?' I shook her gently. 'Mother?'

She has grown unused to living without the false strength afforded her by her fear, Risk volunteered. *Now that she has remembered where her true strength lies she will need much practice in choosing it over that on which she has come to rely.*

And she needs me gone in order to practise. I neither needed nor waited for Risk to confirm my observation, instead calling, 'Father, can you come out here?'

'What the... Mowaya? MOWAYA!' Father came tearing across the paddock with Shif shuffling slowly in his wake to where I sat in the grass, nestling Mother in my arms. 'What happened? Is she... is she...'

'She's exhausted,' I said, only just realising it myself. 'She needs to sleep and for me to be gone by the time she wakes up.'

Chapter Eleven

Father flung his arms in the air. 'Are you at least going to tell me what this has all been about, these past fifteen years? All of a sudden, you're one of the Horse-Bonded and finally leaving the village as Shif advised you to, he's allowed back into the house when I never understood why your mother banned him in the first place, and now your mother's almost comatose out here in the paddock? I mean, what the hell, Devlin? There's only so much patience a man can find.'

It was my father's shoulder that Risk chose as the next place to rest her muzzle. He stiffened but then sagged underneath her, though she burdened him with little of her weight, all his frustration fleeing from her warmth and patience.

'You're going to have to find a whole lot more, I'm afraid,' I told him.

He looked at me searchingly and I paused, unsure of what to say.

The truth, Risk offered. *He will recognise its energy even if its subject is outside his experience and he will accept nothing less. Acceptance of mistakes is necessary for all of you if you are to move past them.*

I took a deep breath and said, 'You know how bad my nightmares were.'

He shuddered and nodded. 'They're another thing I still don't understand, but your mother said that asking you about them would only make things worse for you.'

'She was right, but now I need to tell you I wasn't so much having nightmares as reliving a past life that she and I shared. She was my mother then too. We lived with my father and brother…'

'Pa and Henry,' Father said with a sigh.

I nodded. 'Pa and Henry. Men came to our village. They killed Pa and took me, Henry, and other men and lads of seafaring age to their warship. They killed Henry before it set sail, then forced the rest of us to help sail it. I was killed in a battle on it when I was twenty.'

'You were... you were killed?' Father said. Shif lowered himself painfully slowly to the grass beside me and, despite his advanced years, crossed his legs in front of him and leant on them, looking from Father to me.

'Jimmy was killed,' I said. 'My name was Jimmy then. I sketched it all while it was happening, and Mother was there, watching me. Through her, Jimmy's ma knew what was happening to him – he was skewered by a splinter from the main mast while hanging from his broken wrist and dislocated shoulder. We felt everything Ma and Jimmy felt as he died.' My voice shook and I swallowed for fear I would sob.

Shif placed his hand gently on my shoulder and squeezed it.

'Your last nightmare,' Father whispered. 'You bled from your chest, your wrist was broken and your shoulder dislocated.' He looked suddenly at Shif. 'Did you know about this?'

'I suspected,' Shif said tactfully.

'Why the hell didn't you say? Don't you think I had a right to know?'

Shif shrugged. 'It wasn't my secret to tell.'

'Risk has just helped Mother to realise how to stop being so afraid for me, but she'll need your help,' I said, looking from Father to Shif.

'She'll have it, lad,' Shif said. 'Won't she, Lennon?'

Father crouched down in front of Mother and stroked her hair back from her face. 'Of course she will.' He put one arm under her knees and the other around her back and, with a grunt, lifted her as he got to his feet. 'I'll put her to bed and then we'd better spread the word that your Quest Ceremony has been brought forward, hadn't we?'

He walked towards the cottage, leaving Shif and me sitting in the grass. Risk grazed by my feet.

'You've taken to it like a lamb to the teat, haven't you?' Shif said, his eyes twinkling.

'What?'

'Being Horse-Bonded. You're comfortable around Risk, like you've always known her. You've listened to her more in the single day you've been bonded than you have to me or your father in the past twenty years, and you're passing on her advice in the manner of one who's been doing it for a lifetime. Flaming lanterns, you even look like the human and horse versions of one another!'

I grinned. It was kind of true; I was as slim as Risk was slender, my hair was as black as hers and my eyes were the same dark shade of brown.

'I'm not sure how it's happened,' I said. Then I remembered the effect Risk had on both of my parents during the past half hour, and realised it wasn't true. My Bond-Partner affected people. She reached into them and stripped away their anger and fear so that the best parts of them could shine through. I held a hand out to her and she sniffed it briefly before returning to her grazing. 'I'm not sure why it's happened,' I corrected myself.

'I hoped and hoped it would. Then when I saw the evidence that you were being tugged, I thought I must be having the most pleasant of dreams. When I saw Risk standing outside your cottage – well, there are no words to describe how I felt.'

'You hoped a horse would tug me? You actually thought there was a chance it might happen?'

'As soon as I saw your Skill for the first time, I knew you'd have a bigger part to play in The New than most, lad. When you resisted playing it for so long, I realised it would take one far stronger and wiser than me to help you tread the path you have in front of you. Now she's here, and she's everything I hoped she would be and more.' Shif plucked a stalk of grass and stripped the seeds from its head as he gazed at Risk.

'You've always been such a good friend to me,' I said, 'no matter how I've behaved. I'm sorry for the way Mother and I have treated you. We've just been so…'

'Scared.' Shif discarded the stalk and clapped me on the back. 'I know, lad. And you needn't worry about your mother. Your father is most of what she needs now and the self-portrait you painted on your qualification day will be the rest.'

I frowned in confusion.

'If I can see that you painted your soul into it, she can. With a connection like the two of you have, I'm pretty sure she'll be able to know how you're doing at any time she wants to, just by looking at it.'

I wanted to tell him that wasn't possible but I knew he spoke the truth – I recognised the feel of it in the same way that Risk had told me my father would.

'How do you know these things?' I asked him. 'How have you always known so much more than the rest of us?'

Shif chuckled, his eyes twinkling again. 'There's a little voice that speaks to me from somewhere deep inside. I've learnt to trust it.'

'The voice of your soul,' I murmured. 'You listen to the voice of your soul. Mother knows how to do that too – at least Risk just helped her to remember.'

'The voice of my soul.' Shif breathed the words as if he revered them. 'I've never heard it called that before, but that's exactly what it is.' He slapped his knee. 'Thunder and lightning, I wish you and your mare were staying longer. There's so much I could learn from you both.'

'You could come with us?' I said suddenly. There was no harm in reducing the risk I was taking in leaving by having a friend along, was there?

Risk lifted her head and gazed at me, her lower jaw moving from side to side as she chewed long stalks of grass. *Stifled By Dread. There is an element of risk in everything we do. You cannot know the composition of the air around you yet you breathe it regardless. You cannot know that the ground will not give way beneath your next footstep yet you commit your weight as if it will hold.*

What if it doesn't? My heart pounded. I hadn't considered the unknowns she had just brought to my attention.

You find a way to climb out of the resulting chasm. Confidence arises not from external assurances that you will be safe but from knowing you will find a way to cope with whatever befalls you.

But I don't know I can do that.

Then know we can do it. I will help you hear the voice of your soul. When you cannot then I will ensure you hear the voice of mine.

Once again, the safety net that was Risk closed around me, holding my terror away so that although I was aware of its existence, it couldn't take hold of me. I looked apologetically at Shif, who chuckled again.

'Don't worry, lad, I'll not take it personally. When a bird comes into his full plumage, he needs to fly.'

I got up and extended my hands to my friend and mentor. Once I had pulled him to his feet, I drew him into a hug from which I found it hard to withdraw. He smelt of herbs, transporting me to his workshop and cottage, where I had spent so many happy hours as a boy. His arms felt strong as they held me, even though they trembled with the effort. Rather than standing squarely on both feet, he rested the leg that had resisted my effort to pull him upright. I had always seen him as an old man, but now he was very old and I didn't know if I would see him again. I tried and failed to stifle a sob.

He wriggled out of my arms and held me away from him. 'There's no reason for any of that,' he said, though he blinked away his own tears. 'You've accepted your bond with Risk, so you let her take you away from here and you don't look back. Have you got that, lad?'

I didn't trust myself to do anything but nod.

'And when you have the time, I'll expect you back here with sketches of your travels. Keep them small, mind, so you can fit them all in. You can't be expecting Risk, here, to carry too much weight.' He stroked my horse's glossy black neck, and she made the low, husky noise in her throat that she'd made on seeing me exit the cottage both mornings since she had arrived outside its front gate. 'You're a beautiful girl, in every way,' he told her, then without looking at me, shuffled away, saying over his shoulder, 'It's getting dark, so I'll be off. I'll be back in the morning for your Quest Ceremony.'

Chapter Twelve

*A*s always, I rose with the dawn, early though it was since we were only four days past the longest day of the year. Like the previous morning, the dullness with which I was used to waking was immediately replaced by a burst of excitement for what another day with Risk would bring... followed immediately by intense dread at the very same thought. On this morning, I would have to navigate the unknowns presented by the Quest Ceremony that the villagers of Coastwood had refused to be denied, even though Risk's presence negated the need for me to actually go on a quest... and then I would have to leave the village. Actually leave.

Stifled By Dread. For the second morning in a row, Risk took hold of my attention with her use of the name which I hated and loved in equal measure; hated because it was true but loved because the fact it was true afforded it a greater hold on me than did my panic... which quickly receded as Risk took its place in my mind. *Rise and ready yourself to leave. I await you where we first met.*

I scrambled out of bed and pulled apart my curtains to see that she was indeed standing out on the street before our front gate.

How did you get there? Who opened the gate for you? In any case, you're too early, the Quest Ceremony isn't for a couple of hours.

Your gate was an insufficient barrier to my intention to leave. A ceremony is not appropriate. We will leave now.

I know we need to leave before Mother wakes, but she's so exhausted, she'll probably sleep for a week.

Do not underestimate the strength of the connection shared by the two of you. Your departure will cause her difficulty that will be insurmountable unless she is as far removed from the waking world as she is presently. We will leave now.

Risk's warmth soothed me even as she threw aside the plan for the morning to which I had resigned myself, and my ever-present – if currently held at a distance – panic tried to batter its way past her and take hold of me.

We will leave now, she repeated, her calm intention reaching deep inside me until it found its echo.

We will leave now, I affirmed, shocking myself. How had that happened? She hadn't commanded me or even convinced me; she had repeated her intention and I had known, deep down, that it was the right thing to do, for my mother if maybe not for everyone who was looking forward to Coastwood's first Quest Ceremony in six decades.

I also knew that I didn't have time to think about it. I needed to leave as soon as possible – but my morning routine awaited me. I tiptoed down the hall to the bathroom, relieved to hear two lots of gentle snoring as I passed my parents' room. I stepped towards the bath... no, I didn't have time for that. I turned to the clean, freshly pressed clothes on the stool behind the door... but then couldn't bring myself to put them on because I hadn't bathed first. I stood where I was, paralysed by uncertainty, which in itself brought my panic closer until it poked at me through Risk's warmth.

Riiiiiiiiisk!

You need not give up that which serves you. Merely adapt it to your current circumstances.

Relief flooded me. I ran a bath and sat in it, washing, whilst it was still filling. I decreased the number of heartbeats for which I shaved, combed my hair and dressed, then hurried back to my room, hoisted the back-sack I had packed the previous evening onto my shoulder and tiptoed down the stairs. I hesitated in the hallway, then remembered Risk's counsel. I hurried to the kitchen, made my breakfast and bolted it down before guiltily shoving into the top of my back-sack the food Father had put on the table ready to present to me during my Quest Ceremony. I hastened back along the hallway to the front door, turned its handle... and paused to look back at the place that had been my haven for the past thirty-five years.

My stomach churned uncomfortably, and I allowed the door handle to return to its resting place. What was I thinking, leaving my home behind? Mother was right; I couldn't hunt or gather food and I had no clue what was out there or what might happen. What if I weren't up to being Risk's Bond-Partner? What if she gave up on me and abandoned me? What would I do then?

You would look for a way to climb out of the chasm in which you found yourself, Risk reminded me.

I didn't actually decide to turn the door handle and walk down the front path, but I found myself doing it anyway as my feet responded to the part of me, deep inside, that Risk's gentle patience had reached yet again. When I neared the gate, she stepped back from it and turned to walk up the cobbled street, leaving me to hurry in order to benefit from the added reassurance that I knew walking with a hand on her shoulder would afford me. The faster I walked, the more she increased her pace so that she was always a few strides ahead of me and I couldn't touch her.

The further I got from my home, the more pronounced became my panic and the more intently it reached for me. Risk didn't appear to notice it stabbing at her warmth and confidence, even when it broke through to me, causing me to gasp and stagger to a stop. The pain and terror of drowning whilst suspended from a broken wrist and dislocated shoulder caused me to clutch at my throat and gasp for air. When I could breathe again, agony pierced my chest along with the echo of the stake that had splintered from HMS Royal Sovereign's mast. I fell to my knees, my right hand now pressed to the site of my wound while my left hung limply, its knuckles resting on the cobbles. I had to get up. I had to get back to Ma.

I was vaguely aware of the sound of shuffling footsteps in between the pounding of blood through my ears.

'Here, lad.' Shif dropped a sketchpad onto my lap and pushed a pencil into my right hand. 'Draw it all. Get it out. Then it'll lose its hold on you, like always.'

Sketch? Now? I couldn't. I had to get back to Ma. Why had I ever thought of leaving her? Nothing good ever came of doing that.

Stifled By Dread. Climb out of the chasm into which you have fallen. Risk's counsel was the faintest of whispers in my mind, yet I couldn't ignore it. It grabbed hold of me and held fast, a lone beacon of calm within my thrashing, swirling terror.

My hand moved the pencil around the page in front of me at impossible speed, only stopping to turn the page before doing the same on the next. By the time I had filled three pages with

Chapter Twelve

sketches, the pain in my wrist had decreased enough that I could turn the page with the hand it commanded. By the time I had filled the fourth, my wrist was free of pain and my shoulder was merely aching. When I had filled eight pages with my sketches of Jimmy's trauma and subsequent death, I was pain free and my breathing had returned to normal.

Shif's mottled, gnarled hand gently closed the pad so that I found myself staring at its cover. 'Well done, lad.'

I squinted up at him. 'What are you doing here?'

He chuckled. 'It's a surprise to me too. I woke stupidly early with a feeling you needed me, so here I am along with my Quest Ceremony gifts to you.' He flapped five more sketchpads up and down and pulled a box of pencils from a back pocket of his trousers. He looked up and down the deserted street. 'You're leaving after the Farmers have left for the fields, but before everyone else is up and about. I know enduring a Quest Ceremony would have been difficult for you, but I'm thinking that avoiding it wasn't your idea?'

I got to my feet. 'No, it wasn't.' I glanced at where Risk stood waiting for me.

Shif followed my gaze. 'I'll let everyone know it was her preference, then there'll be no hard feelings towards you, lad. Your horse is wise; I can't think it would have done you or your mother any good for the entire village to witness you going through what you did just now.'

I nodded as the realisation dawned that Risk had known it would happen. 'I... I'm scared to walk any further. What if it happens again?'

I will carry you. Risk blinked slowly.

Panic flared within me afresh at the thought of taking on another unknown. *I can't ride.*

You could not respire until you drew your first breath. Stifled By Dread. We must leave now. I will carry you.

'You should ask Risk to carry you,' Shif said. 'If she agrees, I'll help you onto her back. Hurry up and ask her, lad, you don't have long before this street will begin filling with people.'

I looked between the two of them and nodded dumbly.

'Wait a moment.' Shif dragged the straps of my back-sack down my arms, loosened its drawstrings and carefully slid the six sketchpads inside. He added the box of pencils and a parcel of herbal preparations he took from his pouch, then tightened and knotted the drawstrings and held out the straps for me to put my arms back in. He adjusted the sack on my back, yanking at my shirt in several places to smooth out wrinkles that might rub, as if he were a parent helping a small child. He gently turned me to face Risk and said, 'I've seen this done once before, when a Horse-Bonded sprained her ankle and couldn't mount unaided. Grab a handful of her mane in your left hand, lad, a big one mind, then bend your leg and jump on three. When your belly's level with her back, lean forward and swing your leg over.'

I moved towards my horse in a daze of fear, weariness and confusion, softened only by Risk's warmth swirling gently around in my mind. As soon as I touched her, my mind calmed.

'You can't lift me, Shif.'

He bent down beside me. 'Watch me. Hurry, lad, we don't have time to argue.' I bent my leg and he grasped my knee. 'One, two, three.' Shif heaved and I jumped.

The instant I sat on Risk's back, my mind cleared. We were leaving. It was right and necessary. My horse was right and necessary. Our bond was right and necessary. How could I have doubted any of it? Why did I panic? Because I had walked alone. Risk left me behind.

Why didn't you offer to carry me from the gate, or at least walk

Chapter Twelve

with me so I could touch you? I demanded of her. *Why are you only helping me now?*

We have much work to do if you are to accept the experiences of your other incarnation for what they were and release the emotions associated with them so that you can move forward. We have just made a start.

'You did that on purpose?' I said out loud. 'You knew it would happen and you made me go through it on purpose?'

When there is an opportunity to move closer to balance I will always ensure that we take it, Risk informed me and immediately walked forward.

Unprepared, my upper body was left behind and my left hand, clutching her mane, caused me to skew to the left. Shif gripped my left thigh with both hands, holding me in place with surprising strength whilst tottering along beside me, until I regained my balance.

Like that, you mean? I forgot my anger as Risk carried me so surely, so confidently forward.

We have made a start, she repeated.

'Like a lamb to the teat,' Shif said, grinning. 'Fare you well, lad.' He stopped walking.

'Shif, are you alright?' *Risk, stop!*

I turned to where Shif stood on the cobbles, but was immediately forced to face forward again, grip hard with my legs and grab even more mane in both hands, in order to stay in position on Risk's back. My horse ignored my request and continued to walk towards the end of Coastwood's main street.

'Risk! Stop!' I repeated out loud.

'She shouldn't and she won't,' Shif called just loudly enough to reach me. 'I told you, lad, let her take you away from here, and don't look back.'

Risk was right to keep going. Shif was right to stay where he was. I was right to take heart and strength from the determination I could feel in every muscle, every nerve, every bone in Risk's body as she walked away from everything that felt safe. I knew all of those things with a level of confidence I had never experienced before.

I remembered Risk's assurance from the previous evening. *I will help you hear the voice of your soul. When you can't then I will ensure you hear the voice of mine.* Whilst sitting on her back, I found I could hear it loud and clear.

The only problem was, sitting on Risk's back for any length of time wasn't easy. When she stepped from the uneven cobbles of the street to the level, sun-baked pasture beyond, she picked up her pace and turned suddenly to the left, taking us away from the rapidly rising sun. She stopped just long enough for me to push against a conveniently placed gatepost and right myself rather than continue sliding off her right side, then walked mercilessly onward. When she snorted and side-stepped a low-growing, prickly bush, however, I slid to the ground without impediment, landing on the shoulder whose dislocation my sketches had exorcised only minutes before, and winding myself. By the time I had regained my breath and got to my feet, rubbing my shoulder, Risk was fifty paces distant. Panicked, I looked longingly back towards Coastwood; towards safety.

Yet it didn't feel like safety anymore. It didn't afford me the calm confidence I had felt whilst astride Risk, that whatever happened, I would be able to cope with it. My head swivelled so quickly back to where my horse continued to walk away from me that I cricked my neck violently.

Risk, wait!

Waiting is not moving forward, she advised me without slowing her pace.

But I'm in pain! I landed on my shoulder and my neck hurts. I rubbed the site of the ceaseless, stabbing pain, trying to ease the crick.

Avoiding discomfort is not moving forward. Resist it not. Accept it as an experience from which to learn. View it as a variation of your preferred experience that will afford context and depth to all your other experiences.

Accept pain? My mind spun. *Accept it? But it hurt.*

Accept it for that which it really is. You yet resist. Your village is waking.

I watched her rump getting gradually smaller as she continued to walk west.

Please, Risk, come back for me, or at least wait for me?

Stifled By Dread. You have fallen into another chasm. Only you can climb out. Her instruction resonated with my whole being until I felt as if it had originated with me. I walked after her, wincing at the pain in my neck and kneading it even more firmly. Then I was jogging, despite my back-sack bouncing up and down and causing me even more discomfort. By the time I was running as fast as my legs could carry me, I had forgotten about my aching shoulder, and the pain in my neck was more of a twinge.

When I caught up with Risk, she diverted from her path towards a fallen tree. She sidled into place next to it and looked around at me expectantly.

I was torn. I knew how much calmer and clearer I felt whilst astride her, but I also knew how easy it was to fall off her, and how much it could hurt.

Your next departure from my back will differ from the first in nature but equal it in terms of necessity, Risk advised me calmly. *You have shielded yourself from so many experiences desired by your soul that you have much on which to catch up.*

My soul wants me to fall from your back and hurt myself?

Your soul desires to break free from the restrictions your personality has imposed upon it. Your mentor helped you to discover one method for doing such. You are in the process of discovering another. I will carry you until you fall once more. Accept the inevitable and be little affected or resist it and be affected more.

Chapter Thirteen

It was four painful days before I understood Risk's counsel and realised that bracing myself in order to avoid falling from her back didn't prevent it from happening. It was a further couple of days before I acted upon her advice and accepted that I might fall, by which time far more of my body was bruised than unbruised, I could barely walk due to a throbbing hip, a skinned knee and a sprained ankle, and could hardly bear the pain of sitting on Risk's back due to the constant spasming in my own.

I was no better at riding Risk – I certainly felt no more balanced or secure – yet to my astonishment, once I accepted the possibility that I could slide from her back at any given moment, in any of the painful ways I had already experienced or one of the many I was sure were still possible, it stopped happening. Moreover, the fact that I could remain in place for decent periods of time meant I could hear the voice of her soul more consistently and without interference from the panic that continued to hover at the outskirts of her influence. There were even times when I was pretty sure I heard my own.

When Risk stopped to graze or rest, however, I was vulnerable. The damage my body had sustained meant that I needed to rest whenever the situation presented itself, so remaining near Risk as she grazed, in order to put a hand on her shoulder, rump, back or any other part of her so that I could remain calm and clear-minded, wasn't an option. As soon as I sat down on the ground, whether in open plains, forest glades, scrubby hillsides or the lush grassland sustained by streams, rivers and lakes, my appreciation of the beauty of my unfamiliar surroundings was immediately swamped by my terror of all the accompanying unknowns.

Where were we? If something happened to Risk, would I find my way back to Coastwood? What type of animals lived in the area? Were they dangerous? Would they see me or Risk as food? And on the subject of food, what would I do when the supplies I had brought with me ran out? Nothing I could see looked familiar or even vaguely edible even though Risk happily tucked into whatever nature provided. When we stopped to rest near water, I was relieved of the fear of not finding any, but when there was none nearby, I dreaded having to drink from my pouch for fear I wouldn't be able to refill it.

Risk's counsel was always the same. *Stifled By Dread. When you cannot hear the voice of your soul then allow yourself to see it.*

I would reach for a sketchpad and pencil and allow Risk's use of my name to draw out the part of me that was otherwise smothered by my fear and resistance. When my hand eventually stopped moving across the pages, I would peruse my sketches and, as Risk had advised, see that which I could not hear.

Through my sketches, I discovered which parts of which

Chapter Thirteen

plants I could eat, for they seemed to reach out of my drawings to me. I knew where I was in relation to Coastwood and also where we were heading, though I had never been to the home of the Horse-Bonded for which Risk had informed me we were bound. As I sketched, I knew where there was water, for I sensed it as easily as I had sensed the subjects awaiting my observation as a teenager, and by the same means, I knew there were no predators in the vicinity.

Each time I sketched yet another beautiful vista without even a hint of menace to warn me I had something to fear, I could hear the voice that sang with joy deep inside me. Each time I included in my sketch the slender, elegant black mare who was never far from my side, the voice became all of me, and through it, I knew more of her than I could sense through our bond and even more than she had shown me when I had chosen her name.

Though my sketches were true to the refined features and graceful beauty of Risk's body, they didn't confine her to her physicality, for that would have been a falsehood; she occupied her body but she was also everywhere and everything else. She was the wisdom of the trees, the warmth of the sun, and the strength of the moon. She was ageless in a way I could sense but not comprehend, and sage to a degree that overwhelmed me and convinced me never to question her counsel or judgement.

Whilst I was sketching or perusing my sketches of her, I remembered what I knew about her. Whilst I was astride her, I also remembered. When I was neither, yet able to touch any part of her body, I remembered knowing something that would ease the continuing panic held at bay by her warmth, and remained calm.

So passed the weeks it took us to reach the home of the Horse-Bonded. When we topped a hill and saw paddocks stretching away from us towards distant – and seemingly enormous – buildings, I was stunned to realise that not only had we arrived at our destination having experienced none of the horrors I had been convinced would befall me were I to leave Coastwood, but I was relatively sanguine about the multitude of unknowns that were undoubtedly about to unfold before me.

You will not find it so easy to remain calm once we are apart but events will unfold as necessary, Risk told me.

Sitting more easily upon her back now that I had recovered from my sprains and bruises and relaxed into following her body with my own, I accepted her counsel wholeheartedly. I adjusted my weight as she picked her way slowly down the hill towards the bank of a fast-flowing river and adjusted it again once we were on more level ground.

My attention was taken and held by the water that spat, churned and groaned its way past us as if fighting the inevitability of reaching the sea; I felt an affinity with it even though, astride Risk's back as I was, I knew the futility of its fight. What would be, would be, regardless of fight or resistance.

I wanted to smooth out the water, to help it know that accepting its fate would make the journey towards the sea calmer and more pleasurable, even though Risk's warning was a necessary reminder that I still had much to learn myself in that regard.

You have learnt much and progressed well during our time together, she informed me, and I sat up a little straighter, feeling as if my chest would burst with pride and pleasure. *Were you not ready for all that you have learnt to be challenged then we would not yet have arrived here.*

Despite being astride her and at my strongest, my heart lurched at the thought that everything I had learnt and become was about to be put at risk.

Previous experience has taught you that the absence of risk and variation generates boredom and depression, my horse reminded me. *Recent experience has taught you that embracing that which is unknown renders it not only known but life affirming. Allow that experience to give you the strength that you currently gain from physical contact with me and once more the unknown will become a source of vitality.*

I couldn't help but understand as her body moved mine, ensuring that my mind followed hers. *I have to stand on my own two feet.*

Stand on your feet while knowing mine will never be far away. Risk turned to the left, away from the river and along a stony path that bisected the paddocks.

The first few on either side had sheep and cows grazing within them, some of whom lifted their heads to watch our passage for the few seconds it took them to grow bored of the sight of us, before returning their attention to the pasture. When we reached paddocks containing horses, we caused more of a stir.

A white horse came trotting over to the fence, tossing her head, followed by one the colour of sun-ripened wheat with a white stripe down the front of her nose. They whickered to Risk, their nostrils vibrating in time with their deep, throaty greetings. My horse nearly unseated me when she came to a sudden, rigid halt, her neck held high and her ears pricked in the mares' direction. She took a step towards them and then laid her ears flat back against her head. She stamped a front foot and squealed so loudly, I flinched.

The two horses spun around and galloped away, tails streaming out behind them and hooves kicking up a trail of grass tufts that drifted slowly back down to the ground. I could feel Risk's heart pounding against my left leg as she moved closer to the fence and watched the mares. I sensed her waiting for them to return and complete what seemed to me to be a very peculiar greeting. They raced almost to the far fence of their paddock, then turned, one to the right and the other to the left, and tore back towards us. Risk's heart rate increased until her whole body was shuddering in anticipation of their imminent approach. When they skidded to a halt in front of us, she reached out and touched her nose to the white mare's, then stamped her foot, squealed, and spun in a full circle to face them again.

'That was well sat for an experienced rider, let alone a newly bonded one,' boomed a female voice behind me.

'Barely.' The word only just escaped my lips before Risk touched noses with the wheat-coloured horse and repeated her spin in the opposite direction, reversing the momentum that had left me hanging on to her neck with my arms, and her back with my right thigh, so that I regained my place atop her.

'Bravo!' The woman clapped and Risk, still on her toes, jumped. 'Sorry, love.' A hand appeared in front of my horse's nose. She sniffed it hurriedly, distractedly, and allowed it to stroke her cheek. It was joined by a short body and a plump face with flushed cheeks and a friendly smile. The woman tilted her head towards Risk. 'She'll be wanting to have a play with these two before taking a paddock nearer the buildings, and you'll be wanting to get off her before that happens. You've done well to stay on board this far, but best not to push your luck, eh? Falling off hurts. Believe me, I know it only too well.'

I didn't have the wherewithal to assure her I was guaranteed to know it even better. Play? Risk wanted to play with these two horses? That was why she was behaving so oddly? It was strange to sense from her that playing was exactly what my usually calm, gentle horse wanted, and almost as weird to realise that the woman had known it even as I sat wondering what in the light was going on.

I slid from Risk's back as the woman opened the gate to the paddock. Neither of the mares attempted to leave it but trotted

Chapter Thirteen

back and forth in an arc around the gateway, tails held high and nostrils flaring, waiting for Risk to join them. She needed no further invitation and, without even a backward glance towards me, thundered into the paddock and galloped off, whinnying loudly with the two of them in pursuit.

It was as if my mind split in two. Part of me was mesmerised by the sight of Risk behaving in such an uncontained manner and by my sense of her power, strength and joy. The other part was horrified at her sudden departure and her apparent lack of concern for my state of mind, or even survival. She had abandoned me, just as I had always feared she would. She had brought me to a strange place and then left me exposed and vulnerable.

A sickening pain in my wrist was joined almost immediately by agony in my shoulder and then also by the heaving and gasping that I knew from bitter experience accompanied drowning. As soon as my breathing was easier, it rapidly became laboured again as the echo of a long-decayed splinter once again pierced my chest.

'She's a graceful one, isn't she? Just look at her go. They'll not catch her unless she decides to let… what on earth's the matter?' The woman dropped to the ground beside where I had fallen to my knees, clutching my chest with my right hand while my left trailed on the path, knuckles down, as had happened on the cobbles of Coastwood. Risk had been nearby then, waiting for me and supporting me, as had Shif. This time, I was alone. This time, the end would surely come.

Stifled By Dread. You have merely tumbled into another chasm affording yourself another opportunity to practise climbing back out.

My sense of my horse was very faint, as if she were somewhere far distant. I tried to grab hold of her in my mind and pull her closer, but to no avail. *Risk, I need you with me. You said you'd never be far away.*

Open your ears and you will hear my feet on the ground. Open your eyes and you will see that I am present. Open your mind to your recent learnings and experiences and your physical senses of me will not matter.

My recent learnings and experiences… if I couldn't be within touching distance of Risk then I needed a sketchpad. But all six that Shif had given me were full, as were the twelve I had packed before leaving home. Over the past weeks, I had squeezed tiny sketches in between larger ones until each page of all eighteen sketchpads was a mass of barely intelligible lines, as were their front and back covers. There was nowhere for my sketches to go; nowhere I could expel the echoes of the injuries that I was sure would kill me as surely as the real ones had killed Jimmy.

Accept your memories for what they are rather than what you fear them to be, Risk advised. *Accept them and release their hold on you or resist them and give them strength.*

I sensed, rather than heard, her whinny of enticement to the other mares to approach her for another round of squealing, stamping and tearing around. I sensed the feeling of release their game gave her, and her joy at being with her own kind. Devastation added to my panic and agony.

Hands clutched my shoulders and gently shook them. 'Are you weak from hunger? Nod if it's a yes. No? Then, are you dehydrated from lack of water? Having a seizure? Oh, is it a meltdown because your horse has gone off with the others for a bit? That's common with newcomers, you know. Granted, not usually to this extent, but it's nothing to be embarrassed about… oh, hold on, Mellow has something to say on the matter.'

Her hands disappeared from my shoulders and her feet crunched away from me on the stones and then were silent. I was truly alone again. Just like Jimmy had been. His injuries clutched at me with renewed vigour.

Stifled By Dread. You are ready to accept that which you have so far resisted. Risk drove the notion through my fear and agony and reached the only part of me that was capable of believing her.

I was ready to accept my memories for what they were. They were Jimmy's experiences. My soul's memories of a life lived long ago, from which I could learn. Risk had proved to me that I could survive leaving my mother and travelling an unknown journey to an unknown destination; that feeling safe wasn't about eliminating risk but about finding ways to cope with the unknown. I flexed my wrist and rotated my shoulder back and forth. Both joints ached but otherwise felt normal. I breathed in slowly and deeply. The searing pain of the splinter's echo had vanished.

Risk was right. Acceptance of the past had relieved its hold over me… yet I still didn't feel comfortable being apart from her. My resistance to the idea felt like a lump of iron sitting at the bottom of my stomach. So then, I hadn't fully accepted it, had I?

You have made sufficient progress for now. You will find yourself able to stand. Risk was a blur of black fur and dust in the distance, but her thought was crystal clear and full of conviction.

I got to my feet and staggered to the fence of Risk's playmates' paddock.

'I'd help you, but Mellow told me to leave you alone unless you ask for my help.' I turned at the sound of the woman's cheerful, booming voice and found her sitting on the top rail of the opposite fence, her arm hanging over the neck of a brown horse. 'This is my boy,' she said and hugged him. 'Isn't he handsome? I'm Toolie, by the way. And you are? Besides being newly bonded, a pretty decent rider and clearly in a not insignificant level of distress?'

'Devlin,' I croaked, my head spinning. I felt all wrong. I

wasn't with Risk, I wasn't sketching and I was no longer in fear for my life. None of the three states of existence between which I had flitted since leaving Coastwood were available to me… and I had no fourth state with which to replace them. I was standing at the centre of a giant unknown with no idea how to cope.

On the contrary. There was a pounding of hooves behind me and I turned to see Risk galloping past and then away from me, leaving a cloud of dust in her wake. Her momentary nearness afforded me a moment's clarity in which I remembered her recent counsel. *Embracing that which is unknown renders it not only known but life affirming.*

'I have to stand on my own two feet while knowing hers are never far away,' I murmured.

'What was that? Can I help?' Toolie said.

'Embrace the unknown,' I whispered to myself. I shuddered and felt nauseous. 'Embrace it and it will make my life worth living. Embrace it.' I took a deep breath and turned on unsteady feet back to Toolie. 'My name is Devlin. Could you help me, please?'

Chapter Fourteen

Toolie was by my side in an instant. 'What can I do for you? What do you need?'

I flinched at the loudness of her voice. I needed Risk but I knew she wouldn't come. Risk was known to me and I had to embrace the unknown. Nausea continued to swirl around in my stomach.

'I'm not sure. I don't feel well,' I said. 'I've never felt like this before. I don't really know who I am anymore, or why I'm here.'

Toolie grinned and said a little more softly, 'Believe me, every single person here has felt exactly like you do now. You just about get used to being bonded, spending all your time with your horse and learning that the world isn't as you thought it was, and you think you're okay with it all, then you arrive here, everything changes again and you don't know whether you're coming or going.'

I nodded slowly. 'That's part of it. I've never been good at coping with the thought of change though, let alone it actually happening, and I thought Risk would give me more help than she is at the moment. I thought she'd give me more time to get used to it before leaving me to deal with it on my own.'

Toolie put her hand on my arm and squeezed it. 'Devlin, love, you chose her name. You called her Risk because you recognised what it is you need from her. She'll give you that and more, whether it's comfortable for you or not, and I can tell you from personal experience, it'll be uncomfortable a lot of the time. You know what though?'

I shook my head miserably.

'You'll turn into someone you're much happier being.'

I looked blankly at her.

'Want to know something else? You're not on your own. We're all in this together, we Horse-Bonded. It's why Risk brought you here. All of us were chosen by our horses because we have as much to learn as we have to give to the villages of The New, and all of us struggle with that from time to time. When you need help, ask for it and I guarantee you'll get it. You're absolutely not alone, Devlin.'

'Risk told me I have to embrace the unknown, but I don't know how to.' I blurted the words out and instantly felt relief as my nausea passed.

Toolie laughed. 'Judging by the look on her face, you're doing much better than you think.'

I followed her gaze over my shoulder to where Risk now stood, blowing, sweating and grey with dust, yet calm and peaceful, as if she had been standing there the whole time. She stretched her head towards me and gently rested her muzzle on my shoulder, blasting hot air into my ear along with her approval.

Everything was suddenly alright with the world – in fact, it was better than alright. Now that I was in physical contact with Risk, all my uncertainty fell away and I felt in control of myself and my life in a way I never had before – as if more options had opened up before me from which I could, and would, choose.

No step towards balance is insignificant. No step is too small to render the following steps easier. Risk withdrew her muzzle from my shoulder, took a step backward, and then leapt over the fence to stand at my side.

Toolie side-stepped hastily away from her, chuckling. 'Risk by name, risk by nature, I see. I do love the horses who don't trouble themselves with gates, but there is the possibility of bruised soles from them landing on these stones.'

'We take a risk every time we breathe,' I said without thinking and frowned at myself in consternation.

'Really? How so?' Toolie asked.

'Um, we can't... hold on.' I hurried to catch up with Risk as she walked towards the buildings in the distance. When Toolie reappeared at my side, I continued, 'We can't know exactly what's in the air we're breathing, any more than Risk can know if she'll land on a stone that'll bruise her foot. There are some things you just have to trust or you'd never go anywhere... or... or... do anything.' I sensed deep satisfaction emanating from Risk and couldn't help smiling. *What in the light, Risk... how in the light did I just say... what have you done to me?*

Risk didn't deign to answer. Toolie did. 'Well, I'll consider myself told. That was a quick turnaround. I bet Risk's proud of you?'

I nodded. 'She seems to be. It's easier to remember what she's taught me when she's near me though.'

'And she'll be as close as possible to begin with,' Toolie said. 'She'll take one of the paddocks nearest the buildings so that when you panic, as we all did when we first came here,' she added hurriedly, 'you can get to her quickly.'

'How far away will I be?' My mouth was suddenly dry at the thought.

Toolie pointed to a small gap between two of the buildings. 'The buildings are arranged around a central square just through there, so you'll never be far. The accommodation block is just the other side of the square. You'll be there when you want to sleep or bathe, in the dining hall to the left of the square at mealtimes, in the healing rooms or workshops when you're availing the rest of us of whichever Skill or Trade you're qualified in, and in any or all of the buildings, or out here in the paddocks, when you're doing chores assigned to you. What was your occupation before Risk tugged you, by the way?'

Be mindful that most humans here agreed to share a bond with one of my kind because they are ready at a soul level to address issues they have previously found insurmountable. Risk continued to walk calmly at my side with none of the urgency that accompanied her counsel. *Much of the detail may be unknown to them on a personality level and it may not serve them to see it in your creations before their partners have helped them to gain the strength necessary to fully address and release that which is necessary.*

'Devlin? Oh, sorry, is Risk counselling you? I'll wait.'

I barely heard Toolie because I was so eager to ask Risk, *There are other people like me? I mean, not just Horse-Bonded, but dealing with stuff from a past life?*

Every human alive is processing and releasing patterns carried by their souls into this incarnation from previous ones. Those with more difficult patterns to release require assistance. My kind can provide that assistance.

I was stunned. *But why? Why do you, the horses, do this for us?*

We strive for balance. That which moves one of us closer to the equilibrium we seek moves us all for we are one.

We're one? What do you mean?

Refer to your depictions of me for you have already seen that to which I refer. Show them only to those who specifically ask to see them for only they will be ready to see that which they reveal. Admit your Skill only to those who probe deeply for answers for only they will be ready for those you can provide.

You mean I can't tell anyone I'm an Artist? You heard Toolie, I have to contribute my Skill or Trade. What do I tell them I do?

Tell the truth they are ready to hear until they ask for more.

'Um, what do you do?' I asked Toolie. 'I mean, what did you do before you came here?'

'I was, and am, a Farmer,' she said proudly. 'Did you see the sheep in the paddocks down by the river? It was me who sent home for them so I could prove they cope better with the conditions here than the ones they used to keep. Less susceptible to foot rot, you see. The ground gets soft down here, being in a dip and by the river.' She tilted her face downward and looked up at me as if peering over a pair of non-existent glasses. 'So, is it a secret then, what you contributed to your village, or are you going to tell me?'

My mind raced. Were her questions sufficiently "probing" for me to reveal my Skill?

If you have to ask yourself then you already know, Risk volunteered.

'I worked at the village school,' I said. 'I was a Teacher.'

Toolie pursed her lips and nodded. 'What did you teach?'

'Artistry. I taught people to draw and paint.'

She clasped her hands together. 'Oooh, I've always wanted to do that. We don't get many Teachers here, in fact, I think you might be the only one at the moment. We'll have to get you a workshop set up so you can teach anyone who wants to learn. You mustn't be disappointed or upset if you don't get many people asking for lessons though; what with doing chores, learning from our horses and contributing our Skill or Trade, we're all pretty flat out most of the time.'

'That's absolutely fine,' I said and immediately worried that my voice had betrayed the extent of my relief – which was short lived.

'If you can teach artistry, you must be a pretty good at it yourself?' Toolie said. 'So, you could paint our horses for us?'

'Er, yes, I suppose so. But only if people ask me directly.'

Toolie nudged me playfully. 'Well, that's usually how it works. The Herbalists have only ever given me help I've asked for, and the Tailors don't tend to shower clothes upon people who have no need of them.'

'Yes, that, um, that makes sense. Sorry.'

She smiled. 'Don't be. Now, I wonder which paddock Risk will choose; there appear to be three empty ones down here, although I'm pretty sure Flight was in that one when I passed this way earlier.' Toolie pointed to a paddock to the right of the path, one of whose boundaries was the tallest wall of rock I had ever seen.

'Whoever sang those rocks up there must have been phenomenally strong,' I said, awestruck.

'According to The Histories, there were several phenomenally strong Rock-Singers here when The Gathering was built, but apparently, not all of their strength was inherent. One of them – Ben something, I seem to remember – was recorded as saying it was his horse's belief in him that gave him the strength of intention necessary to lift rocks that high. I like to believe that Mellow's belief in me will give me the strength to…' Her last words were mumbled.

'To what?' I asked.

'Never mind. I wonder whether Risk will wait for us to open a gate for her, or if she'll just... ah, okay, she must want to share with Flight.'

Risk had marched purposefully towards the open gate of the paddock on the right, and dropped her head to graze just inside.

'She doesn't know Flight,' I said – but then sensed that she did. She'd never met him before, yet she knew him and all the other horses in the paddocks we had just passed. How was that possible?

We are all one, Risk reminded me. Something tickled at the back of my mind, as if I knew it was true but had forgotten. I felt a sudden need to look at my sketches of her, but knew I couldn't do that in front of Toolie.

'I'll just shut the gate until Flight and Katie get back here, so no livestock wander in if they're passing. You'll want to check the water barrel's full, morning and night, as Katie's already done this morning.' Toolie pointed at a tall barrel brimming with water in the corner of the paddock to the right of the gate. 'The horses won't need hay at this time of year, but you'll need to clear their field and shelter of dung and soiled bedding and deposit it in there.' She pointed to a wooden enclosure in the corner of the paddock to the left of the gate, out of which poked the handles of two shovels and a pitchfork. 'Then you'll lay a bed of fresh straw in the shelter, in case either of them has a mind to lie down in there. Katie'll show you where to fetch the straw from. Okay? Are you ready to come and choose a room in the accommodation block?'

I wasn't. Not at all. Leaving Risk was the last thing I wanted to do, but I was growing desperate to scratch the itch at the back of my mind that promised understanding if I were to study my sketches of my Bond-Partner.

Risk raised her head, her gaze gentle as always but adding strength to her counsel. *Go.*

'I'm definitely not ready,' I said to Toolie. 'But I also kind of am.'

'That's as good an answer as any newbie is ever able to give,' Toolie said with a wide smile. 'Come on then, you know where she is and you can come to her whenever you want, so we'll go and bag you a room. Then, I'll show you where the workshops are in case you need anything from any of them, and you can choose an empty one for your classes. Oh, and we'll need to see the Overseer so she can assign you chores and put you on the rota. Then it'll be time for lunch…' She stopped talking at the look on my face.

'Can I just find a room and deal with the rest later?' I said.

She rolled her eyes. 'Of course you can. Just listen to me, going on like that. I'm sorry. You see what Mellow has to deal with? He's always telling me to slow my thoughts, but I just have so many of them, I can't stop them all from falling out of my mouth at once. They get me into trouble, you know. A lot.'

Remembering Risk's observation of the Horse-Bonded, I found myself warming to her. 'Don't be sorry. I just need a little time to…'

'Settle in? Calm down? Find your reference point without me bending your ear? There now, I'm doing it again.' She hurried through the gap between the buildings. 'Come on, this way. Then I'll leave you in peace.'

~

I waited until I could no longer hear Toolie's footsteps descending the stairwell. I hated the fact that we had found all the rooms on the ground, first and second floors of the accommodation block occupied, but consoled myself with the fact that the room closest to the stairs on the third was now mine. I closed the door and hurried past the mantelpiece with its carving of a horse in flight, the easy chair standing in front of it and the basket full of dung bricks for which I couldn't see a need this side of autumn, to the bed, upon which I hurled my back-sack. I had long since exhausted the food and herbal preparations I had carried away from Coastwood and discarded all clothes that were in other than perfect condition – which was all of them except those in which I was standing – so the sack was empty but for my sketchpads, my box of now extremely short pencils and a sharp-edged stone I had used to sharpen them.

I spread my pads out across the bed and quickly arranged them in order of use. Discarding the first one lest I catch a glimpse of Jimmy's injuries, I opened the second, ignoring the scrawling all over its cover and flinching at the mess of scribbles inside. I flicked through its pages until I found a sketch of Risk that was clearly distinguishable from those I had squeezed around it.

She stared out of the page at me as if she were right there in front of me. How could I have forgotten that she was all there was?

We are all one. The sentence that joined her image in my mind was no echo of her previous counsel; she was with me, observing herself through my drawings whilst also observing me.

How can that be?

You see it in me as easily as your mother sees it in the depiction of you that you left with her. There will come a time when all humans will be able to feel it but only if we help He Who Can Heal That Which Has Gone Before.

He who can... what?

His pattern pulls at us both though he does not yet have need of us. That is fortunate for we are far from ready to provide the assistance he will require.

I shoved my sketchpads aside and sank onto the bed, my head spinning. *Dare I ask what that is?*

By the time he calls us to him you will know.

But how will I know when he's calling us? I don't hear anyone in my head except for you.

You will know when you know.

And until then, he'll be a massive unknown looming over me.

You can know him any time you wish. We are all one.

I needed paper.

Chapter Fifteen

 $\mathcal{I}$ raced to my bedroom door and down the stairs. Before I knew it, I was standing in the cobbled square of The Gathering with no idea where to go. Toolie had mentioned workshops – I should be able to get paper there, if I could just remember where she said they were. I racked my brains until I was sure she hadn't told me, then cast about, desperately looking for a clue as to where they could be.

'Can I help you at all?' A man of around my age, with surprisingly bushy eyebrows above penetrating blue eyes, stood a few paces to my left, holding a stack of towels.

'Um, I'm new here and I'm trying to find the workshops. It's urgent,' I added so that hopefully, he wouldn't try to engage me in small talk.

He chuckled. 'No spare clothes left after your journey here, eh? You must be desperate for a bath, so I'll not hold you up.' He nodded towards the building opposite the accommodation block. 'That's the dining hall, but if you go to the left of it and around the back, you'll find the workshops. The Tailors carry stocks of clothing so they should have a few bits that'll do for now, but you're taller than most, so I'm guessing they'll need to make you up a new wardrobe from scratch. Not to worry, you're in luck – there are five Tailors in residence at the moment, so they'll have you kitted out in no time.'

'Thank you.' I hurried to follow his directions, leaving him standing, staring after me.

'Make sure you ask them for riding breeches, they're more comfortable for riding in a saddle than normal trousers,' he called after me. 'I'm Mistral, by the way, Apprentice to the Master of Riding. See you around.'

I lifted a hand but could spare him no more of my attention than that. I had been away from Risk for too long, and my need for paper on which to sketch was rapidly progressing beyond just trying to make a single unknown into a known; the square across which I hurried – with its central statue of a man and a horse, its monstrous buildings, and people standing chatting or hurrying from one door to the next – was overwhelming me with its strangeness and unfamiliarity. I cursed myself for not bringing a pencil with me, realising I wouldn't make it back to my room without sketching in order to avoid panicking. I tore towards the gap between the buildings at the corner of the square, and instead of taking the path around the back of the dining hall as Mistral had directed, I headed for Risk's paddock.

When I reached it, my horse was standing at its centre, watching for me. She wasn't alone. A brown horse with a black mane and tail stood by her side whilst being sponged with water by a young woman wearing tightly fitting trousers and long boots. A saddle sat on the top rail of the fence and its accompanying sheepskin pad stank of sweat. I had made no sound, yet the woman looked up suddenly, followed her horse's gaze to me, and waved.

Chapter Fifteen

I was rooted to the spot. *Stand on my own two feet and embrace the unknown,* I told myself over and over until I managed to lift a shaking hand and wave back.

Immediately, Risk left her companions and trotted over to me, her warmth and satisfaction preceding her so that by the time she was close enough to touch, I was already feeling calmer.

You have more strength than you currently believe, my horse informed me, nuzzling my face. *Go now. Return to your task for it will give rise to direction and purpose.*

With another wave to the woman who was now brushing out her horse's tail, I did as Risk bid me. I walked back towards the gap at less than half the pace than when I had come the other way, and turned left behind the dining hall along an extension of the stony track that bisected the paddocks. Unlike the front of the building which faced onto the square, the back was lined with tall windows and glass doors which allowed as much light as possible into the workshops within. I peered into one after another, looking for any sign of a Papermaker.

The more workshops I passed, the lower sank my heart. At work inside were Leatherworkers, Metal-Singers, Tailors, Weavers, Glass-Singers, Chandlers, Dyers, Carpenters, Spinners – and by the look of it, there were even workshops being used by Tree-Singers to grow saplings before planting, and by Beekeepers to overwinter their bees and store honey and its associated products. There was no sign at all that paper was made at The Gathering. By the time I reached the first empty workshop, I could feel my panic returning.

'You're new, aren't you?'

I turned to where a short, stocky man had stepped out of one of the workshops behind me. He wore an apron that covered him from neck to foot and was flecked with different colours of wax, and he was sweating profusely.

'I'm Garry. What are you looking for? Clearly not candles, judging by the look of distress on your face when you looked through my window just now!' He grinned and walked towards me, rubbing his hands on his apron. 'And you are? Apart from lost, overwhelmed and probably doubting your sanity?' He held out his hand to me.

I shook it hesitantly. 'I'm Devlin, and I'm looking for the Papermakers?'

Garry put his hands on his hips. 'There are none here at the moment, I'm afraid. If you're one, go ahead and choose any empty workshop you like, tell the Overseer what you need, and get cracking as soon as you can. If you're not, you'll need to beg paper from the stores like the rest of us – which also means going to the Overseer, since she keeps track of who takes what. She has to make sure there's enough to last of anything we don't make here until a Pedlar gets here with more, you see. So, which is it? Papermaker or beggar like the rest of us?' His eyes laughed along with his mouth and I relaxed a little.

'Beggar, I guess.'

'So, what do you do?' He put a finger on his chin and looked up to the cloudless sky. 'If you need paper, you're a Healer wanting it for your client records?'

A smile twitched at the corners of my mouth and I relaxed further. 'No.'

'A Baker wanting to record all the amazing new recipes you're going to dream up for us to enjoy?'

'Sadly, no.'

'A Farmer wanting to take notes about the state of play so another can be freed to go off visiting the villages?'

I grinned. 'Not even close. I'm a Teacher. Of artistry. I need paper for sketching on.'

Garry flicked away sweat that was dripping from the tip of his nose. 'A Teacher of artistry, eh? So, you can paint as well as draw?'

I nodded.

'Well then, can you use canvas instead of paper?' He tilted his head back towards the Weavers' workshop. 'If you want my advice, you'll use canvas as much as you can and only beg paper from the Overseer when you have to, seeing as it's in limited supply; the Weavers can produce an endless supply of canvas for you. What name did you give your horse, by the way? I know I've been busy lately, but I've missed all talk of your arrival.'

'Her name is Risk, and we only got here an hour or so ago.' I said.

'You're looking for paper when you've literally just got here? You must have a very urgent need to draw – or did you fall for a wind up? Did someone tell you that you have to get to work straight away? You don't, you know. You wait until the Overseer puts you on the duty rota and then see when you can offer your Skill or Trade around your chores and being with your horse.'

'I draw to…' I hesitated.

'Toooooooooo…' Garry spread his hands as if waiting to welcome my answer.

Embrace the unknown. If I could trust that the air around me was safe to breathe, I could trust myself to know what to tell Garry. 'To relax.'

'Ahhhhhh, I'm with you. It's the familiarity, isn't it? I find the same with pouring candles. Come with me.' He turned and headed for his workshop, then held the door open for me to go in before him. I was just about to enter when he put a hand out. 'On second thoughts, wait out here. It's roasting in there, that's why I came outside in the first place.'

He disappeared into a cloud of steam that was heavy with the scent of the lavender, and reappeared shortly afterward with two sheets of paper. 'This is all I can spare, I'm afraid. I've only a little left, I've had that many orders recently. Go and relax, my friend.'

'Thank you.' I took them from him and tried not to hurry away.

'Risk, you say?' Garry called after me.

I stopped short at my horse's name, turned back to him and nodded. 'And your horse?'

'Swift. That'll give you something to chew on.' He winked and waved me on my way with a flick of his hand. 'See you around, Devlin.'

He couldn't have known that all it would take for me to know exactly why he had chosen that name for his horse was to sketch him. He also couldn't have known how little interest I had in finding out. Not when I had a subject waiting to be drawn who would, according to Risk, have a far greater impact on my life.

I was barely aware of the people I passed in the square, or the buildings I had found so imposing such a short time before, and only noticed the statue at its centre because I almost ran into it. Barely allowing myself time to feel silly, I put a hand out to the lifeless rump of the horse half of the statue and propelled myself past it.

By the time I reached my room, I was gasping for breath and sweating almost as much as Garry had been. I grabbed a sketchpad on which to lean and fumbled through my pencil box with a shaking hand, looking for the one that was least blunt, since I didn't want to waste time sharpening one.

When I had a pencil in my hand and a blank sheet on my lap, I closed my eyes. Who was he? I found Risk within my mind, mostly occupied with biting her field companion – no, I corrected myself, massaging his skin and underlying muscles with her teeth while he did the same for her – but also very aware of me and my intention. I felt about within our bond for the sense she had described of the unknown man's pattern pulling at us.

I had him. Through Risk, I felt him pulling at us ever so gently, like a fish nibbling at bait before committing itself to the hook. I focused upon the sensation, waiting to gain more of a sense of the subject I would sketch. Like the stag in Shif's woods, I knew exactly where he was in relation to me. Unlike the stag in Shif's woods, I couldn't go to him to capture his likeness; Risk had told me he wasn't ready, and neither was I.

We are one.

My Bond-Partner's reminder was all I needed. My hand began to move across the page. When it finally stopped, almost rigid with cramp, I gasped. My heart clenched violently, painfully, as if someone had reached into my chest and twisted it mercilessly. I had never in my life seen the man who stared out of my sketch at me, but having recognised Ma in Mother's portrait back in Coastwood, I was quick to identify the aspect of my current subject who lifted one corner of his mouth slightly higher than the other as he smiled, and whose pain stiffened his shoulders. There could be no mistaking him. It was my brother, Henry.

Chapter Sixteen

I stroked his face, wanting to ease the agony that exploded out of his eyes at having first lost Pa and then believing he had lost me. I welcomed the familiar pain in my wrist, shoulder and chest. I wanted to tell my brother that he couldn't possibly have saved Pa, and that he hadn't lost me for I had outlived him, grieved for him and fought as hard as I could to get back to Ma before... No. That wasn't right. I pushed my injuries aside. Jimmy's injuries, I corrected myself and felt a little stronger, for I wasn't Jimmy and... whoever this man was, he wasn't my brother.

But he was. He always would be. And if he carried Henry's pain, then I had to help him let it go.

Not yet, Risk reminded me. *His soul carries pain and anger that have not yet surfaced in his current personality. When they do he will need time to truly experience their depth for only then will he be ready to process and release them. We will use that time to prepare ourselves so that when he requires our assistance we are in a position to give it.*

Will he know me when he sees me? I mean, will he know who I was to him before?

He will not. Knowing will distract him from that which he must address if he is to heal that which has gone before.

So I can't even tell him?

You have two choices. You have begun to accept the experiences of your previous incarnation for what they are. You may continue to learn from them and gather the strength you will need in order to help the soul with whom you have incarnated many times to heal. Or you may allow the knowledge that he is incarnate with you once again to hold you back so that you must both revisit the same lessons in yet another incarnation.

I chewed on my lower lip as I stared down at the man who had been my brother. So many emotions tore at me, I didn't know whether to laugh or cry, holler with delight or bellow in agony, tear around waving my arms at the thought of seeing him again or stamp my feet at the unfairness of it all.

You now understand the amount we must do in order to prepare, Risk advised me. *Your ability to see that which you cannot yet hear the voice of your soul telling you affords you a level of understanding and compassion far beyond that which most humans are capable. Both will be necessary if you are to help He Who Can Heal That Which Has Gone Before but neither are at your disposal when you resist the lessons of your past.*

My mind raced. The quicker I could accept everything she had taught me, the sooner I would be able to help my brother. *I have to get better at accepting new people,* I affirmed to myself as much as her. *At being okay in new surroundings. At not panicking when things change. I have to get better at all of that so I can go to Henry when he needs me. Except he probably isn't called Henry now, is he?*

His name matters not. You will know him when you see him and you will find the strength to conceal the fact.

So where do I start? What should I do right now? I could feel my reticence to engage with all that was strange to me about The Gathering now warring with my desire and determination to race as fast and as hard as I could to be the person I would need to be in order to help my brother.

You have already started. You know what you must do but before that you should hide your depiction of He Who Can Heal That Which Has Gone Before.

Hide it? Why, does someone here know him?

There will come a time when all here will know him.

How? What, you mean... he's going to be Horse-Bonded? My brother will live here, with me?

He is not your brother. But he will spend time here.

Okay, fine, my... my soul brother then. He's going to be Horse-Bonded alongside me! We can be like brothers again!

The news lifted me to a point where I couldn't sit still. I got up from the bed and then didn't know what to do with myself.

I would have a bath. Everything else might be strange to me but that, I knew how to do. The thought of being able to slip back into one of my rituals from home added to my enthusiasm, and I followed the directions Toolie had given me along the corridor to the floor's supply cupboard and bathrooms.

Once I had liberated a clean, fluffy towel and a fresh bar of soap from the cupboard, I hurried to the nearest of the three bathrooms but then paused in its doorway. I didn't have any fresh clothes for when I was clean. Presentable though my current garments were, putting them back on after bathing was unthinkable.

I put the towel and soap on the side of the bath and took a deep breath. I would have to visit the Tailors, as I remembered

Mistral suggesting. I didn't know them, and they wouldn't have the same clothes I always wore. Assuming they worked in the same way as those in Coastwood, they would make any clothes I wanted, but in the meantime, I would have to wear clothes other than the white shirt and brown trousers I preferred. I felt an urge to run back to my bedroom.

Risk, help.

My horse didn't answer because she didn't need to. As soon as I opened my mind to her warmth and calm, I remembered what I had to do. Embrace the unknown, for that was where I would find my soul brother.

I forced my feet to take me back along the corridor to the stairs. When I reached the square and wanted to turn back to my room again, I stood for a few moments, looking at my feet. I remembered Risk's counsel when I had been preparing to leave Coastwood with her.

You need not give up that which serves you. Merely adapt it to your current circumstances.

I took a deep breath and listened to the blood pounding through my ears as it did during my extreme baths. I counted how many heartbeats it took for me to lift my eyes from my feet to the dining hall at the opposite side of the square. Six. It took three hundred and four to reach the Tailor's workshop, eight before I worked up the courage to knock on its glass door, and a further eleven before a woman opened it with a smile.

'Devlin, isn't it? I'm pretty sure that's what Garry said, but I'll admit I was only half listening.' She tilted her red-haired head towards me as if about to share a secret. 'Garry's not known for keeping it short, and I was feeding some particularly slippery fabric through my machine. I've learnt to value my fingers.' She wiggled them at me. 'Anyway, what can I do for you? More paper is it?'

She had clearly been more than half listening. I grinned with relief at the familiarity of human nature; regardless of whether one was Horse-Bonded, news was still news and gossip still gossip.

'No thank you, I really need some clothes.' I looked down at my shirt and trousers. 'These are all I have left.'

The woman looked me up and down with a practised eye and then stood aside. 'Come on in. You're a tall one, aren't you? Are you fussy about what you wear or will anything do?'

'I am a bit fussy,' I admitted as I stepped into the workshop. 'I always wear a white shirt with long sleeves – I roll them up at this time of year – and light brown trousers the same as these.'

She beckoned me to follow her past some long, wooden workbenches, the first two of which were occupied by other Tailors. One was slowly and repeatedly licking her lips as she concentrated hard on pinning two pieces of fabric together, while the other looked up and smiled at me briefly before returning his attention to pushing thick fabric through a loudly protesting sewing machine. We passed three more workbenches empty of workers but covered in a mess of fabric, thread, measuring tapes and completed garments, before reaching the last at the back of the workshop.

Piles of neatly folded garments sat on the far end of it, two sewing machines and a pile of pinned fabric occupied the middle section, and nearest to where the woman waited for me was a large tray with countless different segments containing pins, needles, scissors of different sizes, spools of thread, different fastenings for clothes arranged in order of size, and a vast array of other bits a Tailor clearly needed. After the chaos of the rest of the workshop, the order she had created at her workbench was a balm to my soul. A grin twitched at the corners of my mouth as I realised the woman had rushed to open the door even though she was working the furthest from it. I resolved to be careful to reveal

Chapter Sixteen

only that which I was happy for everyone at The Gathering to know.

'I'm Jue, and I'll be happy to create anything you like,' she said, selecting a tape measure from her tray. She studied my trousers. 'Can I suggest, though, that I make you breeches in place of trousers? They'll be much more comfortable for riding.'

I wanted to say an immediate and categorical no, but then I remembered Mistral giving me the same advice. I had to be able to ride Risk at a speed faster than walking if we were to get to my soul brother when he needed us, and that meant having lessons in a saddle and practising frequently. I would need to be comfortable. I swallowed hard. I couldn't bring myself to speak, so nodded my agreement instead.

'Great.' Jue bent down and measured my outside leg. 'I'll use a thin fabric for your summer breeches and a thicker one for your winter ones, but both will be stretchy, so you'll be able to ride your horse in comfort.' I was relieved when she continued talking, sparing me the need to agree with her when I felt like screaming that I wanted the same fabric all year round, no matter how much I was sweating in my current trousers. 'Risk, isn't she called?' Jue continued. 'Got aspirations to be a bit of a wild one, have you?'

I would have laughed if I weren't so busy trying to hold myself together.

'Well, here's a risk I'm going to suggest,' Jue said. 'Allow me to make you short-sleeved shirts to wear while it's this hot, and save the thicker, long-sleeved ones I'll make for the winter?'

It was a step too far. I shook my head firmly. 'Long-sleeved, please, I always wear long-sleeved shirts.'

'But look at you, you're running with sweat, and if you're going to be teaching people to paint in one of the workshops down the way, you're going to need to dress more appropriately. Lots of light through the windows means a fair bit of heat, unfortunately. You can quickly get dehydrated, you know.'

I was relieved that she believed my sudden profuse perspiration to be the result of my clothes and the room's heat. I gritted my teeth so hard that by the time she wound her measuring tape around her hand and plopped it back into her tray, my jaws ached.

'Give me a few days, and you won't know yourself,' she said. 'Now, we need to find you something to wear until then. What about a pair of shorts for when you're not riding? You'll find them much cooler in this... No?' Her eyes widened as I was finally unable to stop my horror showing on my face.

'Er, no.' I moved my bottom jaw from side to side to loosen it. 'Trousers please. And a long-sleeved, white shirt, like the ones I'd like you to make for me. Please?'

She held my gaze. 'You're a funny one, aren't you?' She waited for me to respond, but I didn't trust myself, so remained silent. 'Right then,' she said eventually. 'I'll go and see what we've got. Don't move, I'll be right back.' She hurried through a doorway behind her workbench, allowing the door to swing shut behind her.

I stood self-consciously, not knowing where to look and willing her to return before any of the other Tailors saw fit to engage me in conversation.

'I thought I saw you disappearing in here,' Garry shouted over the racket the protesting sewing machine was now making. He waved at me from the doorway while frowning at the Tailor who was responsible for the noise. 'Oi, Tevin, are you deaf? That machine needs attention. Want me to knock on the Metal-Singers' door on my way past?'

The Tailor lifted a hand briefly in greeting, shook his head and continued abusing his sewing machine.

Chapter Sixteen

Garry rolled his eyes and beckoned to me to go outside with him. I looked towards the doorway through which Jue had disappeared, and shrugged.

Garry looked wistfully back to the relative cool outside but then made his way over to me. 'Did you come in here voluntarily or did Jue abduct you?' he asked me. 'She couldn't get to me quick enough after you left with the paper; wanted to know all about you, she did.'

'She came to find you? You didn't come in here to speak to her?'

He grinned wickedly. 'You've met her, what do you think?'

I couldn't help but grin back. 'I think she likes to know everything about everyone, and she's a bit flexible with the truth.'

Garry nodded. 'With everyone except Pensive. Watch Jue ride and you'll see she's completely different from how she is normally.'

'In what way?'

'For a start, she's quiet. Sensitive. Watch her sometime and you'll see what I mean. Watch anyone here ride and you'll see a similar thing. We're all different from how we are when we're on the ground. Have you seen the Saddler yet?'

'No. I was just going to have a bath and realised I needed some clothes.'

'Well then, I'll tell her you'll be in to see her this afternoon with Risk. The sooner she gets you both sorted with a saddle, the sooner you can start your riding lessons. Then the fun will really start.'

'I get the feeling that by "fun", you don't really mean fun?' I asked him.

'I mean both meanings of the word,' Garry said with a wink, and jumped as the sewing machine made an alarming grinding noise before descending into silence. 'I'll just let the Metal-

Singers know to expect you, then, shall I?' he said to Tevin, who was trying to wrench what appeared to be a coat from the jammed teeth of his machine. The Tailor glared at Garry, who grinned at him and then at me. 'Well, I'll get back to my workshop. My candles won't pour themselves, will they?'

'You spend so little time in your workshop, we're all beginning to believe they actually do,' Jue retorted from behind the pile of clothes she was carrying. 'Here you go, Devlin. These will serve until I have your clothes ready for you. Feel free to drop in any time to check on their progress, won't you?'

'What she means is, come and see her whenever you're free so she can squeeze you for information about yourself and anyone else you've seen that day,' Garry told me over his shoulder. 'You should have been a Herald instead of a Tailor, Jue.'

'And you should get your lazy backside out of here before I see fit to take my yardstick to it,' Jue retorted. There was no anger or malice in her voice, and when Garry lifted a hand and waved cheerily on his way out of the door, she flushed red and smiled at him.

'Thank you for these,' I said. 'I'll be back in a few days for my new ones.'

Jue jumped as if she'd forgotten I was there. 'Oh, yes, definitely. See you, Devlin.'

I felt calmer as I made my way back across the square, to the point that I made eye contact and exchanged greetings with many of those I passed, all of whom glanced knowingly at the clothes in my arms and made no attempt to waylay me by engaging me in conversation. I realised it was just like Toolie had told me; everyone had been where I was and understood. We were all from different villages and backgrounds, but there was a natural kinship between us, even, apparently, between those who pretended to be at odds like Garry and Jue. The Gathering was an unknown that I was beginning to believe would be easier to embrace than I had thought.

Even so, I bathed, groomed and dressed myself in the exact number of heartbeats I had always afforded the tasks in my bathroom at Coastwood. I also felt the need for an immediate visit to Risk as soon as I had donned a pair of dark blue trousers and a pale blue, short-sleeved shirt; cool, comfortable and well-fitting they may have been, but I felt like a different – albeit far more comfortable – person as a result of wearing them, and needed to be with Risk long enough to remember that was a good thing.

By the time I went to bed that night, congratulating myself that I was indeed in a bed for the first time in weeks rather than out in the field with Risk as I had feared I would need to be, I had plucked up the courage to dive into the dining hall at lunchtime and grab some food that I then ate with Risk; accompanied her to the Saddler, who assured me she would have a saddle made to suit us both within the next three days; introduced myself to the Overseer, who told me I would have almost a full week to settle in before being assigned chores; and visited the Weavers and Dyers to ask them to prepare canvas and paint, respectively, for me.

I was proud of myself but utterly exhausted, and sleep was slow to come, since I had sneaked a peek at my sketch of my soul brother before getting into bed. His face, so foreign to me and yet so familiar, was etched in my mind so that when I closed my eyes, he was all I could see. Eventually, I focused upon Risk and allowed her calm warmth to lull me to sleep.

Chapter Seventeen

It was Risk's warmth and guidance combined with frequent glances at my sketch of my soul brother that propelled me, full of hope and determination interspersed with fear, pain and frustration, through the following months. I was determined to leave Jimmy's pain and fear behind me and open myself to every suggestion made by Risk, as well as to embrace any new situation that I knew would present me with an opportunity to feel curiosity, surprise and excitement, or even afraid, hurt or humiliated. Every time I wanted to run to Risk or to my room in order to hide from a new unknown, my soul brother's face would hover at the forefront of my mind, reminding me that somewhere, he was alive and would at some point need me. I would stay exactly where I was, immersed in the bond I shared with my horse, until I could trust myself to do as I knew I must.

It was fourteen months before I was able to countenance leaving The Gathering. Despite all that time being bonded to Risk and supported and encouraged by my fellow Horse-Bonded, I still couldn't bring myself to hurl myself at change as if it were desirable, but I had at least found ways of being able to embrace it on my strongest days and tolerate it on my weakest.

I would go through my bathroom routine before I went down to check out the new chore rota on a Sunday morning, knowing the comfort gained by my ritual would soften the discomfort I always felt at discovering which new chores had been assigned to me for the following week, alongside which people. I would sit in the workshop I had claimed for my teaching – the furthest away from the square and beyond many empty ones, which no one except Garry and Jue ever found the time or inclination to visit – for hours, painting the horses and people I had surreptitiously sketched, in case anyone ever felt called to ask me to show them the aspects only I could see.

I painted the river, knowing that only I could see it pulling released patterns and emotions away from The Gathering so that its inhabitants enjoyed a constantly refreshed and revitalised environment in which to learn from their horses. I painted the plants and trees I came across while out riding Risk, and the vistas where we would stop to rest.

After each painting session, I would hide my work away in the back room so that there was no evidence of my Skill, leaving easels with Garry and Jue's efforts on display in their place. Both had improved their ability to observe and record as a result of their lessons with me but neither produced anything remarkable, and I suspected their enthusiasm for their art lessons was more to do with having an excuse to spend more time with one another than anything else – a fact borne out as the barbs they continued to exchange gradually became softer and more affectionate.

Whenever I was due to have a riding lesson with Risk, during which I knew I could be instructed to learn any number of new cues, techniques or manoeuvres, I consoled myself first by giving her a thorough groom until she was as spotless as I would be once

I had rushed back to my room to wash and don a clean shirt and breeches. I would inspect and if necessary clean the brown, wide-brimmed hat and boots that Jue had instructed the Leatherworkers to make for me, and only when I was satisfied that I was as immaculate as Risk would I saddle her and consent to enduring the unknown of another lesson.

Once I was astride my horse and subject to her far more intense influence, my concerns and rituals to overcome them seemed utterly ridiculous, and became a source of increased frustration to me as it became apparent that I was incapable of being the person I was when riding, whilst standing on my own two feet.

Embracing change includes accepting that it may occur slowly as well as rapidly, Risk informed me when I was feeling particularly frustrated one morning. *Neither is better and neither is worse. Utilise the methods that serve you until you need utilise them no more. You are doing well.*

Her sentiment was often echoed by Toolie, who was an avid watcher of my and Risk's lessons with the Master of Riding, Astrid, or her Apprentice, Mistral.

'You're such a natural,' Toolie would say, as if it hadn't taken me over an hour to prepare myself to accept the instruction I had just been given, and as if I'd never told her how many times I'd fallen off Risk during our first weeks together in order for me to be comfortable upon her back.

It was she who badgered me for weeks to leave The Gathering with her and Mellow on a visit to the villages, before I finally agreed to leave the place whose unknowns had gradually become fewer and farther between, to the point I could almost relax.

It had been a while since I had given Jimmy's injuries cause to announce themselves within my body and when they had, they were mere whispers of the screams they had been. On the morning I was due to leave, however, they were much louder. As soon as I woke and saw the saddlebags that I had packed the night before draped over the back of my easy chair, my shoulder and wrist ached. When I tried to ignore the pain by carefully collecting the pile of freshly laundered clothes I had laid ready on top of my chest of drawers, and padding past the saddlebags to the door in order to begin my bathroom routine, I felt a stab of pain in my chest. I tore down the corridor to the nearest bathroom – I had forced myself to use the other two occasionally but needed the comfort of using one I usually frequented – pausing only to collect a clean towel, some bath salts and soap on the way, and slammed the door, my heart racing.

A door opened nearby and a sleepy voice said, 'Wassup?'

I cursed myself for making so much noise, but couldn't bring myself to answer. I waited until the door clicked shut again, then took a deep breath and began the routine that I hoped would soothe away the aches and pains of the life lived long ago whose lessons I still hadn't quite managed to accept.

Steam quickly filled the room as hot water blasted from the tap with only a hint of cold to temper it. I relished the water stinging my skin as I got into my extreme bath. Seven hundred heartbeats lying still, allowing not just the heat but its familiarity to soothe me. Three hundred and fifty heartbeats to wash my hair and lather myself with soap. A hundred heartbeats to towel myself dry and a further two hundred and fifty to shave and comb my hair. By the time I dressed from the pile of clothes I had placed on the shelf by the door, my chest was merely aching along with my wrist and shoulder.

I placed the towel in the wash basket in the corner of the bathroom and took the soap with me to my bedroom. As I entered it and saw my bulging saddlebags, realising all over again that I would be leaving the four walls that had been part of my sanctuary for the past two years, the pain in my chest exploded once more.

'These are not... my... injuries,' I told myself through gritted teeth. 'They're... Jimmy's.' The pain lessened. 'Leaving here will be... good for me. New experiences are... good for me.' I wanted to reach for Risk, but I knew what she'd tell me; I'd had plenty of practise at climbing out of whichever "chasm" I had fallen into and this was more of the same. I also knew I could do it without her. I could stand on my own two feet. While I felt in no mood to hurl myself at the day's challenge as if it were desirable, I could render it tolerable. 'My soul brother needs me and... I have... to be able to... help him. I'll be... with... Risk. I... can... do this.'

Determination battered at the pain, which faded to nothing as if it had never existed – which I knew in truth, it hadn't.

Fortified By Trust. I am satisfied with your progress. Risk's warmth exploded not just within my mind but all around me, as if she were actually in the room and curling her body around me so that nothing else could get close. She was more than satisfied; she was elated.

I smiled and then laughed giddily, wondering how I could ever have been afraid at the thought of leaving The Gathering when it wasn't possible for me to be apart from the real source of safety in my life. I quietened all of a sudden. *Fortified By Trust?* Her new name for me had reached the part deep inside that had always responded to the truth of how she perceived me, so it had taken a few moments for me to realise that it had changed.

You have changed. Your trust in me has afforded you the strength to accept that which you resisted. Our planned endeavour will give you further opportunity to practise doing so as you must if it is to feel more natural to you.

A spike of concern penetrated the joy I was feeling at her approval.

Chapter Seventeen

You are Fortified By Trust, Risk reminded me. *Your trust in me. Your growing trust in the variety of life and the opportunities it can offer. Your trust in yourself that you will do as you must in order to be ready to help the one who will need you.*

In all the time I had known her, she never wavered from her devotion to supporting me or her calm confidence that I could, and would, follow her counsel – her love for me, I suddenly realised. She was always ready and willing to carry me when we had a riding lesson or I wanted to practise, or just wanted to be alone with her, away from The Gathering. She was always at the back of my mind, ready to offer counsel if I needed it but content to give me time and space to work things through if I didn't – even if I wanted it. And now she was happy to leave her preferred equine companions in order to take me on a trip to the villages, where she would dispense her counsel to any humans who needed it whilst continuing to support me so that in time, I could help my soul brother.

My chest filled with emotion that made my heart race, then rushed up to my head, making it feel as if it would explode. In the past, only fear had been strong enough to do that – fear that would have incapacitated me. The love I felt in its place energised me. I grabbed my saddlebags and left my room without looking back. I hurried across the square, a broad smile on my face, and jogged along the path between the paddocks to the one halfway down that Risk had taken to sharing with the two mares she had met on our arrival at The Gathering. Draping the bags over the bottom rail of the fence, I climbed between the higher two rails and hurried to where my beautiful mare stood in the dewy grass, the glancing rays of the early morning sun silhouetting her against the lightest of mists that would disperse the instant the rays gained enough strength.

She lifted her head, dew dripping from her muzzle, to watch

my approach. I had never seen anyone or anything so beautiful. Her paddock mates were grazing a short distance away, but I had eyes only for the horse who had dedicated her life to being my Bond-Partner. She may have taken me away from everything I knew, refused to allow me the security of certainty, and constantly challenged me to do that which had been previously unthinkable, but I had never felt so alert, so vibrant – so alive.

I stopped in front of her, my heart feeling as if it would explode with love and gratitude, and suddenly didn't know what to do. No words were enough. No gesture was enough to compensate her for all she had done and was still doing for me.

Step away from your humanness and into all you know me to be, Risk advised simply.

As always, I followed her advice. She didn't need gratitude. She didn't need a grand gesture. She needed nothing from me at all; she did what she did in order to fulfil an agreement – one that was older than time itself yet younger than the present moment. How could that be?

Merely accept it since you know it to be true. Any pondering will be a distraction from what we must do. Fortified By Trust. You should prepare for us to leave. Risk dropped her head and snatched at the grass.

Feeling not at all rebuffed and wondering how that could be when I had run down to see my horse intending to express my love and undying devotion, only to be heading back the way I had come shortly afterward having done no such thing, I left my saddlebags hanging on the fence rail and made my way to the dining hall. As I entered the square, Toolie was leaving the accommodation block, her own saddlebags draped over her shoulder, and we reached the dining hall together. I opened its huge oak door and leant on it while Toolie went through before me into the lobby, whose walls were covered with coat hooks. She hung her bags from a low and very sturdy one and went ahead of me through a smaller door into the cavernous dining hall, which seemed even larger now that it was empty apart from the two of us.

Toolie yawned. 'I suppose having the dining hall to ourselves and not having to queue for breakfast is an advantage of getting up at dawn – believe me, I've been trying very hard to find one in between cursing you for insisting on it.'

I chuckled. 'Granted, it's early in summer, but it's definitely the best time of day all year round.'

She rolled her eyes. 'I'll take your word for it since I have absolutely no intention of finding out. Right, let's see what they've left out for us.'

We made our way between the multitude of long wooden tables and benches to the food table at the far end of the hall, where two tubs with tightly fitting lids awaited us. Inside we discovered enough sandwiches, fruit and nuts to break our fast and sustain us until we reached the nearest village for which we would be heading, which Toolie had assured me we would reach in plenty of time for the evening meal we would be offered there.

I wasn't completely okay with not knowing where we were going, where Risk and I would stay, or what, exactly, we would do when we got there, but Toolie had told me that our first trip would be easy, with no camping, food provided at every stage, and plenty of water and grazing available for the horses as we travelled. I trusted her and I trusted Risk, and I focused hard on remembering that as I half listened to Toolie happily describing the first village we would visit, in between mouthfuls of sandwich.

'You've packed enough clothes?' Toolie said suddenly and grimaced as I looked at her with raised eyebrows. 'Of course you have, sorry. Come on then, let's get going, shall we? Since we're up at stupid o'clock, we may as well make the most of it and get a decent distance behind us before the heat sets in.'

'Now, why didn't I think of that?' I said and immediately raised my hands in supplication. 'I'm just teasing you.'

She sighed as she got to her feet. 'I know. I'm just so used to apologising for being bossy, I forget I don't need to with you. Why is that, by the way? I've often wondered.'

I smiled sadly as Ma's face flashed into my mind. 'You remind me of someone. She was only bossy with people she cared about.'

'Was?' Toolie said, her face full of concern.

'She died a long time ago. Risk has helped me to be okay with it.'

Toolie watched me as I got to my feet beside her. When my eyes met hers, she said, 'But not completely okay, I think. There's still stuff lingering, isn't there?'

I flinched and then nodded slowly. 'A little.' I picked up my tub of food and walked towards the door, saying over my shoulder, 'I know how to clear it, and it's not by staying here where it's safe.' I bit my lip as soon as I had uttered the last word and inwardly cursed myself for being so careless. I may have changed a lot during my time at The Gathering, but I wasn't ready to discuss that which had caused me so much pain with any other than Risk.

As it happened, my slip gave me even greater reason to trust Toolie. In a much softer voice than her usual booming one, she said, 'That's why I need to leave here too. I find it easy to stagnate when I'm around people who know me well and are tolerant of me. When I go out to the villages, I have to watch everything I do and everything I say because if I start being too much, the villagers are wary of asking for Mellow's counsel. I find it exhausting but every time I arrive back here, I feel more comfortable in my skin and I know from everyone's reactions to me that they see it.'

I stopped and turned to her. 'Do you think any of the villagers realise how hard you find it? All I ever heard of the Horse-Bonded when I was back in my village was how amazing they are, how calm and wise, but if the other Horse-Bonded are all like the two of us, how come nobody from my village ever saw it?'

Toolie's eyes shone. 'Because our horses help us be how the villagers see us. The harder the challenge we set ourselves to overcome, the more support they give us so we appear to have life sorted when actually, we can be dealing with bigger issues than anyone around us can possibly imagine. It's just what they do. They're where the real safety is, and not just for us, for everyone.'

I nodded, remembering that I'd already figured that out for myself. 'There's so much to know and remember, isn't there?'

'Always,' Toolie replied. She flicked the fingers of both hands past me towards the door. 'Go on, or I'll start complaining about being up with the sun again.'

I grinned. 'If ever I needed any extra incentive to be with my horse, that would be it.'

Chapter Eighteen

My stomach was rumbling as the first wisps of smoke appeared above a stand of trees in the distance. Despite having rested during the hottest part of the day, sweat soaked my shirt and ran down my temples. My wide-brimmed hat kept the sun off my head, so I was confident my face wasn't as red as Toolie's, but I was far from immaculately turned out as I had grown into the habit of being before facing the unknown, as was my sweaty and very dusty Bond-Partner. Grooming her and putting a clean saddle and cloth on her back, and washing and dressing in freshly washed clothes myself, had always given me what felt like a layer of protection – armour, even – that helped me to cope with uncertainty, and without my ritual, I felt naked and exposed. I wanted to ask Risk to turn around and run for The Gathering.

But I didn't. I sat upon her back as she steadfastly carried me towards the trees, between which gradually came into sight the first cottages of grey stone, so like those of my home village that a lump formed in my throat. My heart lifted. Maybe this wouldn't be as hard as I had thought; maybe the village would be like Coastwood in other ways too, and it would be like being somewhere I already knew.

It matters not, Risk told me patiently. *You have the ability to cope with anything that befalls you. You approach a village that is unknown to you only until it is known. That is filled with humans who are unknown to you only until they are known. Who have issues that are unknown to you only until they are known. When all of it is known you will have more experience from which to draw. Experience that will enrich your life and expand your opportunities. Remember who you are and welcome all that is before you into your life.*

Fortified By Trust. It was the first time I had repeated the new name she had given me, and as I did so, I sat up straighter and pulled my hat further back on my head so that my face was more visible. I looked across at a hot, sweaty, sunburnt Toolie and grinned.

She stuck out her chin and blew her breath upward in an attempt to cool her face. 'Don't smile at me. If I smile back, my skin will split.'

'I offered you my hat,' I said.

She shuddered. 'I'd rather have a sunburnt face than wear a hat soaked in someone else's sweat. No offence.'

'None taken. Hopefully, there's a decent Herbalist in Ashstand who can give you something to soothe the burning.'

'Oh, there is,' Toolie said, 'in fact I stayed with him once before, when Mellow hurt his leg on the way here.' If I had thought it wasn't possible for her face to go any redder, I was wrong.

'And the Herbalist's name is…?' I asked, looking across at her pointedly.

'Um, Jeffers.' She cleared her throat and refused to meet my eyes. 'Oh look, our arrival has been noticed. Thank goodness, the sooner I can get to his... I mean the sooner we can accept the hospitality we'll be offered, get the horses settled and have a nice, cool bath and some food, the happier I'll be. I mean, we'll all be.'

She was saved from her embarrassment by a horde of children tearing between the trees towards us, all yelling at the tops of their voices and waving their arms. Mellow continued walking towards them, but Risk stopped and snorted, her body rigid beneath mine.

I held up a hand and called out, 'Everyone slow down and calm down. NOW!'

Toolie looked at me in surprise as the children all obeyed me. 'Once a Teacher always a Teacher, eh?'

I reached down and rubbed Risk's neck, sensing her innate instinct to flee abating. I dismounted and walked in front of her towards the children. 'Risk and Mellow will be happy to meet you, but they're horses, not people. Approach them slowly and quietly, then we'll walk with them to the trees. They need shade, water and rest.'

All but one of the children walked meekly up to Mellow and Risk. A little girl, aged about ten I guessed, stood where she was, watching the horses intently as they sniffed their admirers and accepted strokes from a multitude of little hands, then she turned on her heels and ran back to the village. By the time we reached the trees, she was on her way back towards us, awkwardly carrying two large buckets, her legs wet with the water that had splashed out of them. She refused with a firm shake of her head offers of help from older children and adults as they passed her on their way to greet us. By the time Toolie and I had unsaddled our horses in the centre of the stand of trees, the little girl was at the back of the rapidly growing crowd, her face redder than Toolie's.

Risk and Mellow gently wended their way through the villagers eager to greet them, ignoring all hands offered for them

Chapter Eighteen

to sniff by those experienced at greeting visiting horses, to the girl. They each sniffed one side of her, from her face down to her feet, before drinking the water she had brought. A smile lit the face that had been on the verge of tears, and she tentatively stroked the horses' necks as they drained the buckets.

'They need more water,' someone said. 'There isn't enough here. I'll get more.'

The girl's face fell. I hurried to where she stood with Risk, and said, 'Thank you for working so hard in this heat to bring water for our horses. What's your name?'

'Rache.' Her bottom lip quivered and she didn't look at me.

'Risk and Mellow really appreciate what you did for them. They were desperate for a drink. They also need a wash down. Would you like to help?'

Her face lit up even as her eyes remained downcast.

I looked around at the sea of unfamiliar faces I suddenly realised were watching and listening to me. My knees almost buckled, but I put a hand out to Risk and remembered who I was. 'Um, the horses will be better staying under the trees until it's cooler. We'll need to wash them down here with Rache's help, as well as give them more to drink, so if anyone else could fetch more water, we'd really appreciate it. If anyone has any spare hay, that would be great too.'

Lots of heads nodded and a group of villagers ran back to the cottages. The rest looked at me expectantly. I turned to see Toolie nearby, chatting more quietly than normal to the crowd of people surrounding her. I swallowed, not knowing what to do or say and feeling an urgent need for my sketchpad even though Risk was by my side.

A man stepped in front of me and held out his hand. 'I'm Fabian, Rache's father.'

I shook his hand gratefully. 'I'm Devlin, and this is Risk.' I felt a thrill as I said my Bond-Partner's name and sensed a surge of warmth from her in response. I remembered the name she had given me and remembered again that it was true. 'This is our first trip to visit villages so we'll be finding our feet, but we'll do our best to help in any way we can.'

Fabian put his other hand over my and his clasped ones. 'Then you must stay with us; Rache, her brother, my wife and me. We have a spare room and a paddock out the back with plenty of grass for Risk when it's cool enough for her to leave the trees, if that will be acceptable?' There was an urgency in his voice that led me to think his offer of hospitality was more of a plea for help.

I smiled at him. 'Thank you, that's very kind. We'd love to stay with you all.'

Fabian gave my hand another firm shake and then released it. 'I'll let my wife know. When Risk has everything she needs, and you're ready for something to eat, Rache will bring you to us, won't you, Rache?'

His daughter nodded enthusiastically, her cheeks now flushed with pleasure as my horse blew gently on her cheek.

∽

I watched Risk through the bedroom window. She was grazing in the silvery moonlight, her tail at rest from flicking at biters now that they had run out of the energy afforded them by the sun and finally let her be. I was relieved to have her close by after an evening alone with Fabian and his family while she rested in the trees with Mellow until the sun finally relinquished its hold on the sky and sank beneath the horizon.

I had employed all my coping mechanisms in order to remain calm whilst being apart from her in a strange place. The heartbeats

Chapter Eighteen

I counted while performing the steps of my bathing ritual were exact and comforting. Donning a clean white shirt and brown breeches calmed me further. A quick sketch of the view from my window revealed a total absence of menace in my surroundings, assuring me further that Risk and I were safe, and giving me the confidence to descend the stairs and join the family in the kitchen for what transpired to be a delicious and satisfying – if unfamiliar – stew of grains, pulses, nuts and vegetables.

Fabian and his wife, Topula, chattered constantly, darting from one topic of conversation to the next, as if nervous. Their son, Zeud, who was Rache's ten-year-old twin, attempted to interrupt them now and then and rolled his eyes at me every time he failed. Rache alternated between staring at me intently and staring towards the wall with a distant look in her eyes, as if her mind were somewhere else. Fabian and Topula glanced at her frequently, the speed and volume of their conversation increasing whenever she was staring at me, until her attention was once again elsewhere.

When they finally stopped talking, I had no idea what it was they had been telling me about, and had a feeling they didn't either. I also felt that it had been anything and everything but the topic they really wanted to talk about, and wondered if I should ask what that was.

They will not be ready to hear the counsel they seek until they find the courage to ask for it, Risk advised me.

Zeud saved us all the discomfort of wondering when that would be by asking, 'When will it be cool enough for Risk to come and stay in our paddock? Can I go and fetch her when it is? Can I wash her down like Rache did? Can I ask her questions so you can tell me her replies?'

'Which word always goes with a request, Zeud?' Fabian said,

his voice suddenly firm and confident where it had been shaky and unsure.

'Please?' Zeud said, looking at me.

'It will be cool enough when she decides it is,' I said with a smile as I sensed her pleasure at Mellow gently nuzzling his way along her back while she did the same along his. 'We'll know when that is because she'll arrive in the paddock of her own accord. She likes to take herself where she wants to go, when she wants to go there, so you won't need to fetch her. You can wash her down if she gets hot again, but that won't be until tomorrow. You can ask her anything you like but be warned, she'll only answer the questions she thinks are worth answering.' I grinned at them all. 'I should know.'

I was relieved when Fabian and Topula chuckled, releasing the tension that had accompanied their discourse.

'How will I know which questions she'll think are worth answering?' Zeud asked.

'Exhaustive trial and error,' I said. 'Once again, I'm speaking from experience.'

'I'll know,' Rache said, suddenly focusing intently on me again.

Her parents stiffened, and Zeud rolled his eyes.

For the first time, I returned Rache's stare. 'I believe you will.' I turned to her parents. 'How about the two of you? Would you like to ask Risk for her counsel before whatever time Toolie announced we'll be ready to receive visitors in the morning?'

They looked at one another, their eyes full of anxiety.

'Knowing Toolie, it's unlikely to be early,' I said. 'I'm always up at dawn though, so there'll be plenty of time for you all to ask Risk any questions you have. You don't have to answer me now, just think about it and let me know in the morning.'

Chapter Eighteen

Zeud bounced up and down on his chair. 'I have questions I want to ask her.'

'You'd like to ask her,' Topula corrected him. 'I want never gets.'

'I'd like to ask her,' Zeud said, still bouncing up and down on his chair. 'Can I go first? Please?' he added hurriedly.

'You can take it in turns with Rache to ask your questions, when your parents say you can,' I said.

'I only have one question to ask her,' Rache said, still staring at me. I realised her parents must be concerned I would find her unsettling, yet there was something about the little girl's manner that made me feel just the opposite.

I smiled at her. 'I know it'll be one she'll be very happy to answer.'

Rache's eyes sparkled. 'So do I.'

I had retired to the room I had been assured was mine for as long as I wanted it, shortly after helping to clear away the dishes, saying I needed to rest following the day's exertions. It was only part of the truth. The fingers of my right hand itched to sketch, not just while I waited for the comfort of knowing Risk was in the paddock outside, but because the part of me that saw more than that of which my eyes were capable had information to discharge, and I was desperate to find out what it was.

The sketch that had resulted from my urge to draw lay on the windowsill in front of me as I watched my horse moving slowly around the paddock, utterly at peace with herself and the night. I didn't need to look at it again to know that Fabian gazed down at his daughter with pinched eyes and hunched shoulders. Topula stood between her two children, one hand resting comfortably on Zeud's shoulder while the other pulled Rache close to her side. Zeud looked away from his mother at something of insufficient relevance to have made it into the sketch, oozing energy and enthusiasm and ready to tear off and engage in mischief at any moment. Rache stared directly out of the sketch at me, her eyes bright with curiosity, intelligence and a confidence far beyond her years. Gone were the awkwardness and strangeness I had witnessed setting her apart from other children. Despite being held so tightly and uncomfortably by her mother, she was relaxed and… waiting for something.

Chapter Nineteen

I racked my brains, trying to think what Rache could possibly be waiting for so patiently, yet so avidly. I was impatient for the family to retire to bed so I could go and spend time with my horse without the discomfort of needing to explain why I was no longer in need of rest; I hoped that being with Risk might give me the clarity I couldn't find on my own.

You are already with me. You know for what she waits. Your inability to hear the voice of your soul when you can so easily illustrate its knowledge infuriates you. Acceptance of the fact will allow you to rest and realise that which you know. Resistance to it will increase its ability to infuriate you. Risk didn't pause her selection of various stalks of long but dry grass from the rest as she dispensed her advice. Had it been new and important, she would have looked up at me, knowing that even in the dark, her gaze would drive the message into me more deeply. The consequence of accepting rather than resisting a situation, idea, feeling or emotion was something of which she reminded me often – sometimes daily – since the challenge of choosing the appropriate response over its antithesis appeared in a myriad of guises and constantly tripped me up. As ever, her patience was rewarded and I cursed myself for not having realised the trap into which I had fallen yet again.

Mellow and Toolie are okay? I asked my horse as I pulled back the sheet on my bed, releasing a pleasant aroma from the posy of summer flowers that a member of my host family had laid underneath.

They rest easily. There was no reprimand in her response, yet I couldn't help feeling chastened.

Then I will too, I assured her. *See you at dawn.*

It took four attempts before I achieved total acceptance of the fact that while I could see more than most through my ability to draw, my inner hearing was, as yet, intermittent. The instant I did, I slept.

~

As always, I was among the first witnesses to the sun's rays breaking darkness's hold. I rushed to the small window of my room, sensing that Risk was also awake and had enjoyed several hours of grazing since emerging from the deep sleep she had entrusted to the goats with whom she shared the paddock, but wanting to reassure myself with the sight of her calm presence – the only familiarity amid the strangeness to which I had opened my eyes.

I jumped as the door creaked open behind me and candlelight threw flickering shadows against the grey stone walls of my room. I turned to see Rache staring at the floor as she pushed the door shut behind her. When the latch dropped into its holder, she said, 'I was waiting for you to move around so I'd know you were up.

Mum told me I wasn't allowed to wake you, and I haven't, have I?'

Relieved at my decision to wear a nightshirt despite the warmth of the night, I noticed Rache was fully dressed in a pair of shorts, cotton blouse and sandals, and she had brushed her dark brown hair back into a neat tail.

'Did your mum also tell you it's polite to knock before entering someone's bedroom?' I asked her.

'I did knock, but I had to do it really quietly so I wouldn't wake anyone else. I always get up when the birds tell me it's time to, but that's really early in the summer and no one wants to hear me crashing around,' Rache said with a sigh that told me she'd heard the second half of her sentence often. 'I want to ask Risk my question. She's awake, so I've just been waiting for you.' She lifted her eyes and looked past me to the window, as if my Bond-Partner were just on the other side of it. She darted towards me and picked up the open sketchpad I had left on the windowsill. 'What's this?'

I hadn't thought to put the pad away or even close it; I hadn't thought I would need to. I cursed myself inwardly for my oversight as Rache held it close to her candle.

The ten-year-olds I had taught back at Coastwood would have, in Rache's position, been excited at unexpectedly seeing a sketch of themselves and their family, and immediately wanted to show as many people as possible. Rache, however, moved the sketch closer to her face and inspected the depiction of herself and her family slowly and carefully, as if she were reading words rather than looking at images.

Then she handed the sketchpad to me and said, 'I want to draw. Like this. Not silly pictures of fruit like we have to at school. I want to draw things that are important, that I can't describe however hard I try. Like this,' she repeated and lifted her eyes to mine. The desperation within them shook me.

A glimmer of understanding flickered in the back of my mind. 'I'd be happy to teach you, but do you want to ask Risk your question first?' I suspected I knew what her reply would be.

She shook her head firmly. 'I was going to ask her how I'm supposed to tell everyone what I can see, because when I use words, they don't believe me.' She grabbed the sketchpad back from me and held the drawing of her family up to my face. 'But now I know. This is how I tell them. I have to draw it, like this.'

Her face looked out at me from my drawing and I saw again that which my Skill had told me. She had been waiting for something.

She had been waiting for me. She needed me to free her from her strangeness – to show her how to channel it into something those around her could understand. She needed me to help her become an Artist.

'I'll teach you to draw like this, Rache, but first, I'd like you to leave this room so I can get dressed, and I need your promise that you won't come back in without permission. Knocking isn't enough. You have to wait for consent before you enter someone's room. Do we have a deal?'

The little girl held out her hand, all four fingers pressed tightly together and her thumb rigidly vertical. 'We have a deal,' she said solemnly, staring at her hand until I shook it. Then she turned and marched towards the doorway where she paused and said, her eyes boring into mine and almost daring me to disagree, 'I'll wait for you in the kitchen.'

I realised I hadn't told her of my intention to bathe and shave before dressing, then realised further, with a jolt, that I didn't care about that this morning. Not when the student for whom I had waited nearly seventeen years had announced herself to me in such certain terms, and we would only have a few hours before the rest of her family were awake. I even pulled on the clothes I had worn after my bath the previous evening in preference to fresh ones from my saddlebags, in my hurry to begin teaching Rache.

I took a new sketchpad from my saddlebag, selected the sharpest pencil from my box, and tiptoed along the landing and down the stairs. When I reached the kitchen, I didn't even think of breaking my fast but instead took a seat facing the window, through which the rays of dawn were rapidly strengthening and bouncing off the kitchen's contents in a rich array of colours. I beckoned for Rache to leave the chair opposite mine and sit beside me.

'The first rule of artistry is to position yourself where you have the most natural light,' I told her, opening the sketchpad and folding the cover back. I laid the pencil atop the first page and pulled a bowl of berries towards us from the centre of the table. I picked out the largest raspberry and put it on the table in front of Rache. 'I know you don't like drawing fruit,' I said before she could protest, 'so don't see this as fruit. See it in the way you see the things you can't make people understand you can see. Don't move your pencil on the page until you've noticed everything about the raspberry there is to notice, then let your hand move the pencil where it wants to.'

Rache stared up at me defiantly. 'I want to draw things that are important.'

'In order to draw everything there is to see in things you think are important, you have to be able to see everything in things you think aren't. I started with a boot, then moved on to a tree. My mentor wouldn't accept I was finished until I'd drawn every leaf in the tiniest detail.'

Rache stared at the raspberry and then back at me, her eyes now showing a glimmer of concern.

'Just be curious,' I told her. 'Look at that berry as if you've never seen one before. Ask yourself questions about it. Why is one of its lobes bigger than the rest? Why is that lobe a slightly paler pink than the others? How did that speck of dirt come to be there? When your mind wants to move on from your questions, let it absorb the information it needs. When it's full, allow it to move your pencil across the page.'

The little girl stared at me as if willing me to change my instructions, then sighed. She lowered her chin to rest on her fist on the table and turned her full attention to the raspberry.

'Take your time, you have plenty of it...' I stopped talking as Rache suddenly lifted her head, picked up the pencil and began to draw, her eyes never leaving the raspberry.

I had never considered how disconcerting it must be for those around me to watch my hand move so fast across a page as to be a blur, leaving a trail of apparently random lines and squiggles behind it, which then suddenly resolved into the subject of my focus. Nor had I ever wondered how my hand knew exactly where it was on the page when my eyes were transfixed solely upon what it was drawing, or vacant as I pictured my subject in my mind.

When Rache's hand moved away from the page, it left a perfect depiction of the raspberry behind. Beyond perfect, I corrected myself, for she had captured every element of its shape and shading, as well as its history and its future. I felt as if I knew the plant from which it had been picked; how old it was, how much sunlight it received, how well nurtured it was by its grower. I felt the richness of nutrition the berry contained, its vitality despite having been plucked from its parent plant days previously, and the energy it would give its consumer. I could see all that there was to know... and so, now, could Rache.

Chapter Nineteen

She sat staring at her drawing, her mouth open in disbelief. 'It's not just fruit,' she whispered. When she looked up at me, her young eyes were hungry. 'What shall I draw next?'

∽

Teaching Rache wasn't teaching as I had been used to. After her first lesson, when I passed on the advice Shif had given me so many years before and encouraged Rache to be curious, it was more like recognising each new aspect of the little girl's Skill as it erupted out of her, and guiding it so that when she stood back from her sketches and paintings, she could be satisfied she had left absolutely nothing out of them. She spent almost every minute of every waking hour darting here, there and everywhere, frantically sketching whatever she could and then racing to transfer to canvas the subjects that had called most strongly to her. I merely intercepted her now and then in order to look over her latest work and guide her as I felt necessary.

In fact, my student needed so little help from me that I had plenty of time to receive the steady stream of villagers wanting Risk's counsel. Although I reverted to my tried and tested coping strategy of adhering to a strict – although slightly altered – morning routine in order to cope with the novelty of doing so, cope I did. I rose at dawn each morning, went outside to groom Risk until she gleamed, then bathed, shaved and dressed so that I was as immaculately turned out as my Bond-Partner. I breakfasted with the family and then went back out to check Risk was still spotless before receiving her first visitor.

For the first three days, that was Fabien. The first morning, he arrived wringing his hands. His voice shook with desperation as he asked how to help his daughter be more like other children.

His offspring has no need of being like any other, Risk told me. *The difference that stands her apart is one that he will come to admire.*

'But she's not happy,' Fabien protested when I relayed her counsel to him.

It is he who is not happy. He should consider the notion that being different gives one the freedom of expression denied to those who would conform. Freedom of expression is necessary if those who sense the truth of existence are to share what they know.

Fabien listened intently as I passed on my horse's response and then stared at Risk as she stood resting a hind leg in the dewy grass, her eyes half closed as if she were dozing when, in fact, she was as aware of everything around her as ever. Eventually, he leant towards me and whispered, 'I have no idea what she means.'

Understanding will come with time, Risk advised.

I felt her approval when I sensed she hadn't finished dispensing her counsel and instantly knew what the rest of it must be. When she didn't confirm whether I was right, I felt uncomfortable. *Risk, what's the rest of it?*

Present your words as my own for that is what they are.

Fabien flicked sweat from his brow as he stared sideways at me, desperate for any words that would make sense of his confusion.

'Risk counsels that understanding will come with time, and that, er…' I cleared my throat, then removed the wide-brimmed hat that was keeping the sun from raising sweat on my own brow. I scratched my head to give myself time to organise my thoughts, then replaced my hat and continued, 'For now, the most important thing is for you to accept her advice, rather than resist it.'

'Accept what I don't understand?' Fabien said.

'Er, yes.' *Risk?*

She didn't reply. I felt her lack of need and remembered who I was. Fortified By Trust. 'Yes,' I repeated more firmly. 'Accept it and you'll open up to it. Resist it and you'll never understand.'

Risk's approval practically exploded in my mind, to the point I was barely aware of Fabien thanking her for her advice, and apologising to me for the lack of shelter large enough to accommodate her in the paddock and advising me to take her back to the trees now that the heat was increasing.

I didn't need my horse's counsel when Fabien came the following morning to plead for help in understanding her previous advice, but merely repeated my words of the day before. When he arrived on the third morning, he was smiling. He unfolded a sheet of paper and showed me a sketch of Risk.

'How could I have ever doubted her?' he said, flicking his middle finger past his thumb so that it hit the sheet with a loud tap.

'Who?' I asked with a grin.

He looked at the sketch and then back at me as if I were crazy. 'Risk!' His expression softened. 'And Rache. I doubted her too. How could I not have seen that she's special? Look at this!' He held the sketch up in front of my face and shook it. 'When she told me you were teaching her to draw, I didn't think she'd be able to do anything like this. This is Risk, but it's more than Risk, and my daughter, my Rache, drew it!'

I gently pushed his arm down so I could see him over the sketch. 'If you think this is good, wait until you see the painting she'll create from it.'

His eyes widened. 'She's painting now!' He turned and ran back to the cottage.

Just as Risk and I were about to leave for the shade of the trees, Topula came out to see us, carrying a glass of cool fruit juice. 'I know you've not long finished breakfast but I thought you'd like to take this with you, seeing as it's getting hot already,' she said and passed me the glass. She wiped her hands on her apron and then clenched hold of the fabric. 'I also, um, I just wanted to say thanks to you and Risk.' The words that followed spilled out of her as if she were desperate to say them. 'My daughter's been unusual since the day she was born. She didn't cry or scream on that day and she hasn't on any day since, even though I know she feels more than the rest of us. It's like she's been closed off in her own little world where she felt safe, and I haven't been able to reach her, or understand what she's been trying to tell me, but thanks to you, she's reached me and at last, I understand.' She let go of her apron and grabbed hold of my hand, which she squeezed tightly. 'Fabien understands too, and he's like a different man. Rache being... unusual is a good thing, isn't it, for all of us?'

I smiled. 'A very dear friend once told me that the most talented minds are often the most sensitive ones. Yes, Rache being unusually sensitive is definitely a good thing for us all.'

Risk wandered over and touched her muzzle to Topula's shoulder. Topula let go of my hand and put both of hers to Risk's cheeks, stroking her gently and whispering, 'I see you now, thanks to Rache. I see you.' When Risk dropped her head to graze around her feet, Topula said, 'It was you, wasn't it?'

I reached out to flick a biter from Risk's neck. 'What was?'

'Your dear friend was talking about you. You taught Rache to show the rest of us what she can see. Only someone who's like her could have done that. You're more sensitive than most, like Rache is? You didn't need Risk to tell you how to help her, you saw her for who she is and you believed in her when no one else ever has.'

Immediately, Shif's face filled my mind. I swallowed hard and blinked away tears. I had recognised Rache's need to express herself through artistry only because Shif had recognised and encouraged it in me.

'Everyone needs someone to believe in them,' I said hoarsely. 'Before Risk came along, my friend did that for me. Now, I'm lucky enough to have her reminding me who I am when I forget.' I cleared my throat, wondering suddenly whether I had said too much; the Horse-Bonded were supposed to appear as self-assured as their horses.

'I'm glad for you, Devlin. And I'm glad for my family.' Topula smiled warmly. 'Thank you for everything you've done for us all.'

As she hopped and skipped back to the cottage like a girl of her children's age, I realised that Shif had been right all along. I was needed in villages other than Coastwood in order to unlock the Skill of artistry in those as desperate to express themselves as Rache and I – and to free other families from their worry about how their "unusual" loved ones would fare in the world. Someday, hopefully soon, I would return to Coastwood and tell him. Thank him. Apologise for not believing in him as he had always believed in me.

I resolved to write down the names of all those who joined Rache and me as Artists, and present it to Shif as a way of thanking him for his recognition of the Skill within me. I actually found myself looking forward – albeit with trepidation – to the uncertainty of the future, for aside from being where I would find my soul brother, it was where I would meet many new people, any of whom could be another name to add to my list.

Little did I know that after nearly four years of travelling around villages, only returning to the comfort of The Gathering to overwinter, I would have just three names on my list, and would still find embracing each new village only marginally less uncomfortable than the first; that I would be in a constant state of self-reproach for my lack of progress despite Risk's endless patience and confidence in me; and that I would be starting to believe I'd never be in a position to help my soul brother.

And little did I know that the task for which I had tried so hard to prepare yet felt so under qualified to fulfil, would blast into my life one summer's day regardless of my feelings of unpreparedness.

Chapter Twenty

I was sitting under a tree, enjoying the shade it offered from the sun that was beating down on Risk as she grazed a short distance away. The cool, knee-deep stream of water in which she stood while snatching at the relatively lush grass growing on its banks negated any discomfort she might have felt at the sun's intensity, but her long tail swished constantly at the biters that were determined to feast on her blood. I was grateful for my obsession with keeping her well groomed; having brushed the individual hairs of her tail free of one another, they spanned out as she lashed it at the biters so that few were out of its reach.

I had eaten a light lunch of fruit and nuts and settled down to sketch the seemingly endless plains across which we were making our way towards a village we had visited several years before. My sketch confirmed there was nothing in our vicinity that was cause for concern and further that – as Risk and I had also decided was sensible – most animal activity on the plains was in a state of suspension until the heat subsided. Though the sketch was in my usual grey pencil, the lack of colour that normally graced the plains was obvious.

The long stalks of the different grasses were brown, brittle and bent at awkward angles rather than green and sinuous. The herbs that had managed to produce coloured flowers were lower growing than normal and peering between the grass stalks rather than exploding in celebration above them. The leaves still clinging to life on the tree above me were a paler shade of green than they should have been, and those that had lost their fight for life were brown and hung desolately, precariously, before drifting slowly through the still air to the hard, cracked ground around me. The cloudless blue sky offered no hope of a reprieve from the drought and heat that seemed intent on extending their hold over us all, giving me an intense opportunity to practise being unaffected by all the uncertainties that travelling long distances in such difficult conditions entailed.

When Risk and I were on the move, mostly at nighttime, I was calm. As her long legs carried us across the desolate landscape, I mostly managed to maintain my trust that at least some of the water courses that fed the plains would still be capable of doing so, and when I failed, I focused on trusting my horse. It continued to pain me that I was still so reliant on her to keep my panic at bay, but I tried to remember the counsel she had given me one day when I was feeling particularly frustrated with myself.

The energy of trust remains the same no matter to what or whom it is afforded. Each time you trust you grow in strength even if you feel weakened by the process of doing so. It is merely the pattern of fear that would maintain its hold on you that is weakened.

Whenever Risk and I stopped to rest and were physically apart – even by just a few feet – I often needed to sketch in order to still my mind and remain calm, just as when we had been travelling to

The Gathering for the first time. When my sketch of our surroundings was complete, I would allow my mind to wander to my next subject. Sometimes, I would shuffle a short distance to where an insect was drawing nectar from a flower, burrowing into a tree trunk or balancing precariously on a leaf as it wafted around in the breeze. Occasionally, I would move with enough stealth to get close enough to larger animals and sketch them feeding, drinking or playing with their mates. Now and then, I would sketch from my mind's eye as I had learnt I could do when I discovered the existence of my soul brother.

As I finished my current sketch of Risk standing in the stream, a beacon of hope and beauty in the desolate landscape, I allowed my mind to search for my next subject in order to prevent myself from worrying about how far away our next water source would be after leaving this one.

I sat up a little straighter. Having expected to be drawn to an insect, perhaps one of those pestering Risk, I was unprepared for the subject who blasted into my mind as soon as I opened it to possibility. My heart thumped in my chest and my breathing hardened so that it was almost painful in my nose and throat. I turned the page of my sketchpad, almost tearing it, my hand was shaking so violently. As soon as my pencil came into contact with the fresh page awaiting its touch, the shaking stopped. My heart rate slowed. My breathing softened.

It was only when my eyes refocused back to my immediate surroundings from my far distant subject, and I looked down at my drawing, that my calm was shattered. My soul brother looked out of my sketch with such agony in his eyes that my breath caught in my throat and I panicked I wouldn't get it back. The emotions my brother had taken to his death had surfaced within my soul brother, just like Risk had told me they would, and he needed me. Right now.

I jumped to my feet and hurried to Risk. I stopped suddenly, realising I should pack my stuff into my saddlebags before preparing her to move onward. I turned back to where my pad and pencil and the remains of my lunch lay scattered at the base of the tree, but then stopped again. We couldn't leave yet. It was too hot for Risk to leave the water and our source of shade, let alone carry me. She needed to stay near the stream and eat as much of the grass growing on its banks as possible, then rest out of the sun before moving on.

But my soul brother needed me. My brother needed me. I could feel him reaching through time for me, as I had so often reached for him. I had to go to him. I turned back to Risk. No. The heat and drought could indeed kill her, but that wasn't my only reason for hesitating. I wasn't ready. She had told me how I would need to change in order to help my soul brother, and I had tried. For five long years, I had devoted myself to trying, but I still hadn't shed the hold my past had over me. How could I help my soul brother be free of the fear and pain that had trapped us both when I was still a prisoner myself?

You have progressed sufficiently to be in a position to assist He Who Can Heal That Which Has Gone Before. Risk stood motionless in the stream, so focused upon me that she ignored the biters now settling upon her black, sweat-streaked coat. *Consider the fact that your relationship with him will be an exchange of energy rather than a donation from you to him. He requires your assistance on his journey through this incarnation but he will also aid you in yours. When the conditions are conducive to travel we will alter our course towards his location.* Having dispensed her counsel, Risk gave her full attention to dislodging the biters covering her body. They were hurting her.

Her discomfort jerked me out of my reverie. I splashed into the stream beside her and threw cupped handfuls of water at the

Chapter Twenty

biters on her neck and belly as her tail drove away those from her back and sides. I stroked them from her face and washed away the trails of blood they left in their wake. When she was free of them all, I set about washing the rest of her body to give her relief from the heat, however brief it might be before the water dried and the sun's rays lashed at her once more. When she was comfortable, I lay down fully clothed in the stream before dripping my way back to the shade of the tree. The water would soon dry, but I would enjoy the cool it afforded me while it remained.

Once seated on a root that had broken free of the soil before seeking the stream, I shook my hands free of water and picked up my new sketch of my soul brother between my thumb and forefinger in order to study it more closely. I knew the man who looked back at me no better than I had the last time I had drawn his face, but the change in him was very obvious to see.

When I had drawn him last, he had smiled an easy smile and been oblivious to the slight stiffness in his shoulders and pain behind his eyes that were Henry's. His eyes had twinkled with kindness and happiness, and his demeanour radiated confidence. Now, he looked ten years older than the five that had actually passed, and a deep wrinkle at the bridge of his nose told of a well-practised scowl. His eyes were full of the kind of pain and misery that could turn to rage in a flash, yet they looked as if they would widen in fear at any moment. Whatever had happened to him in this life had released in full force everything that had been imprinted on Henry's soul; I could see it as surely as I could see Risk standing in the stream in front of me. There was only one way that could have happened without him remembering the past like I had – he must have suffered a significant loss. Again.

My heart went out to him. Risk had rescued me from the past I shared with this man, but I could see in his face that he was suffering alone. How could I possibly be the help he needed? How could I be that for him when I had needed my bond with Risk in order to even begin to accept the past for what it was?

You mistake our role in his life, Risk informed me without looking up from the particularly tasty tussock of grass that she was rapidly depleting. *Our first task is merely to deliver him a message. The challenge to you will be to perform it without divulging who you and he were to one another. For that you must prepare.*

What message?

That there is room in his heart for the one who calls to him but whom as yet he cannot hear.

Understanding flooded through me with relief hot on its heels. *He's being tugged? Now? Thank the light.*

Your eagerness to help him will not decrease the challenge you will face regarding keeping your knowledge of the past to yourself. It will serve you to create as many depictions of him as you can whilst we travel so that you become well used to seeing his face and confident that you will not deviate from your normal attitudes and behaviour on meeting him.

Relief lifted my heart at knowing I wouldn't be alone in trying to help the man who had been my brother, and I couldn't prevent a smile from spreading across my face, despite the condition in which I knew I would find him. It had been so long since I had been with Henry in my dreams; since we had shared a joke at Ma's expense; since he had filched pies from those cooling on her baking rack for the two of us to share; since we had sat with Pa, mending nets while the gulls screeched in the sky above; since he had been beaten to death for losing his mind when he thought he had lost me.

My wrist and shoulder began to ache with an intensity I hadn't experienced for several years, then to throb. It was only when a sharp pain pierced my chest that I pulled myself out of the past and reminded myself for the hundredth time that was all it was; a time when my soul brother and I had incarnated together and responded in a certain way to a certain situation. We would soon be together again, in a present that would give us the opportunity to respond differently; to clear the hold over us both that we had given the past.

I understand, I told Risk and picked up my pencil.

∽

I couldn't decide whether I was glad when, after weeks of travel across the hot plains, Risk and I finally reached the relative cool of a forest, or whether I wanted to turn around and run from it; despite Risk striding into the shade of the trees as if there were nowhere she would rather be, there was a very definite undercurrent of unease to the calm confidence I usually felt from her.

The instinct of my kind warns me I cannot run from danger as easily here, Risk informed me. *Consider that which you sense from me to be increased alertness and nothing more. Do not allow it to distract you from your task for I will not allow it to distract me from mine.*

She walked purposefully between the trees, marginally deviating from the most direct path towards where we both sensed my soul brother to be when the density of undergrowth forced her to, but otherwise crashing through it as if it weren't there. I was constantly forced to duck down close to her neck in order to avoid being swept from her back by low-hanging branches, and to lift one or other of my legs over her withers with little or no notice in order to prevent them being caught on the trunks of the close-growing trees, whilst Risk marched onward regardless.

Not regardless, I corrected myself; with trust. As always, she had complete confidence that I would cope with whatever risk presented itself to my person, and further, that I would be as difficult to distract from our destination and task as was she. She didn't even stop to rest despite the sun having risen shortly before we entered the trees; at least the canopy above us took the intensity out of the rays that would otherwise have hindered our journey.

I was shocked to note that the damp, earthy smell that would have told me we had entered a forest even had I been blindfolded, was muted almost to the point of being undetectable by my nose. Brown leaves crackled under Risk's hooves as if it were autumn rather than summer, and the undergrowth was almost as dry and brittle as the grasses of the plains. I wondered how long the heat and drought would last, for it was clear that the forest too was struggling to withstand their effects.

I reached down to rub Risk's neck and my hand came away sticky with sweat. *Should we stop?* I asked her. *I can pour water into my hands from my pouch for you to drink.*

You should bring your depictions of He Who Can Heal That Which Has Gone Before to the forefront of your mind, Risk replied without slowing her pace. *Feel the emotions to which he has surrendered and practise stepping aside from them. It will be more difficult when he directs them towards you but with preparation you will succeed. You must be as calm as he is irate and as measured as he is irrational otherwise he will not receive our message.*

I immediately did as she instructed and was surprised to find that once my mind was otherwise occupied and dodging branches and tree trunks left to instinct, the task became easier – like dancing with my surroundings rather than constantly trying to avoid a fight.

I judged the sun to be directly above us when we came across a small pool of water fed from a clear and surprisingly fast-moving stream, and Risk finally paused her march through the forest. I slid from her back, removed her saddle before she could protest, and, as she drank from the stream, cupped water in my hands from the pool and threw it over her, rubbing the sweat from her coat and enjoying the immediate relief she felt as if it were my own.

When she finished drinking and started to snatch at some low hanging leaves, I refilled my water pouches then undressed, lowered myself to my knees in the pool and washed away my own sweat and dirt before drinking from the stream until I could drink no more. I cupped my hands and flung the soiled water from the pool to the plants desperately reaching for it, so that the pool would refill with fresh water ready for whichever animals visited it next. Then I selected some slices of the firm, dry travel bread I always carried when away from The Gathering, squeezed them around some rabbit jerky to make a sandwich, and ate standing up while my body dripped and dried. By the time I had dressed in a fresh white shirt and brown breeches, pulled on my brown boots and the wide-brimmed hat I was rarely without, Risk was standing by her saddle, looking at me expectantly.

I didn't bother to ask whether she was sure she didn't want to rest and eat more before continuing, since I knew she wouldn't bother replying to a question whose answer she considered obvious. I rubbed the fur of her back to make sure it was dry, then gently lowered the saddle onto it and slowly, almost apologetically, tightened the girth. No sooner had I sat in the saddle than she was off, striding through the forest once more.

Chapter Twenty-One

The light of the day was diminishing when the faintest waft of smoke caught at my nose and made it twitch. Not my nose, I realised, but Risk's. It wasn't until a few minutes later, when I could actually see the wisps of smoke escaping the ashes of a campfire, that my own nose stung with its scent. I barely had time to register it, or that which could only be described as a hovel standing a short distance beyond it, before my heart lurched with shock and horror at the rest of the scene before me.

My soul brother was sitting on the ground between the remains of his campfire and his ramshackle hut, his face gaunt and his hair lank and greasy. His shirt was filthy and unbuttoned, revealing an equally filthy – and exceptionally skinny – chest and stomach. His trousers, which I guessed may have been beige and well-fitting at one time, were held up by string and as dirty and shabby as everything else that appeared to comprise his life. Remnants of clothing littered the small clearing he had made his home, along with pieces of crockery, rusting parts of old tools

Chapter Twenty-One

and piles of dead undergrowth that had been pulled up and left to rot.

He was staring so intently behind himself at a back-sack that appeared to be moving of its own accord, he neither saw nor heard Risk's and my approach. He suddenly leapt to his feet, took hold of the back-sack and upended it with a yell, as if doing so pained him. A pile of clothes and some food tumbled out of it along with a grey squirrel, who scampered to a nearby tree with its prize of a small net filled with nuts.

The rage that blasted out of my soul brother in all directions threatened to shake me loose from my saddle, even though it wasn't directed at me. I couldn't help but feel his pain – Henry's pain – and flinched at the sudden ache in my wrist and shoulder. I immediately immersed myself in Risk's confidence that I had changed and prepared enough to be whom my soul brother needed me to be. I understood why his pain was so intense and his fury so unfettered, for I too had been overwhelmed by the emotions carried with me from the life he and I had shared before. Where I supposed others may have felt afraid of him or returned his anger, I felt only empathy and a fierce determination to help him. The ache in my wrist and shoulder vanished.

Though the words I said to the man before me were borne of my desperation that he would cease making things worse for himself, I voiced them as if I were commenting on the weather. 'From the look of you, you don't have the luxury of food to spare, to be throwing it all over the ground.'

My soul brother spun around, his eyes wide in fear and then narrowing in anger as he drank in the sight of me astride my Bond-Partner. 'I don't remember inviting you to invade my home, let alone pass comment on how I choose to live.' His voice carried such venom that I had to stare into the depths of his eyes in order to remind myself who dwelt there.

Love for my brother combined again with sadness for my soul brother, allowing me to reply, as cheerfully as I could, 'I didn't ask the woodlice, birds, mice, rabbits or any of the other animals who live here, either, yet none of them seem to be objecting.'

My attempt at a jest served only to make him scowl at me with even more ferocity. I averted my eyes from his and looked instead at his hut. Its walls were made of logs strapped one above the other, some with gaps between them that I supposed had once been plugged with moss, judging by the brown fragments still in place elsewhere. Its sagging roof had saplings growing out of it.

'You've been living here a while,' I said, stating the obvious for want of anything more helpful to say.

'And I'll say the same to you as I've said to everyone else who's tried to impose their presence on me while I've been here,' the man spat. 'Go away and don't come back. And you can tell Morvyr that I meant what I said.'

Morvyr? Should I know who that is? I asked Risk.

We are here to deliver a message, she reminded me. *Do not be distracted by the details of the life He Who Can Heal That Which Has Gone Before has constructed for himself.*

I felt the weariness that accompanied her counsel and felt chastened. I jumped down from her back and rubbed her face, telling her, 'Thanks, Risk. Give me a minute and I'll fetch you some water.'

'Don't plan on making yourselves comfortable,' my soul brother snarled. 'You may be used to adoration wherever you go because you're Horse-Bonded, but I couldn't care less who or what you are. I don't want you here, either of you, so you can get lost. Do you hear me? GET LOST.'

The hate in his voice shook me out of my confidence. This couldn't be; my brother loved me as I loved him. My shoulder and wrist began to ache again and were quickly joined by the familiar sharp pain in my chest. I should remind him of who we were to one another. I should tell him why I was here, how I could help him, how we could both leave our pain behind and move on.

Fortified By Trust. Risk's reminder was patient but tired.

It was all I needed; my aches and pains disappeared as suddenly as they had arrived. What had I been thinking? For want of a distraction to stop me from saying something I would regret, I began pulling at Risk's girth straps.

'GET LOST, I TELL YOU!' my soul brother shouted, advancing on us both.

I might have been thrown from my confidence again but for Risk shaking her head at him in warning, her ears flat back as I had rarely seen her do before. We were there to deliver a message, and she was committed to doing so. I glanced up at him from beneath the saddle flap, to see him halt his advance, one arm still in the air from where he had been gesturing for us to leave, his other held across his chest.

'What's wrong with your other arm?' I asked him. 'Why are you holding it against yourself like that? I'm no Healer, but the Herbalist of the last village I passed through gave me some preparations if you need respite from pain?'

For the first time, anger fled my soul brother's face and was replaced by surprise. 'You don't know who I am, do you? So Morvyr didn't send you?'

I did know. He was my soul brother, and I desperately wanted to tell him so. But I couldn't. I had to deliver the message.

'Not a clue, no,' I said, for in this lifetime it was the truth. 'And sorry, never heard of her.' I turned back to Risk and pulled her saddle from her back, grimacing at the crust of rapidly drying sweat that marked the edges of where it had sat.

'Who are you then?' My soul brother demanded. 'And why are you here? Not that it matters, because I want you to leave.'

'I have every intention of leaving once Risk has drunk and eaten as much as she needs to, and once you've received our message.' I said, lowering my saddle to the ground. I opened a saddlebag, pulled out a brush, and scrubbed gently at the crust on Risk's back.

'It never flaming well stops, does it?' The man who had been my brother paced back and forth behind me. 'However hard I try to remove myself from know-it-all do-gooders, however remote a place I choose to live so I can just be left alone, so I don't have to hear the advice of everyone who knows how to live my life better than I do, it just goes on and on. I DON'T WANT YOU HERE AND I DON'T WANT YOUR HORSE'S ADVICE.'

I found solace in the rhythmical strokes with which I continued to brush Risk's back. 'Her name is Risk. Mine is Devlin,' I said evenly and moved to Risk's other side to brush away the sweat I hadn't been able to reach. My eyes flicked up to meet his as they blazed at me across her back, then lowered to my task when it appeared he had no intention of telling me his name. I continued, 'I'm pleased to meet you, despite your lack of manners and regardless of whether you decide to tell me your name in return. Now, where can I find water for Risk? She's brought me a long way in the heat to find you.'

I scrubbed a little harder at a stubborn patch of dried sweat and Risk nuzzled the back of my shoulder.

My soul brother was quiet. When I risked another glance at him over my horse's back, he was looking between me and her with such anguish on his face, I wanted to run to him and hug away everything that was causing him so much pain.

Risk increased her presence within my mind so that when he turned away from us without a word and strode for his hut, slamming its door behind him so hard it bounced back from the doorframe and hung open forlornly, I was able to watch him without following. His face now contorted with rage, he picked up a bucket by the door and threw it at me and Risk.

I caught it. 'Thanks. I take it that's a water barrel jutting out from behind your shed? I'll just help myself, shall I?'

Risk sniffed the bucket and then raised her head and stared at my soul brother. For a moment, his face softened and he looked ten years younger than I had judged him to be. Then it hardened again. He slammed the door of his hut and this time it stayed shut.

'Come on, Risk,' I murmured, walking towards the water barrel. 'You drink as much as you need from here and then I'll find where he gets his water from and fill it back up while you find something to eat. There's not much around here but leaves and brambles, but hopefully there'll be something better where the water source is.' I lifted the lid from the barrel, dunked the bucket and offered it to her. Still feeling the need to fill the silence left behind by my soul brother, I continued to murmur to her. 'There you go, that's better, isn't it.' I stroked her neck as she drank. 'I'd never have been able to do this without you. Thanks for helping me, and for helping him. I don't think he'll listen to me just yet if I tell him he's being tugged, so I guess I'll have to wait until he seems calmer. Hold on, I'll refill the bucket.'

I had barely put the freshly filled bucket on the ground for her when a scream from within the hut silenced the twilit forest. It went on and on, carrying my soul brother's pain to all within earshot and no doubt halting the animals of the forest dead in their tracks, just as it did me. Risk lifted her dripping muzzle from the bucket but soon resumed quenching her thirst even as the screaming continued. The only way I could bear it was to stand with my hand on her shoulder so that I could completely immerse myself in our bond until it finally stopped.

As soon as it did, Risk moved off purposefully and I sensed that she had scented water. I followed her, carrying the bucket and careful to avoid tripping over the plentiful tree roots and brambles over which Risk stepped as if they weren't there, as the ground sloped downward. When the trees thinned, moonlight afforded us a grey-blue view of a grassy clearing with a small pool at its centre that appeared to be bubbling gently.

Risk picked up her pace, and I was relieved beyond measure to sense her enjoyment of the lush grass when she began to graze. I made my way past her, my boots squelching in the oasis of moisture spreading out from the spring. My heart sank when I reached it; it was way too shallow for me to fill my bucket, and thinking about it, Risk had forged her own path to the clearing rather than followed a well trodden one. I would have to search elsewhere for the water source my soul brother used. That would mean being apart from Risk.

A situation with which you are well able to cope, she reminded me, her awareness of my thoughts diminished not at all by the ferocity with which she was grazing.

But even you're not completely comfortable here in the forest. I can still feel that, you know. And I don't know how far away from you I'll have to go to fetch water.

One can never have too much practice at accepting the unknown, she reminded me for what seemed the thousandth time. She lifted her nose and her nostrils flared in the moonlight as she turned her head. Through her, I knew in exactly which direction to head to find water, if not how far. She dropped her head and grazed on without further comment.

I took a deep breath and turned away from the clearing.

Chapter Twenty-Two

Risk was right. I coped with being apart from her as I found the well trodden path from my soul brother's camp to the stream she had scented, gathered herbs from along its banks in the moonlight, refilled the water barrel, hunted several rabbits and made a large pot of stew, and repacked the food into the back-sack my soul brother had emptied over the forest floor and hung it from a low-hanging branch. I even resolved to settle down and try to sleep by the still smouldering campfire rather than in the glade with Risk, so that I could deter nighttime animals from investigating the stew and be on hand in case my soul brother needed me. That didn't mean I was any more comfortable than I sensed was she. But where my horse focused her attention on her enjoyment of the lush, plentiful grasses and herbs rather than her instinct to flee the forest for the safety of the open plains, I could find nothing with which to distract myself from the unfamiliarity of my surroundings, my separation from her, and my concern for my soul brother.

It was as if the darkness surrounding his hovel – in which I presumed he was asleep – was more absolute than in the rest of the clearing. When clouds obscured the moon, its soft, blue light still cast faint shadows on the forest floor of the tall trees whose leaves rustled in the warm breeze, and highlighted the scraps of clothing, pieces of crockery and tools littered all about. Yet whenever I turned my eyes towards the hovel in the hope of catching sight of it in my peripheral night vision, all I could perceive was a total blackness that seemed to reach out and beckon to me as if wanting to draw me into its grasp.

I wanted to break down the door of the hut and get my soul brother away from its darkness, but I suspected it would only follow him. I wanted to beg him to believe that a horse was attempting to break through his hurt and rage and help him, but I knew, without Risk needing to tell me, that I would have as little success as the horse at reaching him. I wanted to ease the pain that leached through the gaps in the hovel's walls and tore at my heart, but could do nothing but toss and turn sleeplessly on the forest floor until the first promise of dawn relieved me of my turmoil.

I leapt to my feet and gathered dead leaves and twigs with which to relight the campfire, over which I hung the pot of stew I had made the previous evening. While the fire was gathering strength, I collected the crockery that was strewn about, then the cutlery highlighted by flashes of light as the first rays of sunshine reached the forest floor, and scrubbed them in a bucket of water using a handful of thorny undergrowth. Then I stirred the stew as it slowly heated, wondering what the day would bring.

I jumped at a crash from within the hovel and turned as its door burst open. 'Just in time,' I told my scowling soul brother. 'I was about to dish up. Rabbit stew okay for you? I managed a little hunting and gathering before I put my head down last night. I helped myself to a little of your salt, I hope you don't mind?'

'Would it matter if I did?' he snarled.

I immersed myself in Risk and said, 'I gathered your food parcel back together and hung it from that branch over there, else there would have been nothing left by this morning. Mind you, that squirrel has been busy gnawing at the drawstring for the past few minutes, so you might want to take it inside and store it somewhere he can't get to it.'

My soul brother stomped behind me as I sat cross-legged, still stirring the stew that I was hoping might put a little flesh on his bones. 'Well, I'll just do that then, shall I?' He winced as he reached up with both arms to retrieve his back-sack.

'That shoulder still troubling you?' I asked him. 'Shall I add some of the painkilling preparation the Herbalist gave me to your portion of stew?' He tramped back past me towards his hut without replying. 'It really will help,' I called after him.

He banged about in his hut for some time. When the noise finally ceased, a loud stomach rumble reached me and I hoped upon hope that it would precede his appearance. I spooned the stew into two of the bowls I had cleaned and placed one on the ground at a distance from me, as if intending to entice a wild animal, rather than a fellow human, to eat.

When my soul brother stepped out of his hut, he appeared almost hesitant, as if suddenly unsure of himself. I didn't give him a chance to think, but pointed to his bowl of stew with my spoon.

'I washed the crockery and cutlery I found lying around as best I could,' I told him. 'And I promise you, I haven't poisoned the stew, so go ahead and eat, I'm not a bad cook.'

He took a step forward, his eyes alight with hunger... but then stopped as Risk appeared in the clearing. It was as if the sun had just come out from behind the most ferocious storm clouds. Risk's sudden proximity combined with her beauty to fill my heart with love and happiness, and as I watched her approach, all

I could do was smile. When I sensed her satisfaction, my smile widened.

He Who Can Heal That Which Has Gone Before has received our message, Risk informed me.

I turned back to my soul brother to find him looking between Risk and me with an expression of total desolation. It was replaced by one of agony, and he turned and ran from the clearing, leaving his breakfast untouched.

I jumped to my feet, intent on going after him.

We should leave, Risk announced.

I turned back to her. *Leave? He's suffering more than when we got here. He couldn't even find the wherewithal to be angry. He's my brother, I can't leave him.* My wrist and shoulder began to ache.

Only you could have afforded him the level of understanding necessary to tolerate his behaviour long enough for him to receive our message. You have helped him. Now we must leave so we do not hinder him.

I felt like stamping my feet. *I don't understand. How did he get our message? I didn't have a chance to tell him a horse is trying to tug him before he ran off.*

He did not require telling. He saw the bond that exists between us when first we arrived. When he felt it he could not contain his agony.

That was what the screaming was about last night?

Risk ignored my question and continued, *He both saw and felt it just now. Our presence has opened his mind sufficiently for his Bond-Partner to reach him.* She looked at me and blinked. *We should leave.*

I wanted to argue with her but couldn't, for as she held me in her gaze, I couldn't help but know she was right. But I couldn't leave my brother when I'd waited so long to see him again. I just couldn't. A sharp pain stabbed through my chest, adding to the increasing ache in my wrist and shoulder. The pain should have been enough for me to pack my things and leave immediately, but I couldn't bring myself to move.

Henry was my brother. He had died believing he had lost me, and now he was feeling the same emotional torment all over again, presumably at having lost someone dear to him in this lifetime, and I was supposed to just leave him to it?

Fortified By Trust you are not alone in wanting to help He Who Can Heal That Which Has Gone Before. You can assist him best at present by remembering everything you have learnt and trusting the horse who now calls to him in earnest. When it becomes necessary to assist him again we will do so. Risk moved closer, so that the warmth of her body soothed me as much as that of her mind. *We should leave.*

I wasn't Jimmy, I was Fortified By Trust. I would find the strength to leave my soul brother so that his horse could help him as I couldn't. My pain disappeared and I rubbed Risk's neck.

I'm sorry. Thank you.

My horse remained where she was. I leant my forehead against hers until I felt I could do what I must, then in a whirlwind of activity, packed my gear. I left to one side a parcel of herbal preparations and put it on the rickety table in my soul brother's hut, along with the crockery and cutlery I had gathered, and his cook pot containing the rest of the rabbit stew. I shuddered at the mattress of rotting moss on which he clearly slept, and the pile of dirty clothes in a corner of the hut. I couldn't just leave him without letting him know I wasn't disappearing from his life – that I would be there for him if he needed me.

I ran to where Risk waited by her saddle and rummaged

through my saddlebags until I found one of my sketchpads. I tore a strip from a fresh page and then, with a shaking hand, wrote my soul brother a note.

> Risk tells me that you have received our message, so we will bother you no longer. The parcel contains the herbs I was telling you about. I doubt you will use them, but I'm leaving them for you just in case – the dosage is written clearly on the front of each preparation. When next we meet, I truly hope that you will be happier to see us.
> Devlin.

A tear ran down my cheek and landed on the note by my name. I bit my lip as I read what I had written, then folded the note in two. I returned to the hut and placed it in one of the bowls, along with the parcel of herbs. As I emerged into the clearing, a grey squirrel bounding towards me stopped in its tracks and stood on its hind legs chittering, as if cross at discovering me in the hut. I had a feeling it was the same squirrel that had stolen some of my soul brother's food.

I hurried to the campfire and searched the forest floor around it until I found the cook pot lid, then hurried back to the hut and placed it on the cook pot. The stew was for my soul brother; the squirrel could look after himself. After a last look around the hut, I returned to Risk, saddled her and mounted, allowing her to carry me away from the clearing without a backward glance.

I supposed that Risk must have carried me a different way out of the forest from the route we had taken the previous day – I had been too wrapped up in misery and concern to notice – since the sun hadn't even reached its zenith by the time we emerged into the onslaught of its rays.

We should go back into the trees and carry on our way this evening, I told her, shielding my eyes from the brightness into which she had stepped.

We require more distance between us and He Who Can Heal That Which Has Gone Before if you are to properly rest.

My heart sank on two counts. *It's too hot for you to be moving around much, let alone carrying me. And what if he needs more help once he realises we've gone?*

When he requires more assistance then his Bond-Partner will request it of us and we will respond. We will continue on our own path until that time. Risk picked up her pace, walking more surely now that she was no longer impeded by the forest's undergrowth. I dismounted and walked beside her.

Which will be when? I asked. *All this time, I've been working hard at leaving my old self behind so that I'd be able to help my soul brother. What am I meant to do now?*

Your acceptance of the lessons of your past is not yet complete. He Who Can Heal That Which Has Gone Before will help you but there is more we can do to prepare your mind in readiness.

I sighed, sensing her intention. *Starting with travelling through life-threatening heat without knowing when we'll reach shade or water, so I get to practise being okay with a greater level of risk than I've managed before? You're seriously suggesting we risk our lives in order for me to get over myself?*

We risk our lives with every breath we take, my horse reminded me. *Yet the deeper and longer our breaths then the stronger we are and the more open to that which life has to offer.*

That bit was new. I pondered on its meaning for some time until I found it.

Fortified by trust, I announced finally. *It always comes back to that.* I looked up from the brown stalks of grass through which the two of us had been walking for what seemed like forever, but was more likely a few hours, to see a large body of water glistening in the distance. Beyond it was an abundance of trees whose uppermost branches swayed tantalisingly in a breeze we would surely soon feel. Sweat dripped off my nose as I reached out and stroked Risk's sodden neck. No words were necessary.

~

When we reached the lake, I unsaddled Risk and we both waded into its clear blue water. Its bottom fell away sharply, and I was delighted when, instead of stopping to drink, Risk swam at my side. The water's coolness was delicious after the furnace of the plains, and reinvigorated us both within minutes. We turned in unison and swam for the shore, where Risk stood sucking in long draughts of water while I knelt beside her, drinking from cupped hands. When I was sated, I crawled onto the bank and lay flat on my back. I reached for the hat I had abandoned by Risk's saddle, pulled it over my face, and fell asleep to the sound of Risk munching on the oasis of green grass that surrounded the lake.

I woke to a griping in my stomach and a persistent nudging of my arm. I sat up, squinting as my hat slid off my face, even though my horse stood blocking me from the sun. Judging by its position in the sky, it was early evening. My clothes were dry – even the parts on which I had been lying – and so was Risk. I sensed her thirst and discomfort at the heat, and felt terrible. She had shaded me from the sun for hours while I slept, at an increasing cost to herself.

I got to my feet and rubbed her neck. *Thanks for looking out for me. I'm so sorry I slept for so long. Go on, get back in the water and cool down.*

My horse wasted no time in doing as I suggested. While the water cooled her and rehydrated her, it did nothing for her weariness.

I checked the sun's position again, then shaded my eyes as I looked across the water towards the distant treeline. *The heat will be going out of the sun now, but we could move around to the far side of the lake where there is shade, so you can be more sure of being able to sleep without getting too hot?* I suggested to my horse.

I would rest here, she replied. She plodded lethargically out of the water and back to my side, where she immediately folded her forelegs and then landed on her side with a soft bump.

Right, well, I'll shade you as best I can until the sun goes down, I told her.

She closed her eyes, sighed and was asleep.

I stood at her head with the gradually lowering sun behind me, so that my shadow hovered over as much of her as possible. A wave of love and gratitude washed over me, eclipsing the gentle lapping of water at the lake's shore. It seemed there was nothing my horse wouldn't do to challenge my fear of risk, and no limit to her resolve to care for me, even at detriment to herself. I would stand at her head until the sun could no longer cause her a problem, and ensure she rested until she was fully recovered from her exertions of the past few days.

When the sun finally disappeared behind the distant trees, I refilled my water pouches and then took another bath in the lake. I washed my clothes and hat, laying them on the bank to dry. Standing naked while my skin dried, I ate some beef jerky followed by dried fruit and nuts, then donned a clean set of clothes. I sat down by Risk's head, enjoying the sound of her nostrils fluttering gently with each outward breath, and the sense I had of her body recovering from all she had endured in order to help me.

The sketch I produced of her lying, sleeping in our new surroundings assured me not only that there was nothing in the vicinity of which we needed to be mindful, but that we were exactly where we needed to be; it was as if her prone body were as much a part of the landscape as the lake, grass and cloudless sky.

I yawned often as darkness fell, my hours of sleep during the afternoon not having been sufficient to make up for all those that had evaded me the previous night. Risk hadn't slept either, I reminded myself; she never fully rested when she was by herself since the instincts of her kind warned her against it. The fact that she was so soundly asleep now warmed my heart; she trusted me with her life as much as she encouraged me to trust her with mine. And we were both stronger for it. I reached out and gently stroked her cheek in the darkness, wondering how I came to be so fortunate as to have one such as her in my life.

I smiled to myself as I remembered the firm response she had given me when I had pondered the same question before. *Fortune is a human construct and has no part to play in that which we are about.*

It didn't stop me from feeling fortunate and, human construct or not, I enjoyed feeling that way. My joy kept my drooping eyelids from closing, ensured a smile every time a rabbit hopped past, and kept my heart rate steady despite the frequent shrieks of the nighttime birds and animals grazing and hunting under the starlit sky.

∼

Chapter Twenty-Two

The short summer's night was half gone when my horse finally woke. She propped herself up on her elbows and pulled at the surrounding grass for a short while, then got to her feet. She shook herself from muzzle to hoof, stretched both back legs out behind her and wandered down to the lake where she drank and then ate. I forced myself to stay awake and watch her, eager to move on as soon as she was ready, so that we would hopefully reach the shade of the trees on the far bank of the lake before the sun rose.

Several torturous hours passed before I sensed that Risk was ready to be saddled. As soon as I was on her back, she took off at a slow canter, forcing me to push my hat more firmly onto my head lest it get left behind. When her muscles had loosened, she increased her speed, despite the multitude of rabbit burrows dotting the ground. I didn't doubt her for a second, and not because the night was radiant with light from the full moon. If she trusted herself to avoid the hazards in her way, then so did I.

We reached the trees well before the sun afforded them the ability to grant us shade, Risk barely sweating and both of us energised by our moonlit dash around the lake. I unsaddled my horse and brushed her thoroughly before she went to the lake to drink and resume grazing its banks. Leaning her saddle against the nearest tree, I broke my fast with more fruit and nuts, drank from the lake and then sank to the ground, my head resting on my saddlebags.

It was only when I woke that I realised I had been asleep – and not for long enough, judging by the heaviness of my eyelids, the grittiness in my eyes, and my lack of ability to think clearly. It was Risk's unease that had penetrated my slumber and immediately had me sitting up, rubbing my eyes and squinting at the sunlight reflecting off the lake. It was her cantering towards me, spinning on her hindquarters and then cantering away a short distance before stopping with her neck stretched up high and her ears pricked that had me leaping to my feet and grabbing my saddle.

Risk, what is it? I asked her.

We must go.

I hefted her saddle with its attached bags to my hip and put it on her back as soon as she reached my side. She danced on her feet in agitation as I tightened the girth. I had mounted by the time I thought to ask, *But what about the heat? It's, what, mid-afternoon?*

The situation is urgent. It cannot wait, was all she told me before hurtling into a flat-out gallop and heading back the way we had come.

All my joy of the previous evening and night fled and was replaced by a sickening, throat-wrenching dread. Something must have happened to my soul brother. *What's happened to him?* I asked Risk repeatedly, but to no avail. She focused all her attention on her flight around the lake without once stopping to immerse herself in it or drink, before leaving it behind and tearing through the searing heat of the plains.

As her breath became increasingly dry and laboured, I couldn't decide whether my fear for her or my soul brother was greater, because one thing was certain – they were both in dire straits. Yet the determination I could feel emanating from Risk was as great as ever, and not only that, I had a strong sense that as far as she was concerned, the risk to herself and me of heat exhaustion and dehydration was far less than the risk to us all of not reaching my soul brother in time to save him from the situation in which he now found himself.

He Who Can Heal That Which Has Gone Before. I repeated over and over to myself the name Risk had given him. How had I never considered its significance before? How had I never recognised the importance Risk attached to him? Because all I had been able to think about was who he had been to me. I had been so fixated on meeting Henry's reincarnation in this lifetime, I had ignored all the indications Risk had given me as to his importance to far more people than just me.

Risk, why is he so important? I asked my rapidly tiring horse, then felt awful for distracting her when our situation was so dire. I thought back to how she had supported me when I was exhausted and sure I couldn't go on, and tried to emulate her. I extended as much of myself as I could to her through our bond; my energy and strength, my confidence in her, my absolute trust she would get us to my soul brother before it was too late.

She picked up her pace again and, almost riding within her as I was, I became aware through her that another horse did too.

Your trust sustains us both, Risk informed me. While her thought was faint, it rang with pride and significance.

The horse who's tugging my soul brother is trying to reach him too?

He will not be in time. He has requested our assistance, she replied as she crashed into the forest.

Labouring hard now, my beloved horse slowed her pace just enough to avoid trees and pace herself to clear the denser patches of undergrowth. For my part, I continued to give as much of myself to her as I could in order to help her keep going. I saw through her eyes and swerved with her as if I were part of her body rather than merely astride it. I felt the sting of every scratch to her legs as she blasted through barbed undergrowth. The blood pounding so hard it almost hurt, the light-headedness and dizziness, the dryness of nose and throat, all belonged to both of us.

Risk burst into the small clearing in which my soul brother had made his home, and skidded to a halt on shaking legs before his hut. Some food containers appeared to have been hurled out of the doorway; their lids had burst off them, spilling their contents on the forest floor. What appeared to be some of the packets of herbs from the parcel I had left were strewn about nearby. One wall of the hut was charred black and glistened with moisture even as the acrid smell of smoke hung in the air nearby. I didn't have time to wonder how it had caught fire or how long it had taken for the flames to be extinguished, because against the opposite wall, by the water barrel, lay my soul brother.

Chapter Twenty-Three

The first time I had met the man before me, he was a stranger out of whose eyes looked the brother of my soul. Now, as he lay propped against his hovel, his face slack and his mouth open and drooping to one side, he looked exactly the same as the last time I had seen him. Dead. He was my best friend, my partner in mischief, my big brother. My Henry.

Risk shook me out of my horror by stumbling towards the water barrel, almost landing on her knees. I leapt off her back, almost falling on my backside as I landed on unsteady legs, undid the girth of her saddle and practically threw it against a nearby tree. I turned back to her, then to my brother, then repeatedly back and forth between them like a child's wind-up toy with a stuck mechanism, so desperate to help them both that I wasn't helping either.

I will drink and so will you, Risk told me wearily. *Only once your body has regained the fluid it has lost will your mind clear so that you can do that which is necessary.*

Do what was necessary? Bury my brother? My wrist and

shoulder ached abominably and I gasped at the familiar, yet no less fierce, pain in my chest.

He lives, Risk informed me as she tottered closer to the barrel. *The situation will not continue for much longer unless you clear your mind and your past sufficiently to ensure it.*

I staggered to where Henry lay and reached out my hand to his neck, withdrawing it in sudden fear and revulsion as I remembered the coldness of his cheek as he lay dead in the hold of HMS Royal Sovereign. My breath caught in my throat at the increased intensity of the stabbing pain in my chest, and I had to reach out to Henry with my other hand as the injuries to my shoulder and wrist caused the one attached to them to hang limply at my side. I still couldn't bring myself to touch him. I couldn't risk touching my brother and finding him dead all over again.

Fortified By Trust. Something stirred within the pain, horror, dehydration and exhaustion that were causing me to convulse. *Fortified By Trust,* my horse repeated wearily. *It is time for you to make a choice. Accept fully the lessons of the past so that you and He Who Can Heal That Which Has Gone Before can have a future or resist them and ensure that you both perish once again.*

I... want... us both... to have a... future.

Then choose to remember once and for all who you are now over who you were. You have practised enough. Remember who you are above all else to the extent that you will never again forget. Risk's legs buckled and she collapsed to the ground by the water barrel. *Remember.*

It was the sight of my slender, elegant, beautiful mare, her black coat grey with rapidly drying sweat, her eyes rolling behind their closing lids, her breaths too fast and shallow, that pulled me out of the past and into the present.

'I'm Fortified By Trust,' I said urgently and with conviction.

My pain fell away as if it had been a pullover I had chosen to wear, but was now warm enough without. I crawled to the water barrel and pulled on it, expecting its weight to support me as I got to my feet and surprised when it tipped towards me until it was almost horizontal. It was almost empty! I scooped out a handful to drink, then pushed it around to where Risk lay.

Drink, I urged her.

She didn't respond. I heaved on the barrel until its lip was underneath her muzzle, relieved that its inward curve allowed water to pool there. *DRINK! RISK, DRINK!*

My horse shuddered and then, to my immense relief, sucked at the water.

I crawled to my saddlebags and relieved them of the water pouches I had filled from the lake. I drank from one until my muscles stopped spasming and my dizziness receded, then crawled back to where Risk and my soul brother lay. I put the pouch from which I had drunk on the ground beside the man whom I now realised looked nothing like the brother I had left behind me in the past, then poured most of the contents of the other pouch into the rim of the barrel for Risk, splashing the remainder on her belly and between her hind legs to help cool her.

I returned to the food that was strewn about in front of the hut and found the packet of salt from which I had taken a pinch when preparing rabbit stew on my previous visit. I poured some of the salt into Risk's water and swirled it around with my finger until it dissolved, knowing that water alone wouldn't be enough to ensure her recovery. Relieved that, slowly but surely, she was still drinking, I returned my attention to the man on the ground beside me.

I felt for a pulse beneath his jaw and found one, albeit a weak one. I pulled back his shirt roughly, looking for any sign of the injury that had rendered him unconscious, then felt all over his legs before pulling him upright as gently as I could to check his back. It was as I was carefully allowing him to rest back against the wall that I noticed again the herb packets strewn on the ground by the door of his hut. They had not only been torn open, but were empty.

My breath caught in my throat as I reached for them, hoping upon hope I wouldn't find that which I had a sinking feeling I would. Sure enough, there was no sign of any herbs having spilt to the ground. And sure enough, one of the empty packets had contained ten doses of a powerful painkiller, and the other five doses of a sleep-inducing herb. The dosage was clearly marked on both packets, yet he had consumed the entire contents of both in one go?

I threw the packets to the ground and forced open my soul brother's mouth, wincing at the smell of the herbs lining his cheeks and throat and stuck to his tongue. My heart, which had been lurching about wildly, sank at the realisation that the man before me had been so desperate to escape his suffering, he hadn't even stopped to fetch a mug of water to make his attempt less unpleasant.

I glanced at Risk and felt immense relief that her eyes were now open and she was drinking with increased vigour. I didn't know what to do next. My horse needed far more water than I had to hand, and somehow, I needed to cause my soul brother to vomit up the contents of his stomach.

Remember who you are. Risk's gentle brown eyes swivelled over to me, but I found it wasn't just their warmth and confidence that made it easy for me to obey her; there was no longer any impediment in my mind to doing so.

She would be okay. As soon as I remembered that I trusted myself as much as her, I knew it. She would need more water soon, and plenty of rest, but she had what she needed in the present moment. I, on the other hand, needed to drink more so that

I could think more clearly and then focus on my soul brother. I took a swig from the water pouch – grateful that I had brought such large ones on our current trip – then several more.

I cast my mind back to all the times I had been in Shif's cottage, sketching or painting while he tended to patients in his treatment room. The faintest of memories resonated with my current situation, like a voice tentatively singing in harmony with another and then becoming stronger as its presence is recognised and applauded. A mother in a high state of anxiety had brought her young, barely conscious child to Shif, suspecting he had eaten berries she knew to be poisonous, and he had asked for my help in saving the child.

I had the answer I needed to save the unconscious man beside me. I grabbed the packet of salt and emptied some into one of the mugs on the table in the hut, added water from my pouch, and stirred it until the salt dissolved. I hurried to my saddlebags and withdrew the tube I sometimes attached to a water pouch so I could drink more easily whilst in the saddle. I knelt down by the prone man's side, put one end of the tube into the salt water and sucked on it until the fluid entered my mouth. Quickly spitting it out before I retched, I fed the tube into his mouth and down his throat, mindful of selecting the opening that led to his stomach and not his lungs, whilst also holding his tongue so it didn't follow, as Shif had asked me to do for the child whilst his hysterical mother looked on. The salt water passed into his stomach via the tube, which I left in place in case I needed to give him more.

'We need him a bit more awake before he vomits.' I could hear Shif telling me what we needed to do for the child as easily as if he were standing right behind me. 'Pass me that bucket of water, lad.'

I reached for the empty bucket still lying by the water barrel and emptied the rest of the water from my pouch into it. Then, trying to put aside my shock at how light my soul brother was, I pulled him up and forward until he was on his knees. Supporting him with an arm around his waist, I slapped him hard, then dunked his head in the water. He began to choke and when I pulled him back out, his eyes flickered open briefly before closing again. I slapped his face with no less force and intent than the first time, desperate for him to come around more before he vomited, and the damn man actually smiled as he went limp again. I shoved his head back into the water until I felt him convulsing, then pulled him upright and quickly pulled the tube out of his throat before flinging him back down on his knees, where he vomited a puddle of herbs and salt water.

He continued to throw up the contents of his stomach until he dry retched, at which point, feeling weak with relief, I said, 'Good. Now don't you dare go back to sleep. Don't. You. Dare.' I hauled him to his feet and pulled his uninjured arm around my shoulder while I continued to grip him firmly around the waist. He sagged against me and a pang of fear shot through my stomach that he might have digested and absorbed enough of the herbs to still be at risk of losing his life.

I decided there was nothing I could do about it other than to stick to my intention of keeping him awake until the danger had passed. 'Come on,' I told him, 'we need to walk.'

Relief almost had me on my knees again when he moved his feet beside mine, and then again when Risk heaved herself to her feet. She shook her whole body, liberating a cloud of dried sweat and debris from the forest floor. My fingers itched to splash water over her and wash her down.

I will go to where there is water and address my needs, she announced, her thought as strong as her body was weak. *You should do the same.* She walked slowly, falteringly, towards the glade that had provided for her needs two nights previously. I heaved my soul brother around, intending to follow her. She stopped and looked back at me. *The needs of He Who Can Heal That Which Has Gone Before differ from mine. You should take him to where you can do that which is necessary for him. And for yourself,* she added pointedly before continuing on her way.

But it'll be dark before too long, and I can feel you're no more comfortable in the forest than you were the last time we were here. Will you be alright on your own?

When the answer to my question settled in my mind, it felt as if it came not from her, but from inside me. *There's an element of risk in everything we do. That doesn't mean we should avoid doing it.*

You have cleared that which prevented you from hearing the voice of your soul, Risk informed me as she disappeared between the trees. *Fortified By Trust you chose well.*

Where her counsel had always carried her gentle and infinitely patient confidence in me, now it was stronger. Firmer. Like I would speak to a young adult human once they were no longer a child. The love and pride that accompanied it gave me the added strength I needed to keep my soul brother on his feet whilst I leant down to pick up my saddlebags – which I heaved over my spare shoulder – then the bucket, and walk him to the stream from which I had refilled his water barrel the previous day.

Once there, I stripped him and sat him in the water, splashing it in his face every time his eyes stopped fluttering. I rummaged in my saddlebags and found my soap, then scrubbed him clean with it and some stems of grass I twisted around one another. When there wasn't a speck of grime left on his skin, I lay him on his back in the stream, supported his head above the water, and washed his hair. When no more dirt flowed away from him in the gentle current, I heaved him out of the water and dragged him to lean against a tree.

I went to fetch my saddlebags from where I had dropped them and found I couldn't lift them, such was the intensity of trembling throughout my body. I glanced at where my soul brother lay, naked and pitifully thin. His eyes were fluttering and he had begun mumbling to himself. I judged I had a little time to tend to myself, and I knew I should if I were to continue being of use to him. Risk's approval wove its way through me, along with her sense of renewed invigoration now that she had drunk her fill from the spring, rolled in the sitting water that surrounded it, and was grazing lush grass.

I filled the bucket upstream from where I had bathed my soul brother and put it on the ground before him so I could splash him if I needed to shock him back awake. Then I pulled my mug and a food parcel from one of my saddlebags and ate and drank until I could do no more of either. Feeling better, I selected a set of fresh clothes, in which I dressed my soul brother. Then I rummaged through my things until I found a piece of cloth I had packed for use as a sling, bandage or tourniquet, and bound his arm across his chest so its movement wouldn't further irritate whatever injury it was that he had sustained to his shoulder.

When I was satisfied that I had done as much for him as I could, I stripped and washed myself in the stream, keeping a close eye on him all the while, then washed my clothes and lay them on the bank to dry in the warm night air. I couldn't bring myself to even touch the rags I had peeled off my soul brother, so instead poked at them with a stick until they hung from its end, and flicked them into the undergrowth to rot.

As soon as my clothes and I were dry, I redressed. Concerned at not being able to see my soul brother's condition in the failing light, I repacked my saddlebags and heaved them back onto my shoulder, then hauled the man, whose face I barely recognised now it was clean, to his feet.

'Time for more walking, my friend,' I told him.

I was gratified that he walked a little more steadily and without the need to lean against me so much, despite his eyes still fluttering rather than being of any use to him, but I still judged him far from ready to be allowed to sleep. When we reached the clearing, I dumped my gear by Risks' saddle and resigned myself to a long night.

I lost track of how long or how far we walked, my soul brother and I; only that we made sufficient trips to the stream to remain cool and hydrated, enough trips to the glade where Risk grazed that I learnt the position of every tree root that could trip us, and enough circuits of the clearing full of his misery that I couldn't wait to leave it.

It was when I began tripping in the absence of any roots or undergrowth that a black shape appeared between the moonlit trees.

I will carry you both. You will rest, Risk informed me.

No way. There's no way you're taking us both after the day you just had. I stopped walking and held my soul brother in place while I moved to his other side so I could change my supporting arm, flexing the hand of the arm that felt as if it didn't belong to me.

I have recovered sufficiently to carry you and He Who Can Heal That Which Has Gone Before to meet his Bond-Partner but we must leave now. Should we wait any longer then the heat will rise and he will be awake.

I shuddered at the thought of trying to take my soul brother to his horse in either scenario, let alone if both were happening at the same time. My sense of Risk told me that, remarkably, she had indeed recovered well and was very determined to fulfil her agreement with the horse who had let her know of my soul brother's predicament. I found myself way too tired to argue with her.

I lowered my soul brother to the ground by my saddlebags and felt around in them until I found my grooming brushes. When I sensed Risk's impatience to leave, I told her, *I can do this by feel, and I'll be quick. There's no way I'm saddling you until I know there's no dirt on you that will cause a rub.*

She stood far more patiently than I would have, had I been experiencing the same urgency to be on our way, but the instant I wedged myself into the back of her saddle, having heaved my soul brother into the front of it, she walked with the sense of purpose that was so familiar, so dear to me, as if her double load were no more than half of one.

My soul brother mumbled something incomprehensible, but in a definite tone of surprise and consternation. I tightened my arms around his waist, relieved that he seemed to be coming around more, whilst hoping upon hope he didn't fully wake before we reached our destination; I wasn't at all confident I would be able to subdue his temper when he realised we had taken him from his home. I focused on keeping him in the saddle, pushing his upper body forward or pulling it back in order to avoid low-hanging branches, and protecting his legs with my own when Risk was forced to squeeze between closely growing trees.

By the time we emerged from the forest onto what smelt like grassland, my eyes were refusing to stay open for more than a second at a time, my arms felt as if they were laden with metal and my backside as if it had deserted me. Risk marched onward, as sure of her direction as her footing, so I forced my eyes open, my arms to keep holding my muttering soul brother in place, and my backside to endure further torture.

It was as I raised my hand against the first of the sun's rays to break the horizon that Risk finally came to a halt. She was definitely stationary – however numb my backside and limbs were, I was sure of that – and yet I could hear the pounding of hooves. How could that be?

I squinted at the orange-tinged grassland and was just about able to make out a white and brown blob hurtling in our direction.

Chapter Twenty-Four

I couldn't find a way to dismount. I couldn't lean forward in order to swing my leg over Risk's back, because my soul brother was in the way. I couldn't lift my leg between him and me because, wedged into the rear of the saddle as I was, I couldn't create any space between us.

How on earth had I mounted? I tried to remember, but my head was fuzzy, and my thoughts seemed to twist around one another so that I couldn't make any sense of them. I tried to knock the stirrup from my soul brother's foot, hoping I could step into it, stand up and get my leg over Risk's back that way. He grunted as I kicked his ankle instead. I could only think of one thing to do.

Risk, I'm sorry about this. Bear with me, I'll be as quick as I can. I pushed against my soul brother's back and slid over the rear of the saddle onto Risk's rump. I lightly grasped his arms, waiting to right him if he swayed to either side, but he sat in place, muttering about someone called Bronwyn. I pushed against the back of the saddle so that I slid backwards towards Risk's tail, then down its length to the hard, cracked ground, where my legs

Chapter Twenty-Four

gave way and I landed on my backside. Thanking my good fortune that it was still too numb to register any kind of sensation, I pushed myself back to my feet and moved on wobbly legs to my soul brother's side.

I reached up and pulled him from Risk's back, then supported him as he staggered alongside me to the trunk of the large-leafed tree under whose canopy my horse had come to rest. As I lowered him to the ground, he mumbled something about never letting anyone down again. When his back rested against the tree trunk, he finally fell silent. His head lolled to one side and he began to snore.

I hurried to Risk and lightly pinched her skin between two of my fingers. My heart sank as her skin remained pinched for more than a couple of seconds after I released it. *You need water, right now, and plenty of it,* I told her. *Will you drink from my hands if I pour it into them from my pouch?*

There is water not far distant. Give your water to he who approaches for his need is greater. Then we will leave him and He Who Can Heal That Which Has Gone Before to consolidate their bond. Risk lifted her head and whinnied shrilly as the sound of pounding hooves became almost deafening.

I turned to see a huge, heavily built horse whose feet were more than twice the size of Risk's, slowing to an ungainly trot, his legs seemingly everywhere at once. His largely white coat was almost transparent with sweat, rendering his pink skin visible beneath. Sweat ran down his legs in rivulets, dripped from his belly and poured down his face. His sides heaved and the lining of his flared nostrils was such a dark pink, it was almost red. His legs trembled so violently that his hocks were almost knocking together, but despite his condition, his large brown eyes were deep pools of serenity – as if they belonged to a body other than the exhausted one before me. He didn't stop flailing his legs around until he was almost on top of my soul brother, and for a moment I feared his lack of co-ordination would have him crush the man he had travelled so far and fast to find.

I needn't have worried. The enormous horse stopped just short of my soul brother and whickered softly. He lowered his head and dripped sweat on the prone man as he sniffed him all over, from the top of his head to his booted feet, pausing only to nuzzle his injured shoulder and the area of his chest enclosing his heart. Then the horse whickered again, nuzzled the top of his Bond-Partner's head, and lifted his head to look at me.

I knew without knowing how that he wouldn't leave my soul brother's side while he slept, and as Risk had told me, he was in even more desperate need of water than was she. I pulled my soul brother's salt packet and one of my water pouches from a saddlebag and knelt on the ground before the horse. I sprinkled a little salt into my hands, then put the pouch between my legs, pulled off its stopper and squeezed it with my knees so that water filled my cupped hands.

A profound sense of peace stole over me as two enormous hooves appeared on the ground before me and a pink muzzle gently brushed my hands, draining them of the water as quickly as it flowed into them. I forgave my past self for choosing two of the largest water pouches the Tailors at The Gathering could provide, despite the increase in weight for Risk to carry. When the first of the two was empty, I stood, intending to fetch the second so that the horse could continue to rehydrate.

He would that you leave that for his Bond-Partner, Risk announced. *He has had sufficient to sustain him until he can visit the source for which we will now head.*

What he just drank wouldn't have been enough to rehydrate you, let alone a horse of his size, I argued, waving a hand towards the horse who stood before me.

Chapter Twenty-Four

He was staring at me. I couldn't hear him in my mind like I could Risk, but I didn't need to.

He'll be okay, I told Risk as if she didn't already know. *He IS okay. He might be a young horse but he knows how to look after himself. He also knows what's best for his Bond-Partner, and that's for us to be gone by the time he wakes.* I nodded to myself even as a faint pang of grief stabbed at my heart at the thought of leaving my soul brother again.

The enormous white and brown horse held my gaze, and I knew with absolute certainty that I had no cause to fear. He would be everything to my soul brother that Risk was to me, and if we were needed again for any reason, he would let Risk know.

I chose to trust him. Risk's pride and approval bolstered the strength my decision afforded me, and my mind cleared despite its exhaustion. We needed to leave, but first there was something I had to do. My soul brother would wake in the middle of nowhere, confused and disoriented, and undoubtedly furious. Who knew how long it would take for him to accept his bond with his horse when he had resisted it so ferociously, let alone heed his counsel, and in the meantime, he would be vulnerable. It wasn't just my water that I should leave for him – it was pretty much everything I had.

I unbuckled my saddlebags and pulled from one of them the back-sack I always had with me in case I needed to carry extra supplies. I filled it with all my clothes except those in which I was standing, my hunting gear, all my food and that of his which I had rescued from the ground by his hut, and the cook pot, bowl, plate, mug and cutlery of his that I brought for him to use. I attached the full water pouch to a handle of the back-sack and then lay it on the ground by his side.

He looked so small as he lay there, propped against the tree trunk in the middle of the vast wilderness that contained little aside from grass and rabbit burrows. I bit my lip hard to stop tears filling my eyes. He wasn't Henry and I wasn't Jimmy. We weren't brothers; we were soul brothers, here in the present in order to heal the past – ours and that of many others if the name by which Risk referred to him was any indication.

I had done all I could for him and now it really was time to go; Risk and I needed water, and my soul brother and his Bond-Partner needed to begin their lives together. I held a hand out for the white and brown horse to sniff, noticing again how young he appeared to be – his head and legs looked far too big for his body. But as he breathed hot air over my hand, I felt again the sense of serenity that suggested an age far greater than I could comprehend, and when he looked at me, I knew all over again that he was all my soul brother would need.

'Until we meet again, my friend,' I said out loud to the horse. Before I turned and walked away, I couldn't help whispering, 'Look after him.'

I didn't trust myself to look back. I focused on matching my stride to Risk's as I stumbled along at her side, so that I didn't slow her equally weary trudge to the water she had scented.

It was only later, as I watched Risk slake her thirst at the watering hole, that I realised I'd left behind – without thought or even a second glance – everything that would keep me alive. I now had no food and no means of hunting any; no water or means of carrying any; and no spare clothes. All I had were some sketchpads and pencils, Risk's grooming brushes, my cook pot, bowl, mug and spoon, and my soap.

My mouth twitched into a grin at the thought that if I were going to die out in the wilderness, at least I would be clean. My smile widened further as I realised that, bizarrely, I felt absolutely no fear whatsoever at the massively increased possibility of death

I now faced, and no regrets other than that I had left my soul brother's side without learning his name.

I was now as comfortable with risk as I was with Risk.

My gentle, beautiful, incredible Bond-Partner lifted her head, water dripping from her chin, and stared at me. *Having cleared the hold over you that you afforded your past you are now well placed to help the others involved do the same.*

I knew what she meant and not only because I sensed her intention; the voice of my soul could not have been clearer in confirming that there would be a time when we would need to find my soul brother again and support him further on his path, but in the meantime, there was someone else we needed to help. We should return to my home village. We would return to Coastwood.

Chapter Twenty-Five

We travelled directly to Coastwood without diverting to visit any other villages along the way. The drought continued, the heat remained fierce, the distance between water sources increased and food was scarce – for me at least, if not for Risk whose digestive system allowed her to take sustenance from even the driest grasses – but it was due to none of those factors that we made haste for my home village. After realising that I was needed at home, I had allowed my body as much sleep as it required, then used the time that Risk spent resting and grazing near the waterhole to sketch those I had barely allowed myself to think of since leaving Coastwood, let alone draw.

My brothers and their families almost burst out of my sketches with their joy for life. Joplin now had three children, all of them the image of him, and the swelling of Kaplin's wife's belly told me she was expecting their second child. My father looked as if more years had passed than the five since I had last seen him, but his smile was relaxed as he held my mother close to him, one hand on her waist and the other on his own hip. Mother leant against rather than into his side, her smile narrower than it had used to be and her eyes staring out at me. I was relieved to see that they were her eyes and not Ma's, but I could see the effort it was taking her for that to be the case.

I felt a sudden surge of pride. It had been excruciatingly difficult for me to step aside from the past, and I'd had Risk's understanding, guidance and patience. My mother was doing it alone – however much it was taking out of not only her but clearly my father, she was definitely doing it. Every time I looked at my sketch of my parents, I itched to get back to them, to help my mother as I was sure I now could. Guilt stirred in the pit of my stomach and rose like bile into my throat at having been too scared, too weak, to spare her more than a passing thought before.

As the weeks passed and we edged closer to Coastwood, I learnt to release my guilt more quickly by remembering the counsel Risk had given me when it first emerged.

Had you allowed yourself to focus upon even your recent past then you would not now be in a position to offer assistance in the present. Do not give energy to that which serves no one. Conserve it for that which lies ahead.

Risk didn't just mean helping my mother, for she wasn't the only reason we were making as much haste as possible as soon as the light of each day surrendered to darkness. Much as I loved Mother and was desperate to ease her suffering, it wasn't because of her I barely noticed the hunger pangs that seemed to be trying to chew their way free of my body, or the thirst that at times had me swaying in the saddle even as my beloved mare battled on to the next waterhole despite me. It was because of Shif.

Though he stared out of the likeness I had drawn of him with as much intensity as Mother, his eyes were even cloudier than I remembered and he carried so little flesh as to be almost skeletal;

strong as his will may still have been, his body was failing. That was the description I tried to focus upon when I thought of him, because it was preferable to the one I knew was more accurate. He was dying. He didn't have long left – in fact, he hadn't had long for what must have seemed like an eternity to him, judging by the strain causing him to clamp his jaws together and the blood vessels to stand proud at his temples. His expression was a rictus of concentration as he clung to life, waiting for me.

Of course, he knew I was coming, just like he had always known. I felt him reaching for me, willing me to hurry so that he could know everything he was desperate to know before he let go. So he could see for himself that the boy he had guided and encouraged, the boy he felt such kinship with and yet who had held him at such a distance for so long, the boy in whom he had never lost faith, had achieved everything of which the voice of Shif's soul told him I was capable and had need of him no more.

My heart burned with love for the old man who had given me so much whilst asking for nothing in return… until now. I would ask no more of Risk than she was willing to offer freely, but I would give everything of myself to reach him in time – to read him the list, short as it was, of Artists who would still be struggling with life were it not for him; to apologise for my abuse of his friendship; to thank him, from the bottom of my heart, for opening up my world so that it had room for Risk; to tell him I loved him.

At no point during our four-week-long journey to Coastwood did I fear that my beautiful Risk and I would perish, despite the difficult travelling conditions. When we left one water source, I trusted her to find the next. When she stopped to graze or rest, I trusted I would either find something to eat, or my body's strength and resilience would allow me to survive until I did. I sketched because I wanted to, not because I needed to. I bathed and washed

Chapter Twenty-Five

my clothes when doing so wouldn't pollute our water source, because it felt nice, not because the ritual gave me a sense of security – for security as I had perceived it no longer existed for me. How could it, when there was nothing about which to feel insecure?

So it was that when Risk and I arrived in Coastwood, I barely recognised the village in which I had grown up. It was a shock, since when I scrutinised the details of my surroundings in a way so few others could, I could see nothing that was different. The grey stone cottages lining the cobbled street were as similar in construction as they were different in the tiny ways their individual inhabitants had requested. One had small, coloured stones interspersed between the rocks that made up its walls. Another had a large porch surrounding its front door while its neighbour had a bay window in which the resident Glass-Singer's wares were displayed.

Everything was the same as when I had left, yet where the street had seemed wide and eternally long, now it seemed narrow and comfortably short, as if everyone and everything was within easy reach. Where I had felt the cottages looming over me, imposing their presence and potentially their inhabitants, now I perceived them as pretty, cosy retreats for those no doubt currently eating their evening meal within. I remembered hurrying between my home and the small number of places I'd needed to be, as if something terrible would happen were I to be caught out in the open, and couldn't reconcile those memories with the sense of calm confidence that now pervaded my body as Risk carried me along the cobbled street.

When a front door slammed just in front of us and a boy came running down the path, I smiled at him and lifted a hand in greeting. 'Hello, Shane, how are you?'

He stopped at the front gate of his friend's home and stared at me astride Risk, his mouth hanging open. I was aware I looked a fright but didn't waste time wondering whether it was my appearance, or the fact that a Horse-Bonded had just arrived in Coastwood, that had stopped him short.

'I'll take that as "very well thank you, Mr Bakewell", shall I?' I said with a chuckle. 'Get on home now, or you'll be late for your dinner.'

Without request from me, Risk stopped to let the boy onto the street in front of her, then resumed her way to my parents' cottage once he was running down the street ahead of us, tripping every time he looked back over his shoulder.

We had timed our arrival well; having rested nearby during the heat of the day, we endured the sun's assault for the hour it took to reach Coastwood when I knew that its fisherfolk inhabitants, whose body clocks ran to the strict schedule necessary for their Trade and influenced the daily schedules of those working in the other Trades and Skills, would likely be indoors. Much as I looked forward to catching up with all those I knew and meeting those I didn't, I couldn't afford to be diverted from the reason I had come home.

Risk was hot and tired despite the short distance we had travelled since last resting, but it wasn't because of her keenness to reach the water and shade she knew she'd find in my parents' paddock that she picked up her pace as we neared it; it was because we both knew that it was in my parents' cottage that I would find Shif.

I dismounted on the street outside, and Risk and I made our way soundlessly between my old home and its neighbouring cottage to the paddocks behind. Even had I not sensed Risk's weariness, it was obvious by her uncharacteristic pause to wait for me to open the gate to my parents' paddock rather than sailing over it in her usual elegant fashion. Once inside, she made straight for the water trough, which was always kept full for the chickens and goats. I unsaddled her while she drank, then fetched a decent quantity of hay from the store shed to supplement the scorched, sparse grazing. My parents' four goats looked on hopefully, clearly wanting some hay but cautious about approaching Risk, so I hurried to fetch more hay for them so they could all eat and rest in peace.

I glanced at the cottage, then back at Risk, torn. My concern for my horse won out; her coat was streaked with both wet and dry sweat and I would see her completely comfortable before facing that which awaited me in the cottage. I splashed her with water and rubbed away the evidence of her labour until her black coat shone. I checked her hooves and brushed her mane and tail, then, satisfied that she was comfortable and had everything she needed, I carried her saddle and my meagre belongings to the back door of the cottage. I turned its handle and when it creaked open, dumped my saddle and bags on the flagstones inside where they were safe from the goats, and headed for the kitchen.

I reached for the handle of the kitchen door just as it was flung open. 'I promise you, there's no one here, Shif,' Father said, looking back over his shoulder into the kitchen. 'We'd have heard him and Risk if they were back. I'll let you know as soon as...' His entire face froze as he turned back towards me.

I grinned. 'Hello, Father.'

'Devlin?' he whispered, then made me jump as he grabbed my arms. 'Is it really you?'

'Who's there, Lennon?' Mother appeared at Father's side. She slapped her hands to her cheeks and pulled them downward with such force, her face turned white.

From within the room emanated a faint, raspy chuckle. 'Don't just stand there, lad, come in.'

Chapter Twenty-Six

From the instant I had realised I was needed in Coastwood, I never doubted I would be strong enough to face my family and friends – to be the person I had become whilst in the company of those who knew the person I had been. For a few moments though, the horror in my parents' eyes as they stared at me, the weakness of Shif's voice as he invited me in, and the smell of death emanating from the hub of our family home, caused me to hesitate.

What if I only thought I was strong enough to leave the past behind when it was still part of my mother's present? What if I crumbled back to being the person I used to be, now that I was back with those who still saw me that way? What if Shif died disappointed in me? Should I leave before I made things worse for everyone? Before I proved to myself that I wasn't as strong as I had thought? Before I reverted to feeling terrified all the time? My heart pounded when I reached the question that scared me the most, and I almost turned and ran. But where would I run to?

Risk.

Chapter Twenty-Six

My horse made no attempt to reassure or support me. She was focused on meeting her own needs, her confidence in me absolute that I could do that which was necessary without her. I trusted her and I trusted myself. I had all the strength I needed.

I gently shook my father's hands off my arms and gathered both my parents close to me. 'I probably stink and I know I'm a bit thin, but yes, it's really me,' I said as I hugged them both.

Father hugged me back briefly and then took a step back. 'You're not just a bit thin, Devlin, you're extremely thin, and you're filthy and your clothes are in tatters. You're in a terrible state. What happened to you? And where's Risk? Is she okay?'

I put my now free arm around my mother, who was clinging to me as if her life depended on it, and hugged her even more tightly. 'It's nothing a decent bath and a few good meals won't sort out,' I told my father over her head. 'Honestly, I've never felt better. Risk has dropped a bit of weight too, but she'll soon put it back on now she has access to hay. She's tired, but she can rest for a good while now we're finally here. Everything's fine, honestly.'

I felt Mother relax in my arms and released her. She looked me up and down with an intensity that was almost unsettling – especially since Ma flicked into her expression a couple of times – and then stared into my eyes, searching for what only she, of all my family would be able to see there. I held her gaze as unblinkingly as I could, even when Ma looked up at me, her hope quickly turning to shock and then grief that sent a torrent of tears down my mother's face.

Mother wiped them away and smiled. 'It's true,' she whispered. 'You're better than well. I looked into your portrait at least every few hours, every day, to get a sense of you and know you were alright, but I had no idea this was happening to you.' She waved her hand down the length of my body. 'That you were getting so much better inside while looking so terrible on the outside.'

My father looked between the two of us in consternation. 'What do you mean?' he asked my mother. 'How can he be better on the inside if he's let himself get into that state?' He looked at me. 'How have you got yourself into that state, Devlin?'

'Rushing to get here in time to catch me before I go,' Shif murmured huskily. 'And I'm still not getting any younger, you know.' He chuckled again and then coughed.

Mother rushed to his side, giving me space to step into the room.

Father moved in front of me and said, 'Brace yourself, he's in a bad way.' I nodded and he stepped aside.

Mother was holding a beaker to Shif's mouth whilst catching the water that was dribbling down his chin with a cloth. He lay on a makeshift bed behind the kitchen door, propped up with what appeared to be all the cottage's pillows and covered with a single white sheet.

I glanced back at my father. 'Wouldn't he be more comfortable in one of the beds upstairs?'

Father shook his head ruefully and said in a low voice, 'He wouldn't hear of it. He only agreed to stay with us on the condition that he could sleep right there. He's been holding something of a vigil by the back door, convinced you'd be back soon and that was where you'd come in. We thought it was just the rambling of a dying man, but it turns out he was right.'

He looked surprised when I nodded. 'I knew he was waiting for me. I got here as soon as I could.'

'Risk told you?'

I shook my head. 'He did. Through my sketches of him.' Before my father could say anything else, I moved to Shif's side.

Chapter Twenty-Six

Mother moved away, allowing me to kneel down beside my old friend.

His long hair was now white, and his skin mottled as it hung from his bones. His pale blue pyjamas seemed much too big for him and had a couple of pink stains above their top button.

'Your mother keeps feeding me raspberries,' Shif told me, his rheumy eyes following mine and the edges of his mouth twitching. He still missed nothing.

My eyes flicked up to his and the strain and exhaustion of fighting death fell away from him as he smiled. Holding my gaze with his own, he raised a shaking hand to my cheek. I took it in mine and held it there to save him the effort.

'I knew you had it in you, but I wanted to see it with my own eyes – the man you've become,' he whispered. 'Thank you for granting me that privilege.'

I squeezed his hand. 'I wanted to be here, to thank you for everything you did for me and to apologise for making it so hard for you to help me.'

He flapped his other hand dismissively. 'I'm sure you know yourself by now that nothing is one-sided; I had to become a better man in order to help you. I'm grateful to you, Devlin, for so many things, not least pushing me to discover everything I was capable of. Now, I think, it's time for you to discover the same thing?' He glanced at my mother and then back at me.

I grinned. 'Nothing gets past you, does it? You're not wrong, but that can wait. I have so much to tell...'

Shif shook his head frantically and clamped his jaws together with the effort of pulling my face nearer to his. 'It can't wait,' he mumbled. 'I can't wait. I can't hold on much longer and I would see your mother restored to health before I go. I've supported her as best I can with my friendship and my preparations, but I'm not you, Devlin. I can't heal her in the way you can.'

A feeling of urgency stole over me, followed by panic. I had envisaged sitting quietly with Shif in his last hours, telling him all about Risk, reciting the names of my fellow Artists and maybe recounting my experiences with my soul brother, then having time to grieve before attempting to help my mother – and I hadn't even decided where to start with that.

Fortified By Trust. You need merely heed the voice of your soul.

Shif continued to hold my face close to his – his hand now shaking violently within mine – so that I couldn't mistake either his need for me to act, or his confidence that I could do that which was necessary. Without thinking, I lowered his hand to his chest and made for the door, saying, 'I just need to fetch something, I'll be right back.'

I hesitated briefly as I pulled my sketchpads from my saddlebags. Was I mad? My mother was sensitive and fragile. I had thought to treat her gently, to coax her along the path I had taken, but this would be the equivalent of pushing her to a cliff edge and seeing if she'd topple off. A faint ache arose in my wrist and shoulder as I thought of avoiding the risk. No. That wasn't who I was anymore. I turned on my heel and strode back to the kitchen.

'Mother, Father, come and sit over here with me and Shif,' I said, dragging a chair to my mentor's bedside. 'I have something to show you all.'

'But you need to eat first,' Mother said, 'and so does Shif. He can only manage tiny amounts, so they need to be frequent. And you need to have a bath and…'

'This can't wait.' I sat down on my chair and looked up at them both expectantly.

Ma flicked across Mother's face in panic. Before Mother

Chapter Twenty-Six

could push her to one side, I said, 'Believe me, you're going to want to see this.'

Ma's eyes widened and she moved a chair next to mine.

I turned my attention to my father. 'Whatever happens,' I told him, 'know that it's for the best. I'm here to help.' I barely recognised my own voice; it held the same calm confidence that Risk's thoughts had always carried into my mind. It was the voice of my soul.

My father heard it too. He pulled up a chair and sat down without comment, his focus on me intense. Shif smiled at me as if I had granted him his greatest wish. Mother looked wearily hopeful when her strength allowed her to, before Ma shoved her aside, her eyes full of hunger.

I opened the sketchpad and found my most recent drawing of my soul brother. I resisted holding my breath as I turned it around for Shif and my parents to see, instead breathing slowly and deeply.

All three of them stared at it. Ma reached out and grabbed it. She ran a finger down the face staring back at her. 'Henry?'

'His soul lives on in another,' I said gently. 'He's Horse-Bonded, like me.'

She reached a hand out and stroked my cheek. 'Jimmy.'

I shook my head. 'Devlin. Jimmy's experiences set me up to find a strength in this lifetime that I'd never have had reason to go looking for otherwise, but I'm not him. Henry's experiences likewise imprinted on his soul. If his soul's reincarnation can get past the challenges they've left him with – and with the help of his horse, he will – he'll have the ability to help all of us of The New. It was tough, what happened back then, to Jimmy, Henry, Pa and Ma, but it was perfect. Thank you for loving me, Mother Of My Soul.'

Mother's eyes widened and she looked past Ma at me.

'You loved me enough in our previous lifetime together to fight for me, and you loved me enough in this one to let me go,' I continued. 'You remembered you were Ma to Jimmy so you could help me survive my nightmares, and you've suffered so much as a result. You don't need her fear anymore. It's time to let it go.'

Ma grabbed my arm. 'No, Jimmy, no!'

'Mother Of My Soul.' The voice of my soul reached hers in the same way Risk had always reached mine, and it was Mother who let go of my arm. 'It's time to let go of the past,' I said.

'I don't think I can.'

'I'll help you.'

'I'm coming with you.' I almost didn't hear Shif, his voice was so weak.

I will carry him, Risk offered immediately.

'To where?' Father sat up straight in his chair suddenly, as if coming out of a trance, and looked between Shif, Mother and me.

Mother shook her head slightly and slowly, as if afraid that any more of a response would allow Ma back out.

'It's best if we just get going,' I said. 'Shif, Risk has offered to carry you, but are you sure you want to come?' I didn't question whether he knew the details of my plan, for the voice of his soul had always been stronger than mine.

'I'm sure, lad. I wouldn't miss it. You hurry along and saddle your mare while I get some proper clothes on. Lennon, may I ask for your help?'

Father stood up. 'This is madness. You can't stand up without help, but you're going to ride a horse?'

'Can you think of a better way to travel?' Shif wheezed.

'But where are we going? And how is it you know when Devlin didn't say?'

I left them arguing, amused at my certainty that Shif would

hold his own even as I swallowed down a lump in my throat at what it would cost him to do it.

I opened the back door, my saddle on my hip, to find Risk waiting for me, her front feet placed neatly together and her normally gentle eyes full of intent in the failing light. *He Who Heeds The Wind cannot resist its calling for much longer. We must make haste,* she told me.

Suddenly, this was about more than Shif being able to die knowing that neither Mother nor I needed him any longer; I could feel it in the unusual urgency attached to Risk's counsel, as well as see it in her eyes. I rubbed my hand over her back to check she had gathered no dirt from rolling, then saddled her.

We must make haste. Her advice rang in my mind. We couldn't afford to be waylaid by anyone wanting to welcome Risk and me to the village, or question me about our ragged appearance, or ask what Shif was doing on Risk's back instead of his deathbed.

I hurried back to the kitchen, where Father was supporting Shif upright while Mother fastened his trousers – which she appeared to have pulled on over his pyjamas – below a woollen pullover.

'We'll go out of the lower gate and along the back of the paddocks,' I told them. 'This way.'

I propped the door open as wide as it would go and then when Mother and Father reached me, each with an arm around Shif as they half carried him, I bent down and put one arm behind his knees and the other behind his back.

'Devlin, you can't carry him. Look at you, you're not in much better shape than he is,' Father protested, but not in time to stop me lifting my dearest friend and carrying him towards the one who had taught me that strength is only a small part physical.

'Thanks, lad, I was worried I was going to prove your father right for a second there,' Shif murmured, his voice cracking with the strain.

'Risk calls you "He Who Heeds The Wind",' I whispered, 'and I know that as always, you're going with the way it's blowing. You'll have the time and strength to do whatever it is you need to do. I'm going to lift you up onto Risk's back as best I can. Are you ready?'

He smiled faintly and nodded.

'Devlin, wait, I'll help,' Father said.

Between us, we heaved Shif into the saddle.

'Hold on to the front of it, and Father and I'll support you from either side,' I told him.

He didn't waste any of the energy he had left in replying, but curled his fingers around the pommel of the saddle. I turned to Mother. 'Could you go in front of us and open the gate? Risk isn't going to want to jump it this time.'

As soon as she had passed Risk, my gentle mare turned slowly and followed her. I stood away from Risk as far as I dared, my hand firm against Shif's thigh in order to ensure he didn't slide to the side, but wanting to drink in the sight of the horse I loved so much carrying the man I loved so much. She walked with as much determination as always, but her movements were more careful than normal so that Shif needed to expend no energy in order to remain in place.

Once we were through the gate, I held out a hand to Mother, who took it. She didn't ask where we were going and her movements were almost as careful as Risk's, as if she didn't want to agitate the emotions inside her that she knew she would find difficult to control.

I drank in every detail of every moment as the five of us moved slowly and almost silently in the twilight, alongside the fences of the paddocks adjoining the cottages of Coastwood. When we reached the last one, Risk veered away from it, along a well established path.

Mother gasped, but it was Ma who said, 'No! Not the beach!'

Chapter Twenty-Seven

I had allowed myself to believe I had released all of Jimmy's fear – that I couldn't have saved my soul brother's life had any of it remained. But with Ma gripping my hand and trying to pull me away from the beach, and the sound of the sea's gentle lapping on its shore as darkness was falling, just as it had been when Jimmy and Henry were press-ganged, my footsteps slowed. An echo of the all too familiar pain in my wrist was joined by one in my shoulder and another in my chest.

Risk stopped beside me as I stood, frozen to the spot, causing my father to walk on by himself for a few moments before realising he was alone. He turned and asked, 'Is this it? Are we here?'

'No,' Ma said, 'and we're going straight back home.'

This wasn't right. This wasn't me. Not anymore. 'Um, we're not there yet, Father. Mother, we're not going home. You know we can't.' The echoes disappeared.

Shif's hand fell lightly on my shoulder. 'That's it, Son. That's the way. I knew you could do it.'

Chapter Twenty-Seven

I looked up at him in shock, even as Ma rushed to his side and clung to his leg.

'Pa?' I said at the same moment Ma squeaked, 'Fred?'

Shif smiled and nodded. 'We've had an extraordinary time together this time around, haven't we?'

Father said, 'What the hell, Shif?'

I stared up at the dying man clinging to Risk's saddle. 'It's true,' I said, my voice full of awe. 'We've had an incredible time.'

Risk began walking again and, safe in the knowledge that Ma's strength would keep Shif in place, I hurried around her to walk with Father. I laid an arm across his shoulders and said, 'Remember, this is for the best. I'm here to help Mother, and so, apparently, is Shif. Trust me.' My words rang with confidence not only that he should, but that he would.

He sighed. 'I don't have any other choice, do I?'

I pulled him to me in a hug as we walked. 'You've always put all of us before yourself, no matter how weird things have got. It's one of the reasons Mother loves you so much. Let her do this, okay?'

His voice was small as he replied, 'I don't know what "this" is, but I trust you and Risk. And... Shif?'

'He's still Shif, he just knows a lot more than most of us. You can still trust him, Father. Just keep hold of his leg so he doesn't slide off before we reach the sea, okay?'

When he nodded, I returned to my place at Ma's side. 'How can this be?' she was sobbing. 'How can you be here? How have you been all this time without me knowing? Without even Jimmy knowing?'

Shif chuckled and then wheezed, 'I didn't allow Devlin to see the sketch he did of me back when he was a teenager, and I never allowed him to draw me again after that. I knew I could never let either of you see what was better kept hidden.' He coughed and folded over in the saddle, his forehead resting on Risk's neck. He waved a hand at Ma as she fussed over him, and somehow found the strength to continue. 'I couldn't let knowing who I was to you before distract you from accepting my help.'

'I sketched you on the way here and I still didn't see it,' I said and immediately knew why. 'Because it didn't matter. I was following the voice of my soul and it knows all the aspects of you. It didn't allow me to get distracted by any of the others when the one that matters now was calling to me.' I looked up and saw Shif with fresh eyes. I'd always known he was wiser than the rest of us, but I'd had no idea just how much.

He returned my smile, his cheek now resting on Risk's neck as she slowed her steps and picked her way between rocks and tufts of grass, down the path to the beach. I took hold of Ma's hand as she pulled at Shif's leg, trying to stop Risk's advance towards the root of her fear.

She turned to me, her face taut and the whites of her eyes glistening in the moonlight that danced off the waves. 'No! We have to stop! The sea took you away from me before and I won't let it happen again.'

'Mother Of My Soul.' The words reached her as I knew they would, and Mother let go of Shif's leg. 'We have to continue.'

She ground her teeth together and stood where she was, shifting from one foot to the other. I put one hand to Shif's leg and gently took one of hers with the other. 'Come on, Mother. You're safe. I'm safe. We always were.'

Ma pulled back at my hand. 'Henry isn't. He's alone.'

'The man who was Henry isn't alone. He's with his horse. And once you're okay, Risk and I'll go back to him and stay close in case there's anything he needs from us. But I can't do that, Mother Of My Soul, until you let me help you. Until you trust me.'

Chapter Twenty-Seven

It was Mother who sighed and said, 'I trust you now, Devlin. I'm just... scared.'

The fear in her voice reminded me of that which had gripped me for so long, and my heart thumped more strongly in my chest. What if I were wrong about doing this? My footsteps slowed even as Risk's continued onward, as sure as ever, towards the waves that splashed gently upon the shore. Risk. Without it – without her – there was no curiosity, excitement or achievement. There was no rejection, pain or failure. Life was boring. Depressing. Meaningless. Risk was everything to me.

'It's not your fear, it's Ma's,' I told Mother, almost dragging her with me in my hurry to catch up with my horse and hold on to Shif's leg as Risk splashed into the water. 'The more you trust me, the less scared you'll feel.'

She started to cry. 'No, no, I can't do this. I can't go into the sea. I can't swim!'

'Ma couldn't swim,' I said. 'You can. And you need to; it's the only way you'll leave her and her fears behind.'

Suddenly, I was forced to release her hand and pull hard on Shif's leg as he slid away from me. There was a lot of splashing as I righted him, and Father appeared at Mother's side, telling her, 'Go with them, Ma. Come back to me, Mowaya?'

I reached back and pulled on her hand again. 'Trust me with every breath you take,' I said, fighting to keep hold of my own. 'With every stroke. Stay with me and Risk, Mother Of My Soul.'

Mother followed me as I continued to pull her hand, and Father gently pushed her away from himself.

We were soon waist deep as the shore descended sharply away from us, and then we were swimming, Risk, Mother and me. Shif chuckled faintly as he lay along Risk's neck.

Suddenly, Ma screamed, then spluttered and choked as salty water lapped into her mouth. My heart nearly stopped as she disappeared beneath the waves. I grabbed hold of her and lifted her head above the water. Risk, having rapidly left Mother and me behind, turned and swam around us in a circle.

'Swim, Mother,' I urged her. 'You can swim. You're not afraid to. You don't have Ma's fears.'

Ma flailed her arms around, spluttering. We both went under the waves and I kicked frantically with my legs until we broke above them again, both of us gasping for air. As soon as her lungs were full of it, Ma shrieked it all back out, along with her pain at losing her sons to the sea and her terror of drowning in it herself. I held her close whilst continuing to kick hard against the water that would pull us both under. A hand grabbed the collar of my coat and Pa towed me beside him and Risk with a strength there was no way Shif possessed.

When Ma's screams turned into sobs, I gasped, 'Trust me, Mother Of My Soul. With every stroke.' I let go of her but kept my hand outstretched, ready to grab her again if she faltered. 'SWIM!' I bellowed.

Shif released his hold on me as Mother took her first hesitant stroke. 'Swim,' he echoed faintly.

Mother took another stroke, then another. I swam just ahead of her, urging her on as her strokes gradually became stronger and faster. When she surged forward, her strokes powerful and confident, Shif wheezed, 'Yes!'

I put more strength into my own swimming so that I kept pace with her. Risk circled us both again and then swam at Mother's side, Shif smiling in the moonlight as his hands trailed in the water on either side of my horse's neck.

It was Jimmy who drifted away first. Ma followed him willingly, and Pa was swift to go with her.

I'll look out for my soul brother, I told them as the water took them from me.

Chapter Twenty-Seven

We know you will.

Without speaking, Mother, Risk and I turned in unison and swam for the shore, Mother staying close beside Shif and me swimming frantically to reach my horse's other side, so that I could ensure he remained in place atop her once we reached dry land.

Neither Mother nor I could spare the breath to speak as we swam towards the lone figure waiting for us on the beach made silver by the moonlight, but as I swam next to my strong, determined mare, I felt a sense of elation such as I had never felt before. It was as if every cell in my body were exploding with life and with the joy of knowing that life could never die. Despite not having eaten well for weeks or having swum since I was a child, I found more than enough strength to keep pace with Risk as she swam for the shore, and was almost disappointed when we reached it.

Father splashed out to meet us, first taking Mother's hands and pulling her to her feet, then helping her to keep Shif in place whilst Risk gained her footing on the sand.

'Alright, Devlin?' he called out to me.

'More than alright, thanks,' I called back, leaning against Risk in order to keep hold of Shif's leg as the wet sand shifted beneath my feet.

'Mowaya?' He asked Mother cautiously.

'It's over, Lennon. I've let Ma go.'

Father choked on a sob and then said, 'Shif?'

I looked up at my friend as he lay along Risk's neck. His face was turned towards me and clear of the strain and tension that had distorted it. His mouth was set in a radiant smile even as his eyes stared lifelessly. He had gone.

'Help me, Father?' I said, the urgency in my voice causing him to rush to my side.

He helped me to ease Shif's body from Risk's back and lay him on the beach. I loosened Risk's girth and then joined my parents as they knelt on the sand, their arms around one another and holding Shif's hand in theirs.

Mother's voice shook as she said, 'I feel so different, like a young girl again with no fear, because of what he, you and Risk, just did for me.'

'It's an amazing feeling, isn't it,' I said. 'I'm the same, because of all of you.' I looked from her to Father, to Shif and then reached up behind me to stroke the muzzle I knew was there. 'We're going to miss him so much, aren't we.' My voice broke and my sobs were joined by those of my parents.

He Who Heeds The Wind lived well and moved on well, Risk informed me. *He would that you make optimal use of your lives now that you have freed yourselves from the echoes of the past.*

I passed on her message to my parents a few words at a time, barely able to speak for the grief that was choking me. It was only as I began to shiver that horror at my lack of consideration for Risk pierced my heartache, and I got to my feet.

'We need to go back,' I said. 'I need to wash the seawater off Risk and rub her down, and we need to prepare for Shif's funeral.'

Still snuffling, my parents nodded. Father stood and then bent down to lift Shif.

I will carry him, Risk offered.

Between us, Father and I draped him across her back, then removed our shirts and covered him. It was only as we were making our way back to the cottage that Mother said, 'So, Risk can talk to Shif even now he's dead?'

I chuckled. 'I think you and I, of all people, know there's no such thing as death. I think it's more the case that he can hear her now he's where he is.'

'So, can she communicate with him for all of us?' Mother

asked. 'There'll be people in the village who'll want to ask him things and tell him what they never got around to saying.'

He Who Heeds The Wind would be no more of a distraction to you now that he is discarnate than the knowledge he carried would have been whilst he was incarnate, Risk tells me. *Remember well his parting wish.*

I repeated her reply and added, 'I think we should concentrate on organising his funeral and then doing what he wants us to.'

'Would you do a painting of him for us, Dev?' Father asked suddenly. 'I didn't know him in the way you two did – from before and everything,' he added awkwardly, 'but I know if you paint him, everyone in the village will be able to remember who he was to them.'

I couldn't think of anything I wanted to do more.

~

My painting of Shif rested against the stern of the boat in which lay his body. I had completed a new sketch of him by candlelight as soon as I had made Risk comfortable on our return from the beach, and begun painting as soon as the sun's rays had sufficient strength to assure me I could do his portrait justice.

Mother, Father, Joplin, Kaplin and I stood to one side of the boat, glad to have got it into position on the beach just minutes before the first villagers arrived to pay their respects. They arrived in a steady stream, every one of them studying the painting into which I had put the full extent of my Skill and then finding themselves moved to speak to him as if he were standing before them, rather than lying lifeless just beyond. It wasn't lost on me that while I may have created the strokes that comprised the painting, it was Shif who had ensured I could, and therefore unwittingly given himself the means to reach out to his friends from the other side of death.

When they had said everything they wanted to Shif, the villagers placed flowers and leaves of every description in the boat around him, in recognition of his life's work and contribution to the village, before moving to stand behind my family and me.

I didn't know whom or what anyone else saw when they looked at the painting of the man who had nursed them through their ills, but I saw Shif, my friend and mentor; Pa, my father and protector; and a thousand other aspects of his soul. It was no wonder he had heard its voice so clearly when he'd dedicated so many lives to listening for it.

When the last of the villagers had paid their respects, and Shif was almost completely buried beneath flowers and leaves of all hues and scents with just his face still visible, Mother stepped forward and retrieved my painting so that Father, my brothers and I could take our places along the stern of the boat. We leant into it, driving it through the sand towards the much larger boat bobbing about beyond the shallows, waiting to tow it out to sea.

I thought to begin with that the thrumming in my ears was caused by my blood pounding through them with the effort of pushing the boat. As it got louder and the villagers – who had been silent apart from the odd escaped sob – began murmuring to one another, then shouting in delight, I couldn't help but smile, realising exactly what was causing it.

I wanted you to graze and rest, I told my rapidly approaching horse. I should have known better than to believe closing the paddock gate would ensure that happened.

Risk thundered down onto the beach behind us, and my brothers, father and I paused our effort to get the boat to the water in order to turn and watch her. She galloped away from us along the shore until she was a dot in the distance, then turned and galloped back towards us as if she'd been resting for weeks, whinnying shrilly all the while.

A tingle went down my spine with every whinny, and my skin prickled with goosebumps. It was as if she were charging the air as she galloped along the beach, singing with joy for Shif's life and all he had achieved.

I looked around at my family and friends to see them holding on to one another as if the ground would give way beneath them, whilst laughing hesitantly, as if unsure why they were doing it. It wasn't just my bond with Risk that allowed me to sense her resolve that we should celebrate Shif's passing rather than grieve it; she was using all her power to ensure that everyone could feel it.

The laughing became louder and more confident, and some villagers began to sing. Others rushed to fill in the spaces between my father, brothers and me, and heaved alongside us as we continued to push the boat towards the sea. It began to float just as Risk reached us. She stood on her hind legs and pawed the air, still whinnying. More hands appeared down the sides of the boat, not really helping but keen to be involved in sending Shif to join the waves. Those of us at the stern gave the boat such a strong final shove, it cut through the water as if it weren't there, straight into the hands of a waiting Fisherwoman, who reached for the rope attached to its bow and wound it around a hook on her boat's gunwale.

Everyone cheered and Risk reared and whinnied for a last time before coming to stand beside me. As we all watched the two boats heading out to sea, we sang, we laughed and we hugged one another. When fire erupted from Shif's boat, we cheered again for our friend, for his life and all he had been to us.

The returning Fisherwoman and her crew swam ashore after anchoring their boat in the spot in which it had previously waited, and joined in with our celebrations until the fire out at sea was no more. Silence fell amongst the villagers, unsure what to do now that they had abandoned the decorum normally observed at a funeral. I vaulted upon Risk's back and she cantered slowly through the crowd and then up the beach towards the village. I raised a hand and shouted over my shoulder, 'Come on, Shif would want us to be drinking ale by now!'

A cheer went up from the villagers and they surged up the beach in our wake. I hadn't touched a drop of ale since my qualification ceremony, when Shif had advised me to leave Coastwood. It was way past time to raise a glass to my old friend now.

Chapter Twenty-Eight

*R*isk and I slowly recovered our weight and condition during the weeks that followed Shif's unorthodox funeral, and the village recovered its spirits more quickly than anyone could remember following the loss of someone so prominent and loved as was he. I passed on Risk's counsel to all those who came to see us, and sketched and painted those who asked it of me. I spent enjoyable time with my brothers and their families, and with my parents. I cleaned my saddle repeatedly – but not obsessively – until it was free of sea salt and the leather was supple once again.

When a storm finally broke the weather and opened the way for daily rain showers that revitalised the pastures and gave us relief from the continuing heat, I began to feel restless.

It's time for us to move on, isn't it. I wasn't asking Risk as I groomed her one morning, but confirming that which we both knew. We were fit and well and had served the villagers of Coastwood as best we could. There were other villages that needed us, and I felt duty bound to visit all those we had bypassed on our way to Coastwood. But more than that, I had an itch that I couldn't scratch; I knew Risk would tell me if my soul brother needed me, but I felt as if I were too far away from him. In order to scratch my itch, I should head back towards where we had left him.

It is always wise to heed the voice of your soul, Risk agreed.

∼

Our departure two days later was marked by my previously avoided Quest Ceremony. Since I had arrived in Coastwood with so few belongings, my parents – and indeed the rest of Coastwood – insisted that I left the village properly equipped for travelling. It was, according to my mother, important that I didn't arrive in any other villages "looking like something the cat dragged in" – not that she had a cat, or indeed any idea what anything the village cats may have taken home might look like.

I was touched to discover that, unlike with a normal Quest Ceremony – where the family of the person leaving supplied most of the food, clothes and equipment that might be needed on the quest – the villagers insisted that each household would put something in my saddlebags, as well as throw petals over me or hang tiny horseshoes made from glass, metal or fabric on my clothes and bags. It meant that it took an age for me to make my way along the tunnel formed by two lines of villagers facing one another from my parents' doorstep to where Risk waited patiently for me, but when I finally emerged, I felt as if something had settled deeply into place inside me; wherever I went and however long it was before I returned to Coastwood, it would always be my home – something I had never felt about it before.

My parents and brothers were standing with Risk when I reached her, my mother leaning her head against my horse's neck.

Chapter Twenty-Eight

There was a bucket of water at Risk's feet, as well as a pile of hay from which she had only recently stopped munching, judging by the strands of hay protruding from her mouth.

Broad-shouldered Joplin slapped me on the back. 'Great turnout to see you on your way, eh, Dev? You deserve it.'

Tall, lean Kaplin offered me his hand and then drew me into a hug. 'Don't leave it too long before you come back to see us again, little bro'. It's been good having you here.'

Father was next to pull me into a hug. 'I'm proud of you, Devlin. You'll never know how much,' was all he could say before his voice cracked. When he finally released me, Mother stood waiting.

She held out both hands and I took them in mine. Her eyes glistened above a smile that told me everything I needed to know.

'Thank you for everything, Mother Of My Soul,' I whispered. 'Remember Shif's advice, won't you? Fill your life with everything you love. Do everything you've ever wanted to do. Don't think about it, just do it. You know Father'll be right behind you. It's time for us both to live in the present instead of the past.'

She nodded, biting her lip. 'I will. But what about you? You're going back to… to… the man who was Henry. The past still has a hold on you.'

I shook my head. 'It has a hold on him, and I'm going to do everything I can to help him past it. It has to be me, you know that. Even if it didn't, I'd want it to be me.'

Her smile returned. 'I know. I feel as if I should help, but…'

'But you know it's not your place this time around,' I finished for her. 'You've done all you needed to do for us both by being such a wonderful mother to me. Enjoy the life you have now, and I'll do the same. Goodbye, Mother.'

She released my hands and allowed my father to gently pull her away from me so that I could mount my ever patient horse.

As I rode away from Coastwood, jangling with all the tiny horseshoes hanging from my clothes and saddlebags, and my shirt beginning to stick to me as a result of the lightly falling rain, I had an intense sense of purpose and determination. Previously, I had always associated those feelings with Risk, but now, they were very definitely mine. Whatever happened, whatever it took, I would be there for my soul brother.

He Who Is Risk you have come far, my horse told me, her thought enriched with love and pride.

I almost sobbed in my saddle.

∽

Our month-long journey from Coastwood was infinitely easier than that which had resulted in our dishevelled arrival. Not only was I well stocked with food, but the grazing available as we crossed the plains was nutritious and satisfying for Risk, and the rain showers allowed us to travel during the day as well as the night. Our visits to the seven villages that we had regretfully bypassed when travelling in the other direction delayed our progress by a few days at a time, but the delays were barely noticeable in the long run since we easily made up the time by travelling faster and for longer. I didn't feel in a hurry as such, just eager to be closer to the one who, in my daily sketches of him, seemed to be looking for me out of the corner of his eye.

I sensed us to be several days distant from him when Risk told me, *We are needed once more.*

Is he okay? Is his horse okay?

He has experienced difficulties but it is with another matter that his horse has asked for your help.

What matter?

Risk didn't answer, but sped up into a trot in the direction of

Chapter Twenty-Eight

some distant hills. I knew her well enough to be confident that if she hadn't answered me straight away, there was little likelihood of her doing so at any time in the future, so I focused on being as light and balanced a passenger for her as I could, as she picked her way between rabbit holes and the larger tussocks of grass. Shortly before we reached the hills, she stopped to graze on the lush grass of the plains that I could see petering out as the land rose and being replaced by tougher grasses dotted with bushes.

The two days and nights that followed were arduous, to say the least. The hills were neither steep nor shallow, but packed so densely that we always seemed to be either climbing or descending. Long, coarse grass hindered our progress almost as much as the plethora of bushes between which we were forced to weave our way. I walked as much as I rode and craved level ground under my feet.

I was astride Risk, since the hill we were climbing was blessedly small compared with most of those we had recently encountered, when her ears swivelled forward and her heart thumped so violently that it caused my left leg to shudder. She let out a deafening whinny and sped up from a walk into a canter, causing me to grab my hat and push it down further on my head. She crested the hill and maintained her speed, darting between the tall bushes that blocked our view of where we were going. I relaxed into my saddle, easily absorbing Risk's sudden changes in direction and grinning from ear to ear, despite not knowing what sort of welcome we would receive from my soul brother.

All of a sudden, we rounded the last of the large bushes and there he was, standing a short distance away by a stream with a water pouch in his hand. I barely recognised him. Where his skin had seemed to hang on him, it now covered flesh and muscle. His previously lank, dirty hair now shone as it rested on his shoulders. Where his face had been contorted with rage and pain, it was now relaxed, and his green eyes had a twinkle in them. He was even smiling at me, although judging by the way he was fiddling with the stopper of his water pouch, he was apprehensive.

There was a heavy thudding to my left, and Risk slowed to a walk as my soul brother's enormous Bond-Partner came trotting in our direction, around some low-growing bushes. She halted when he reached us and allowed him to touch the side of her nose with his own. I jumped as both horses stamped a front foot and squealed, then laughed, sensing Risk's delight at reacquainting herself with the huge white and brown horse. I quickly jumped down from her back and unsaddled her, dumped my saddle and saddlebags on the ground, and strode towards my soul brother, as keen to be reunited with him as Risk was with his horse.

'We'll leave those two to catch up, shall we?' I said, holding my hand out to him. 'It's good to see you. My word you look different and so does he. Hasn't he grown and filled out?'

My soul brother took a firm hold of my hand, yet shook it tentatively. I wondered whether I had presumed too much; whether I had misread him and he wasn't as pleased to see me as he had initially appeared. But then Risk and his horse reared in unison, swiped at one another upon landing as if intending to bite, and cantered away, racing one another around the bushes.

My soul brother's voice was gentle but full of pride. 'He has.'

Sensing that his horse was the safest topic of conversation for now, I said, 'He'll be strong enough for you to ride soon. I must admit, when I first saw him, what was it, three months or so ago? I thought it would be a while before he'd be able to carry you, but he's grown into himself quickly.'

'Err, I have ridden him briefly already,' my soul brother told me, still watching his horse and Risk thundering around the bushes. 'It wasn't by choice though, exactly, but because I couldn't walk.' There was a sense of vulnerability about him as he spoke, as if his horse had reached inside him, past his pain and anger, and pulled him out to where he had no protection other than his belief in his Bond-Partner. Well, he now also had me.

'Much like when I left you, then?' I said, intending my observation as a jest but immediately worried I'd spoken out of turn. 'Sorry, you probably don't need reminding. Risk told me you've had a difficult time. By the look of things, you're over the worst though.' I changed the subject to safer ground. 'What's his name?'

The huge white and brown horse chose that moment to slow from a canter to a halt by bouncing on all four legs like a newly born lamb, making us both grin and relax.

'His name is Peace and mine is Adam,' my soul brother told me, still watching his horse. 'I'm sorry I didn't introduce myself when we met before. Thank you for saving my life and taking me to him. And thanks for leaving me with what must have been pretty much all your food and clothes, and for being kind enough not to mention how abominably I behaved towards you.' He turned to me. 'The worst is indeed over, but I have a huge amount to do to undo all the damage I've caused.' His eyes lost their twinkle and were full of regret.

My heart went out to him. Like me, he had brought a heavy burden with him into this life, and it wasn't his fault that he'd had no idea how to cope with it. But he had called his horse Peace, and that meant he recognised what he needed. He would be okay now that we were all here to help him.

I kept my voice light as I said, 'Pleased to meet you, Adam. Peace, eh? Well, whatever you're on your way to do, Risk and I are here to help. She hasn't seen fit to enlighten me as to what it is, exactly, that you need help with, only that your horse, sorry, Peace, asked us to be here, so here we are.'

The twinkle returned to Adam's eyes. 'Oh, he did, did he?

Well, I'm glad it's not just me who gets kept in the dark. Does Risk give you answers that leave you with more questions too?'

I laughed, delighted to talk to him about something we had in common that was joyous rather than painful and difficult. 'Adam, welcome to the world of the Horse-Bonded. The rewards are huge, but they're equalled in magnitude by the frustrations of being guided by those so much wiser than we are.'

Our attention was grabbed by a loud snort. Risk and Peace now appeared to be showing one another how slowly they could trot whilst bouncing as high in the air as possible.

'I see you've found water,' I said to Adam. 'Good news, because I'm running low. Wouldn't you think Risk would rehydrate herself before carrying on like that in the heat?'

Adam continued to watch the horses, a smile on his face that was full of love for the one who had clearly had an enormous impact on him during the months we had been apart.

'Do you have food?' he said suddenly. 'I have plenty if not, and this might be a good time to stop for a bite?' He nodded back towards the horses. 'They can cavort as long as they feel is necessary and then have a chance to drink and graze. Not that the grass is as good here as on the plains.'

'It's good enough,' I replied. 'Yes, that sounds like a plan. It'll give us a chance to catch up.'

Adam didn't reply and his face was suddenly tight with worry. Then his eyes glazed over in the way that was common to all Horse-Bonded whilst being counselled by their horse. I waited quietly until he relaxed again, then followed his gaze to where Peace was doing a succession of little bucks, pretending to kick out at Risk while adeptly missing her while she looked on, unimpressed. I couldn't help but grin. When I looked back at Adam, he was grinning too. He beckoned me to follow him to where he had left his back-sack in the shade of a bush, then sat down on the ground and unpacked some parcels of food. He opened them and placed them between us so we could share their contents, which appeared to be a mixture of fruit, nuts, cake and sandwiches. Then he talked.

I listened, spellbound, as he related his experiences of the past few months. To begin with, he appeared awkward, ashamed even, as he recounted the tale of his slow acceptance of his bond with Peace. As he continued to speak, his voice gradually became softer, more confident, and I got a sense of everything he had learnt and achieved; whom he had become in just three months of being Horse-Bonded. I also got a sense of whom he would become.

He Who Can Heal That Which Has Gone Before. That was what Risk had always called him. She had helped me to find my strength because it was important to me – to my soul – that I did so. Peace was helping Adam to find his because it was important not only to him, but to all of us.

I felt chastened. Who had I thought I was, exactly, riding into Adam's life like I was some sort of saviour? He had already moved mountains without me and would no doubt continue to do so whether I was "helping" him or not. He didn't need me.

When he finished speaking, I picked up my water pouch and handed Adam's to him. 'We should drink a toast,' I said. 'You've come further in these last few months than I have in the five years I've been bonded to Risk. To you and Peace, and all you have and will achieve. I'm glad to know you.'

Adam stared at me. 'How can you be, after everything I've just told you?'

I shrugged. 'We're none of us perfect, and if I've understood counsel Risk's given me correctly, we wouldn't be here if we were. You've made mistakes, you're on a mission to correct them and hopefully, many will benefit from your efforts. Risk and I are here to help you in any way we can. You've been talking a long time, you should eat. I'll rub those two down now that the sweat's finally dry on their coats.'

I selected a few brushes from my saddlebag and went over to where the horses were grazing. Risk whickered to me before continuing to snatch at the coarse grass. Peace sniffed the hand I offered him, then my arm up to my neck, before flicking my hat off my head with his top lip.

I chuckled. 'So, you're a joker then, huh?'

I rubbed his forehead and then began to brush the sweat from Risk's coat. *I've offered to help Adam, but he doesn't need me*, I told her. *How can he possibly, when he's capable of so much more than me?*

His Bond-Partner disagrees, Risk reminded me. *The path he has chosen will be difficult to tread. He will require the support of one who fully understands his motivation. Who will assist him without question or concern. Who will offer him companionship devoid of need or distraction. He Who Is Risk you are uniquely placed to offer all those things to He Who Can Heal That Which Has Gone Before. In the process you will discover more of those who need your help to express themselves without words and you will reveal to those who are ready that there is more to life than the eyes can see.*

I felt a mixture of relief and sadness. *But I can never reveal anything to Adam. I mustn't ever distract him from what he has to do.*

Risk gently nuzzled my back as I brushed hers. *It is difficult to show love to another in a way that they will never acknowledge or even recognise. He Who Is Risk the time has come for you to embrace the greatest unknown of all.*

Epilogue

I am breaking the first rule I always used to teach my students before even letting them pick up a pencil, but I don't need natural light in order to paint Adam and Peace; I could paint them with my eyes closed. Time is limited though, so I've switched on all the lanterns dotted around the living room in order that I can swiftly cover one of its grey stone walls with the exact combination of coloured brushstrokes that I know will comfort my soul brother.

As the hours pass, my wrist, elbow and shoulder ache with increasing intensity – not because I have succumbed to the past that held us both captive for so long, but because I am old. I don't dwell on how old, exactly, because that would mean remembering how long it is since Risk's body finally gave out and she passed on without me. I have often thought of following her, but each time, something – or rather someone – has stopped me.

Adam.

I succeeded, you see, in welcoming that to which Risk referred as "the greatest unknown" into my life, to the extent that it became part of me. I've spent most my life since I met my soul brother supporting him from a place of understanding and devotion about which he is still completely unaware. And I have resolved to not let go of this life until I know for certain that he has no need of me still.

It's been years since I've seen him, for when Risk passed and my years finally caught up with me, I only slowed him and Peace down. But I kept sketching him in order to know how he was faring, and I kept travelling, slowly, on foot and usually by myself, in order to stay as close to him as I could in case he should need me.

It pained me to the depths of my soul when, for the first time, my fingers refused to guide my pencil to draw Peace's outline beside Adam's, and each day that has passed between then and now has pained me further. Adam was there to comfort me when Risk left her body, but my old, creaking body wouldn't allow me to reach him in time to comfort him when Peace left his. So, I'm doing it now, in the best way I know how.

My heart wants me to put everything I know of Adam and Peace into the mural that is coming to life upon Adam's living room wall. The time has come for me to answer the question I asked myself over and over during the years I travelled with my soul brother. Will I allow my heart to tell him that which my soul knows could distract him from his purpose, thereby doing him harm?

I glance down at the sketch from which I'm painting, and my heart lurches, desperate for me to transfer it in its entirety to the wall so that Adam will know everything he is, was and will be – and also know the same about me. All this time, I've loved Adam as he should be loved; uncompromisingly, unselfishly, bravely even, just as Risk advised was necessary for him to achieve his purpose. If I paint the full extent of that which I have sketched, he'll know what I, myself, have achieved... but then I will no longer have achieved it.

I think, as I do at least once in every hour of every day, of Risk, and it strikes me suddenly that she advised me to do no more than she ever did herself. She dedicated her life to being with me even though she so obviously enjoyed the company of other horses; she chose to be my Bond-Partner when doing so deprived her of so much of what it is to be a horse. I quell my heart's desire and listen to the voice of my soul as I know she would want. I scrunch up my sketch and stuff it into my trouser pocket.

Even though my Bond-Partner is no longer with me, her influence remains; there is an element of Risk in everything I do.

∽

The first birds are calling their sleepy questions to the dawn as I step back from the finished mural. I am satisfied with it even though it is so much less than it could be. Peace lies in a meadow rich with summer flowers, and Adam sits between his front and hind legs, leaning back against him with his legs crossed, as he so often did. While so much is missing from the painting, the strength of the bond between the pair, and their mischievous yet gentle personalities, are plain to see. More importantly, the peace emanating from them both is palpable.

I smile in approval of myself for painting the mural of my soul in favour of the one of my heart, for in focusing above all else on that which my soul brother achieved with his Bond-Partner, the painting has rendered the sketch in my pocket an overwhelming irrelevance and has told me what I want to know; my soul brother doesn't need me.

I won't recount what Adam and Peace have done for all of us of The New, for it is Adam's story to tell, and I would be away from here before he wakes in his bedroom upstairs. I pack up my paints and brushes and raise the latch on his front door. I flinch as the door squeaks open and hold my breath until it is closed behind me with its latch back in place. I shuffle along the cobbled street, feeling lighter than my slow, awkward movement would suggest.

We did it, Risk. I'll be with you very soon.

Thank you for reading *An Element Of Risk*!
If you would like to read Adam's story, he tells it in
In Search Of Peace.

Books by Lynn Mann

The Horses Know Trilogy
The Horses Know
The Horses Rejoice
The Horses Return

Sequels to The Horses Know Trilogy
Horses Forever
The Forgotten Horses
The Way Of The Horse

Origins of The Horses Know Trilogy
The Horses Unite

Prequels to The Horses Know Trilogy
An Element Of Risk (Devlin's story)
In Search Of Peace (Adam's story)
The Strength Of Oak (Rowena's story)
A Reason To Be Noble (Quinta's story)

Companion Stories to The Horses Know Trilogy
From A Spark Comes A Flame (Novella)
Tales Of The Horse-Bonded (Short Story Collection)

Tales Of The Horse-Bonded will take you on a journey into the lives of some of your favourite characters from *The Horses Know Trilogy*. The book is available for purchase in paperback and hardback, but is also available to download for free. To find out more, visit www.lynnmann.co.uk.

A regularly updated book list can be found at
www.lynnmann.co.uk/booklist
(The QR code below allows quick access!)

Did you enjoy *An Element Of Risk*?
I'd be extremely grateful if you could spare a few minutes
to leave a review where you purchased your copy.
Reviews really do help my books to reach a wider audience,
which means that I can keep on writing!
Thank you very much.

∼

I love to hear from you!
Get in touch and receive news of future releases at the following:

www.lynnmann.co.uk

www.facebook.com/lynnmann.author

Acknowledgments

A massive thank you, as always, to my editorial team for their invaluable insights and suggestions that make everything I write so much better than it would otherwise be – Fern Sherry, Caroline Macintosh and Cindy Nye, I would be lost without you!

There was sadly someone missing from the team this time around, since Leonard Palmer passed away on 22nd March 2024. As my line editor and also my dad, he was and will always be hugely missed. He had been unwell for some time before his passing, but every time I had a manuscript ready and asked whether he felt up to editing for me, he was adamant he wanted to do it, even working on the second half of *The Forgotten Horses* from his hospital bed in 2022. Thanks, Dad, for everything.

I am grateful to Amanda Horan for her fabulous cover design, and feel blessed to have a designer who nails the brief every time.

As this book was being edited, our beautiful Braveheart, who was the inspiration for Peace's character, went to sleep for the last time. He was my husband's partner in mischief for twenty-five years, and was everything I wrote into Peace's character: goofy, funny and mischievous whilst also loving, wise and full of peace. The term "giving it large" described him perfectly, for his huge emotions were expressed without reservation, his enormous, expressive paces dropped jaws, and his capacity to love his herd and humans was immense. I loved writing about him and will always miss him.

Printed in Great Britain
by Amazon